Graham Greene's Fictions

Graham Greene's Fictions

The Virtues of Extremity

Cates Baldridge

University of Missouri Press

COLUMBIA AND LONDON

Copyright © 2000 by
The Curators of the University of Missouri
University of Missouri Press, Columbia, Missouri 65201
Printed and bound in the United States of America
All rights reserved
5 4 3 2 1   04 03 02 01 00

Library of Congress Cataloging-in-Publication Data

Baldridge, Cates.
Graham Greene's fictions : the virtues of extremity / Cates Baldridge.
   p. cm.
Includes bibliographical references and index.
ISBN 0-8262-1251-4 (alk. paper)
1. Greene, Graham, 1904—Criticism and interpretation.   I. Title.

PR6013.R44Z6315   1999
823'.912–dc21   99-047291

♾™ This paper meets the requirements of the
American National Standard for Permanence of Paper
for Printed Library Materials, Z39.48, 1984.

Text designer: Elizabeth K. Young
Jacket designer: Susan Ferber
Typesetter: BookComp, Inc.
Printer and binder: Edwards Brothers, Inc.
Typefaces: ITC Veljovic Book, Helvetica Neue Extended

For Tricia,
who single-handedly vanquished
the Ministry of Fear

Contents

Acknowledgments ix

Abbreviations xi

Introduction: The Virtues of Extremity 1

1 The Mediated and the Absolute: A Genealogy of *Brighton Rock* 10

2 Waning Power and Faded Glory: Greene's Conception of God 49

3 Love, Pity, Charity: Passions at the Heart of the Matter 90

4 Comedians, Commitment, and *Commedia* 129

5 The Honorary Marxist: Political Philosophy in Greene's Novels 169

Bibliography 199

Index 207

Acknowledgments

The writing of this book was aided considerably by the generous leave policy of Middlebury College, which allowed me to devote myself wholeheartedly to finishing the project during the 1996–1997 academic year. For two very pleasant weeks during that time, I was a guest of the Harry Ransom Research Center at the University of Texas at Austin, which holds a large proportion of Greene's papers. Although relatively few passages from the Ransom Center's holdings appear in this work, the chance to soak up the unpublished productions of Greene did much to increase my knowledge of the man and thus to refine the arguments in *Graham Greene's Fictions.* Everyone connected with the Ransom Center was unfailingly helpful.

Grateful acknowledgment is made to the Harry Ransom Research Center and to David Higham Associates for permission to use material in this book.

Upon my return to Middlebury's English Department, several of my colleagues—among them Jay Parini, Alison Byerly, and Steve Jensen—read parts of this manuscript and offered valuable comments. Jay Parini, who seems to know everyone in publishing, also lent a helping hand in finding a proper home for the book. Just as Jay promised, the University of Missouri Press has been a model of courtesy, professionalism, and dispatch throughout: my dealings with the acquisitions editor Clair Willcox have been especially pleasant, and Julie Schroeder has rescued me from a number of errors and inconsistencies. All blemishes that remain are entirely chargeable to myself.

Back home once again, I owe a debt to the students in my senior seminar on Conrad and Greene, who ably and rigorously tested—and contested—in the crucible of a classroom ideas hitherto extant only on paper.

Finally, and foremost, I must thank my wife, Tricia Welsch, who, through the distances of our commuter marriage and the intimacies of our concurrent leaves, supported and nourished me in a hundred ways, practical and spiritual, while all the time working busily at her own academic labors. Throughout the last four years she has been my toughest critic and my biggest fan, and every page of this book bears some mark of her wisdom and empathy.

Abbreviations

(BR)   *Brighton Rock*

(BC)   *A Burnt-Out Case*

(CE)   *Collected Essays*

(TC)   *The Comedians*

(CA)   *The Confidential Agent*

(EA)   *The End of the Affair*

(HM)   *The Heart of the Matter*

(HC)   *The Honorary Consul*

(HF)   *The Human Factor*

(IB)   *It's a Battlefield*

(LR)   *The Lawless Roads*

(MF)   *The Ministry of Fear*

(MQ)   *Monsignor Quixote*

(OM)   *Our Man in Havana*

(PG)   *The Power and the Glory*

(QA)   *The Quiet American*

(RE)   *Reflections*

(SL)   *A Sort of Life*

(ST)   *Stamboul Train*

(TA)   *Travels with My Aunt*

(WE)   *Ways of Escape*

(YE)   *Yours, Etc.: Letters to the Press*

Graham Greene's Fictions

Introduction

The Virtues of Extremity

Some of Graham Greene's happiest moments were spent under aerial bombardment, as the British capital was systematically turned to rubble: "The nightly routine of sirens, barrage, the probing raider, the unmistakable engine ('Where are you? Where are you? Where are you?'), the bomb-bursts moving nearer and then moving away, hold one like a love-charm" (*CE,* 450). Even decades later, his memories of that unhalcyon age had lost none of their clarity or fondness: "During the Blitz one loved London particularly. Awful as war was, one is nostalgic for the feeling of that period. London became a series of villages. During a blackout you could see the stars and the moon even on Oxford Street, and flares dropping like chandeliers. In the morning there was the sound of broken glass being swept up. It wasn't white, as you'd think, but blue-green."[1] Graham Greene loved the blitz because it suddenly and continually turned the familiar markers of a routinized bourgeois existence into so many macabre heralds of an urgent existential confrontation. This buoyed him because he was a man who could not fully breathe within the confines of middle-class normality, who could only find firm footing upon a moral precipice or pinnacle, and who craved contact with final, awful, and absolute questions—matters of life and death, good and evil, salvation and damnation—as people of a different temper crave quiet, rest, and stability. When he could not catch a boat or a plane to such precincts of extremity, he visited them through the narratives he created; but, in the fall of 1940, the absolute had conveniently come to him, remaking London in its own image, demonstrating nightly that nothing is so ephemeral as normality and confirming his long-held belief that "there is no peace anywhere where there is human life," only "quiet and active sectors of the line" (*LR,* 33). He had never been so happy before; he would never be quite so happy again.

1. Graham Greene, "Places," 1.

1

Greene's affinity for extremes, his hankering after absolutes, is the prime mover of his narrative art, driving him to make heroes of conventional pariahs, to devise his own idiosyncratic theology, to debunk many of our popular illusions about love, and to imagine a tragicomic political drama that is salvational in both a secular and a religious sense. Likewise, it is his angry impatience with the lives of safety and security that most of us long for and strive to attain that lends the world of his fictions its most distinctive and disquieting tone, for to enter fully into his novels is to understand that, in a very real sense, comfort and stasis are always already deadening complacency. Greene's vision of life is an unreasonable one, explicitly and unapologetically so; it stretches our credulity at times; it leads to contradictions; it is not an easy one to live out, even in part. But then surely the tragic spectacle of the twentieth century justified and perhaps demanded such a radical revaluation of values, such a thoroughgoing reimagination of our individual and collective existence. And if Greene's response to the era he lived through is itself full of a violence and an extremity that is both attractive and repellent, then this is only indication the more that he is the century's most representative English novelist.

Greene's fiction has been written about frequently, which makes it especially incumbent upon anyone taking up the subject at this date to justify his enterprise. The 1980s, for instance, saw the publication of a number of valuable general studies of Greene, including those by Roger Sharrock, Grahame Smith, Paul O'Prey, and R. H. Miller. Since then, convincing books on specific themes in the fiction have been produced by Daphna Erdinast-Vulcan, Brian Thomas, Robert Pendleton, and Brian Diemert. Furthermore, all this work of the last two decades lies atop a goodly foundation of earlier assessments by Allott and Farris, Peter Wolfe, and others.[2] Greene has, on balance, been well served by his commentators, though as

---

2. Roger Sharrock, *Saints, Sinners, and Comedians: The Novels of Graham Greene*; Grahame Smith, *The Achievement of Graham Greene*; Paul O'Prey, *A Reader's Guide to Graham Greene*; R. H. Miller, *Understanding Graham Greene*; Daphna Erdinast-Vulcan, *Graham Greene's Childless Fathers*; Brian Thomas, *An Underground Fate: The Idiom of Romance in the Later Novels of Graham Greene*; Robert Pendleton, *Graham Greene's Conradian Masterplot: The Arabesque of Influence*; Brian Diemert, *Graham Greene's Thrillers and the 1930's*; Kenneth Allott and Miriam Farris, *The Art of Graham Greene*; Peter Wolfe, *Graham Greene the Entertainer*.

others besides myself have noticed, there are shortcomings enough, for while "Greene is one of the most interpreted and discussed authors in 20th century British Literature[,] . . . much of that criticism remains redundant"; indeed, as another critic complains, "there is a surprising uniformity in the major evaluation[s] of Greene."[3] In addition to this frustrating sameness—from which the present study will in any case radically depart—the critical literature has, with notable exceptions here and there, evidenced what I would consider a more serious problem: a tendency to water down and domesticate Greene, to flatten out the peaks and valleys of his uncompromising vision of life, to overlook the extremity of his novels as if it were an embarrassment instead of a glory. If I could sum up my intentions in a single sentence, I would assert that this book has been written to correct this critical disservice—it has been written in order to let Greene be Greene, no matter how "unreasonable" or immoderate the result. And while I am not claiming that every aspect of his thought is characterized by proximity to an existential abyss—his vision of romantic love, for instance, is informed by a calm and worldly pessimism—I am claiming that his most dangerous topography has too frequently been admired from a safe and obscuring distance.

Much of the attempt to mainstream Greene has involved his religious views (though no aspect of his thought has wholly escaped the regularizers) and time and again one hears commentators of the last few decades scoffing at earlier reactions to our author that accused him of heresy—most often of the Jansenist or Manichean variety. What these later critics are often at pains to show is that Greene was in the main an orthodox communicant of the Catholic Church, if only we will consider his work from the proper angle. My quarrel with this endeavor is straightforward: any attempt to paint Greene's religious views as conventionally Catholic, or even Christian, does a disservice to the uniqueness—nay, the sheer strangeness—of his religious imaginings. Nor do I wish to return to the position of the forties and early fifties and box him into some sort of recognizable category of historical Christian heresy. Let it be said clearly: Graham Greene was a Catholic in the manner that William Blake was a

---

3. Carolyn Scott, "Review of R. H. Miller's *Understanding Graham Greene*," 189; Peter G. Christiansen, "The Art of Self-Preservation: Monsignor Quixote's Resistance to Don Quixote," 41.

Protestant—he occasionally attended the Sunday services, but in his literary works he created his own personal and powerful religious system. If it yet remains fruitful to examine Greene's thought in juxtaposition with the dogmas of the Catholic Church, it will not do to call him a mere heretic: he is properly nothing less than a heresiarch, for as we shall see, his attack upon orthodoxy is startlingly fresh and modern. And while this book's subject encompasses much more than Greene's religious views, one of its implicit arguments is that the word *heresy* most fittingly describes the tenor of his outlook on many of our common—and supposedly "commonsensical"—assumptions about the way we live now.

One of my models for this attempt to deduce an overarching system of thought from Greene's novels is that enduring classic of literary criticism, J. Hillis Miller's *The Disappearance of God: Five Nineteenth-Century Writers.* In that work, Miller is content to regard each of his authors' intellectual and emotional visions on its own terms, and not to worry overmuch at how idiosyncratic they appear or how difficult they might be to square with the more established and institutionalized religious, social, and psychological theories of their day. Also, he is unembarrassed when two particular ideas implicit in an author's oeuvre contradict each other—indeed, his whole approach seems to accept that any literary mind worth exploring will produce some notions that are in active tension with others of its own manufacture, and that a complex structure of intellection and feeling will always contain a vital element of dialogical self-testing within it. The result of these assumptions on Miller's part is that his portraits of great nineteenth-century figures emerge as representations of minds *in motion,* unquietly searching after a consummation or a reconciliation or a reintegration that they can never quite—or at best only fleetingly—realize. And while in what follows I will attempt, like Miller, to present my subject's body of thought synchronically wherever possible, a tolerance for contradiction and continuous evolution is vital to understanding the ongoing construction of Greene's worldview as it appears, disappears, and reappears in his novels.

I also feel emboldened to claim this book's kinship with *The Disappearance of God* in matters of subject as well as of method. I say this because it strikes me that Greene can profitably be seen as a twentieth-century descendent of those great Romantics and Victorians covered by Miller, who desperately attempted to find—

or rediscover—some spiritual point of contact with a fast-retreating and evermore unfathomable God. In this century, many of the practitioners of high Modernism assumed that the game was simply over and that any endeavor to search for hints of a vanished deity was a futile one, unlikely to repay the enormous effort it required amidst an era marked by so many other great abandonments of one kind or another. Greene, who was of the next generation, annoyed and even scandalized many by once more taking up the dubious search of which De Quincey, Brontë, Browning, Arnold, and Hopkins seemed to have written, each in his or her turn, the excruciating final chapter. Because he did so, it is understandable that some cannot help but see Greene as a kind of throwback or anachronism, though those who hold such a view can certainly be accused in turn of holding to a conception of literary and intellectual history that is dangerously shortsighted, embarrassingly mechanical, and naively progressivist. After all, nothing about Greene's sexual morality or his politics or his psychology reeks of musty Victorianism, and each is deeply intertwined with his conception of God. As I hope will become clear, his religious vision is one that could only take shape in, and for, the harrowing world of the twentieth century.

This book is intended to be about Greene's thought as it emerges through his novels, which means that my presentation of evidence, in the context of his complete range of writings, will be selective, and that in one sense at least the above-mentioned easygoingness concerning our author's self-contradictions will not apply. Greene was, to take one category of example, perfectly capable of sounding like an orthodox Catholic in some of his stage plays, essays, journalistic pieces, and letters to the editor, whereas in his fiction "Greene, the artist, always overrides Greene, the church-goer."[4] And so, where the ideas expressed in the nonfiction genres appear to clash with the more heretical, disturbing, and interesting notions put forward in the novels, the latter will trump and the former will simply be ignored. This strategy is justified by the simple fact that Graham Greene will be remembered as a novelist, not as a dramatist, essayist, or journalist. It is the novels that are his highest achievements, and thus we should be most vitally interested in the world that they construct. This is an unremarkable position to take in literary studies, for many

4. S. K. Sharma, *Graham Greene: The Search for Belief,* 217.

a writer puts forward a vision of life within her creative works that is in some ways incompatible with her utterances in other media—and we, as individuals primarily interested in things literary, are not confused about which vision will and ought to garner our primary attention. In Greene's case, I think one is further justified in allowing the voice from the novels to occasionally drown out that emerging from the other genres because it seems to me that his fictions in many instances represent the advance guard of his thought. More than once, important positions he arrived at only late in life within essays, articles, or interviews were strikingly anticipated in even some of his earliest novels. The act of crafting fiction apparently released extraordinary intellectual crosscurrents within Greene that did not blow as strongly when he was engaged in other kinds of writing—from the novels emerges a voice not only more passionate and anguished, but often self-prophetic.

The overall structure formed by the five chapters that follow is, I hope, straightforward. Each chapter focuses upon a major aspect of Greene's thought as expressed in the novels, and though all of the chapters range widely about his canon in the course of constructing their arguments, each one is also primarily concerned with a partic-ular work of fiction. Not incidentally, the five novels I thus single out as being peculiarly illustrative of Greene's most important themes—*Brighton Rock, The Power and the Glory, The Heart of the Matter, The Comedians,* and *The Honorary Consul*—are also, in my opinion, the masterpieces of his literary career. However, since all such rankings eventually come down to matters of taste and ultimately prove more divisive than illuminating, I do not wish to insist upon this view with any stridency—those who disagree with me will, I hope, find their own preferences no impediment to a dispassionate assessment of my arguments concerning his fictions as a whole and the body of thought they put forward. By the end of this book, most of Greene's novels will have been touched upon in some manner, and just as the five major subjects I explore interpenetrate one another at many points, so the great majority of Greene's canon is drawn upon to illuminate his overarching portrait of life.

I suppose it is also incumbent upon someone writing a book of this kind to explain why certain subjects that one might rea-sonably expect to encounter are not in fact to be covered. The two absences that come most readily to mind are Greene's attitude toward questions of gender, and his place in twentieth-century literary history—especially his relationship to the high Modernism he reacted so strongly against. The first topic is bypassed because there seems to be remarkably little to say about it. The fact is that Greene was almost exclusively interested in male experience, that most (though not all) of the women in his books play at best supporting roles, and that his attitudes toward questions of gendered power were unselfconsciously conventional for a man of his time. Thus, any chapter-length exploration of the question would largely consist of an iteration of negatives and a belaboring of lacunae that would strike even readers vitally interested in issues of sexual politics as predictable and unrewarding. In his severely limited imaginative engagement with female ways of knowing, as in his early flirtations with anti-Semitism, Greene is all the more—and sadly in such instances—the representative writer of his time.

Our author's relationship to the Modernist and Postmodernist movements, however, presents an opposite kind of problem. Not only is the proper placement of Greene within the literary schools of the passing century too large and complex an undertaking to fit within a single chapter, but such an endeavor, if done conscientiously, would necessarily dilute the focus of this book, since it would lead me into extended comparative investigations concerning the thoughts and methods of dozens of other writers, as well as into complex issues of reception theory, the influence of the cinema, and the history of publishing. While I do undertake, in the first chapter, to sketch out a genealogy of influence quite different from that usually assumed to have shaped Greene's concerns, that attempt is meant to be suggestive rather than exhaustive. To describe with any kind of completeness and detail the world constructed by Greene's novels, as I have here tried to do, is subject enough for any single book. A full and just description of his place in literary history, while a worthy and worthwhile subject, must simply await another occasion.

What I hope *has* made it into this book is a sense of why I fervently believe that Greene matters. To me, what is most attractive about his novels is that, when preserved from critics who would sanitize him, they are so patently *unsafe*—they do not "affirm life" in any uncomplicated or unqualified way; they offer at best a tenuous redemption often indistinguishable from damnation; they demand that we radically change our lives. Greene's vision of the modern world is one of endemic and excruciating extremity, and his lack of tolerance for our ongoing efforts to paper over and avert our eyes from this profoundly important fact makes him more of an existentialist than a humanist, and thus an unfit companion for those who, while willing to be made genuinely uneasy during the course of their fiction reading, demand a "reconciling" or "healing" vision at the end of it all. Greene has scant comfort to offer such an audience, and this places his novels among a select group even within the ranks of first-tier literature. Furthermore, surely few if any novelists can lay claim to a comparable breadth of what might be called "ironic moral range": that ability to find—or better, that insistence that we always *do* find—what is noblest and bravest and most charitable about ourselves amidst back-alleys, brothels, and sewers, both physical and figurative. In this deliberate, contrarian, and ultimately convincing refutation of our familiar and comfortable moral compasses, only Dostoyevsky— that other crafter of absolutist fictions—has any pretension to be his peer. And finally, perhaps most importantly, what a wonder it is for Greene to have accomplished such grim cerebral business while at the same time so unashamedly—nay, delightedly—deploying all the loud and unrefined and un-Jamesian ordinance of "popular" novel writing. What "canonical" author, his mentor Conrad included, is so consistently a master of suspense and sheer narrative momentum? To paraphrase a literary adage, who else among novelists of the passing century has succeeded in so thoroughly delighting while at the same time so tough-mindedly instructing?

Roger Sharrock, writing of this virtuosic double game of Greene's, asserts that while "learning his trade during the major phase of the modern movement and the highbrow novel[,] he has never ceased to be a popular writer in the ordinary sense of one who communicates to a wide uncliqueish public while retaining the full force of his personal vision and technical accomplishment. . . . [H]e is there on the revolving bookstall in the airport or supermarket alongside the books of disaster movies and the paperbacks with soft-pornographic covers."[5] This is no hyperbole, since I myself first hurriedly picked up a novel of Greene's at an airport bookshop as I left on a vacation to Italy. Eventually I wound up on a hotel balcony a thousand feet above Amalfi, but I almost might as well have stayed home, for

5. Sharrock, *Saints*, 11–12.

the book had unexpectedly gone off in my hands, its sad beauty blinding me to perhaps the most gorgeous prospect on earth and my first, long-awaited view of the Mediterranean. Greene's fictions have continued to detonate in my life ever since, and this book is above all an attempt to wreak—even among his veteran readers and critics—as much collateral damage as possible.

1 The Mediated and the Absolute

A Genealogy of *Brighton Rock*

I

Reading Graham Greene and the critical literature devoted to him, one quickly discovers the existence of a certain handful of passages that time and again provoke annoyance and even anger from his commentators. One of the scenes that rarely fails to irritate is the following exchange from *Brighton Rock,* in which the do-gooding and good-timing Ida Arnold is attempting to convince young Rose that Pinkie, her murderous coreligionist, will eventually bring her to grief.

> "He wouldn't do me any harm."
> "You're young. You don't know things like I do."
> "There's things *you* don't know." She brooded darkly by the bed, while the woman argued on: a God wept in a garden and cried out upon a cross; Molly Carthew went to everlasting fire.
> "I know one thing you don't. I know the difference between Right and Wrong. They didn't teach you *that* at school."
> Rose didn't answer; the woman was quite right: the two words meant nothing to her. Their taste was extinguished by stronger foods—Good and Evil. The woman could tell her nothing she didn't know about these—she knew by tests as clear as mathematics that Pinkie was evil—what did it matter in that case whether he was right or wrong? (*BR, 199*)

This and similar episodes incite critics to accuse Greene of granting his Catholic characters a larger and deeper moral capacity—for things both benign and malignant—than he confers upon the various nominal Protestants, zealous atheists, facile spiritualists, and feckless liberals who otherwise people his fiction. George Orwell, for instance, complains that in Greene's novels "Hell is a sort of high-class night club, entry to which is reserved for Catholics only, since the others, the non-Catholics, are too ignorant to be held guilty, like the beasts that perish." This idea is echoed by Robert O. Evans, who asserts that for Greene "the Catholic is closer to God and at the same time closer to Satan" than other types of characters.[1] What assessments like these seem to share—and what gives some of them their note of tartness—is an implicit assumption that Greene "favors" his Catholic characters in this way out of a straightforward prejudice toward his own religion—as if he had in mind no more than a desire to propagate the faith by depicting its adherents as all possessing strikingly capacious moral organs. Now, while it would be futile to deny that the protagonists of Greene's middle period tend to be Catholics, I would like to argue that Pinkie's Catholicism is best seen as part of a larger theme that runs through many of Greene's novels, even those in which the Catholic Church is only the most peripheral concern. In the end, we will be able to see Pinkie and the other Catholic characters' preferential proximity to absolute good and evil in proper context, and to understand Greene's placement of them there as something more interesting and ambitious than mere cheerleading for a religion in which he only fitfully believed.

Tracing this larger theme will first involve placing our author within a genealogy of influence that might at first seem a bit surprising. As has long been understood, the major figure among Greene's literary progenitors—aside from the popular thriller writers of his childhood such as Stevenson, Haggard, and Buchan—is Joseph Conrad, whose mark is clearly visible in various precincts of "Greeneland." The Assistant Commissioner of *It's a Battlefield,* for instance, seems to bear an almost plagiaristic likeness to the character of that same name in *The Secret Agent,* and Greene famously gave up reading Conrad when he came to believe his own books were being bullied out of shape by his mentor's too-powerful example. My alternative genealogy has the virtue of retaining Conrad, but it would frame him with the figures of Emily Brontë and D. H. Lawrence.

This trio of authors must be viewed together when considering Greene because, I believe, all four mount a very similar kind of attack against the habits, norms, and imaginative boundaries of bourgeois society. Briefly put, these writers implicitly or explicitly accuse middle-class orthodoxies of constricting our moral imaginations and

1. George Orwell, "The Sanctified Sinner," 105–9; Robert O. Evans, "The Satanist Fallacy of *Brighton Rock,*" 160.

cutting us off from vital sources of emotional, intellectual, and spiritual energies in the name of stability, efficiency, and rational control over a world of threatening—but also potentially exhilarating and illuminating—contingency. It is their contention that the way we live now blunts our minds, deliberately excluding experiences at the dangerous high and low ends of life's spectrum in order to create a world of anodyne mediocrity. According to such a view, the great majority of us have made a kind of anti-Faustian bargain, turning away from explosive gnosis at the cost of a lifetime of crimping stasis. This charge having been made, there is one other element that distinguishes this particular line of authors: their insistence that the only cure for our present condition lies in turning decisively away from the mediated world that we have constructed to enthusiastically embrace the world of the absolutes, despite—or rather, because of—all its attendant perils.[2]

This last point needs some clarification. By "the mediated world" I refer to those bourgeois habits of mind that tend to value the community's interest in stability over the individual's in liberty, to insist that most situations can be negotiated by means of reasoned choices, to foreground questions of manners and etiquette, and to construct love as merely one emotion among others, thus seeing it as subject to the usual array of communal pressures. In other words, there are a wealth of "mediating" structures between the individual and the large, terrible, final questions of life. The absolutistic world, on the other hand, consists of that mental orientation which valorizes individual freedom over social restraint, sees life as rife with mysterious riddles and excruciating paradoxes insoluble by appeals to reason, foregrounds large existential questions rather than everyday concerns, and portrays love as a transcendent force beyond the writ of social restraints.[3] In this realm, to paraphrase Camus, you don't need to wait for the Last Judgment—it happens every day. To make the distinction clearer, one might nominate Jane Austen as the quintessential novelist of the mediated world, for no one in the pages of her fictions ever steps outside the ordered

2. The use of the terms *mediated* and *absolute* as tools of literary classification was first suggested to me by Anthony Winner.

3. These elaborations on the terms *mediated* and *absolute* are largely, though not wholly, taken from the terminology of Joseph Wiesenfarth in his *Gothic Manners and the Classic English Novel*, 11–15. I employ some of his categories fully realizing that I am lifting them out of context.

frame of bourgeois normality to ponder the ultimate meaning of life. By contrast, the premier exemplar of an absolutistic novelist might be Dostoyevsky, whose tortured or ecstatic characters seem to pose such dire questions with harrowing frequency. Of course for our purposes these two categories are only descriptive and no value judgment is implied. However, they are oftentimes implicit fighting words for those authors involved in the forging of such divergent fictional worlds, for the two camps are frequently engaged in an intertextual struggle over what the novel as a genre should properly be and do. As Jane Austen's narrator says near the close of *Mansfield Park:* "Let other pens dwell on guilt and misery. I quit such odious subjects as soon as I can, impatient to restore every body, not greatly in fault themselves, to tolerable comfort, and to have done with all the rest." It is relevant to note in this regard that Greene has admitted that he "do[es] not like Jane Austen" and has "never been able to read her. . . . Jane Austen is [his] blind spot in the novel."[4]

A brief survey of Greene's predecessors in this absolutistic campaign against middle-class normality will provide us with an idea of where and why our author begins his own critique of the bourgeois cast of mind. Basically, all the novelists in the tradition under discussion posit a kind of gnosis (not to be confused with the teachings of Classical Gnosticism) that is available only through the experience of extreme states of feeling and moral apperception located beyond the pale of what middle-class orthodoxies deem seemly, prudent, and ethically acceptable. This gnosis is dangerous to both mind and flesh—the threat (or promise) of madness and death attends it at all times—but this is seen as the wholly necessary risk that the individual must run if the energizing illumination that awaits in the realm of the absolutes is to be gained. Indeed, it is only a life situated on the thin edge of peril—physical and psychic—that can partake of the exhilarating forces that render existence sufficiently heroic and tragic to fully satisfy our aesthetic faculties. As J. Hillis Miller says in connection with Brontë, "unmediated relations with others may be a mortal danger to the self, but such relations are also a way of living a deeper and more authentic life."[5] This mode of existence, of

4. Jane Austen, *Mansfield Park,* 466; Greene is quoted in A. F. Cassis, ed., *Graham Greene: Man of Paradox,* 239.

5. J. Hillis Miller, *The Disappearance of God: Five Nineteenth-Century Writers,* 169.

course, is open only to a tiny elite (though *not* an elite possessed of political power), and a good deal of scorn is directed at the plodding majority who sleep and feed and know not the invigorating danger.

Wuthering Heights, that strange and troubling book that inhabits the point of unstable equilibrium between Romantic and Victorian sensibilities, introduces into the English novel attitudes that Greene will extend and transform a century later. In Emily Brontë's case, the absolutistic gnosis she offers her chosen characters takes the form of a faculty of communication between individuals so comprehensive and intense that it almost constitutes the fusing of identities: as Catherine famously explains to Nelly Dean, "I *am* Heathcliff." That this heightened state of spiritual interpenetration is no mere extension of the bourgeois desideratum of rational affection, and is in fact a state of being wholly distinct and fiercely antithetical to it, is made clear when Nelly foolishly attempts to equate the two in Heathcliff's presence. Remarking on how Catherine's illness has marred both her looks and her mind, the housekeeper opines that any friend of the invalid's must "sustain his affection hereafter by the remembrance of what she once was, by common humanity, and a sense of duty!" The response she receives is illuminating:

> "That is quite possible," remarked Heathcliff, forcing himself to seem calm, "quite possible that your master should have nothing but common humanity, and a sense of duty to fall back upon. But do you imagine that I shall leave Catherine to his *duty* and *humanity?* and can you compare my feelings respecting Catherine, to his?"[6]

In the absolutistic milieu that distinguishes the Heights from Thrushcross Grange, the words *duty* and *humanity* are the equivalent of curses, for they synoptically represent the kind of rational/rationed affection and delayed gratification that is the hallmark of mediated love. Indeed, when Catherine wishes to torment Heathcliff, she hits her mark directly by spinning out an imaginary future for him that corresponds to a bourgeois ideal—that of romantic love's eventual diminution through a mourning process that reconciles one to continuing domestic responsibilities:

6. Emily Brontë, *Wuthering Heights,* 74, 125 (Brontë's italics; italics in all quotations are in the original, except where noted).

"Will you forget me—will you be happy when I am in the earth? Will you say twenty years hence, 'That's the grave of Catherine Earnshaw. I loved her long ago, and was wretched to lose her; but it is past. I've loved many others since—my children are dearer to me than she was, and, at death, I shall not rejoice that I am going to her, I shall be sorry that I must leave them!' Will you say so, Heathcliff?"

"Don't torture me till I'm as mad as yourself," cried he, wrenching his head free, and grinding his teeth.[7]

As if to pointedly refute this prognostication of his attitude toward Catherine's gravesite, Heathcliff eventually exhumes and embraces her corpse.

It is a distinguishing feature of Brontë's absolutistic gnosis—as it will be later of Greene's—that the *intensity* of emotion it demands, creates, or entails is more important than the *kind* of emotion that is experienced. It is as if love and hate were chemicals that, at the room temperature of middle-class normality, have widely divergent qualities, but which, under the plasma-producing heats of the absolute realm, come to possess many more properties in common. In *Wuthering Heights,* the familiar Christian yardstick that damns wrath while valorizing love and forgiveness has been displaced from its horizontal axis to the vertical, and consequently only weakly felt emotions are denigrated while all vehement ones are lauded, be they those of affection or enmity. For instance, when Edgar confronts Catherine over Heathcliff's unauthorized incursion into the Grange "without any anger in his voice, but with much sorrowful despondency," and questions her calmly, Catherine is offended by his tone: "'Oh, for mercy's sake,' interrupted the mistress, stamping her foot, 'for mercy's sake, let us hear no more of it now! Your cold blood cannot be worked into a fever; your veins are full of ice-water, but mine are boiling, and the sight of such chilliness makes them dance.'" Likewise, when Heathcliff imagines the future for himself and the now-deceased Catherine, he is quite willing that it be a thoroughly painful one, for it appears that in such circumstances only the most intense suffering will ensure their continued spiritual commingling. When Nelly, that embodiment of bourgeois reasonableness, insists that "her life closed in a gentle dream—may she wake as kindly in

7. Ibid., 133.

the other world," Heathcliff replies in tones that might belong to *The End of the Affair*'s bereaved lover, Maurice Bendrix:

> "May she wake in torment!" he cried, with frightful vehemence, stamping his foot, and groaning in a sudden paroxysm of ungovernable passion. "Why, she's a liar to the end! Where is she? Not *there*—not in heaven—not perished—where? Oh! you said you cared nothing for my sufferings! And I pray one prayer—I repeat it till my tongue stiffens—Catherine Earnshaw, may you not rest, as long as I am living! You said I killed you—haunt me, then! The murdered *do* haunt their murderers, I believe. I know that ghosts *have* wandered on earth. Be with me always—take any form—drive me mad! only *do* not leave me in this abyss, where I cannot find you! Oh, God! it is unutterable! I *cannot* live without my life! I *cannot* live without my soul!"[8]

We shall find that Greene has likewise "re-identified the villain[s]" to include the lukewarm of any moral stripe, and redefined our conventional moral vocabulary until "the big terms expressing their cold virtues [are] bad, whereas the big terms expressing the warm emotions—Revenge, Jealousy, Passion, etc. . . . [are] good."[9]

As the above passage strongly hints, it is difficult to celebrate an absolutistic gnosis while retaining a religious conception that is even nominally orthodox. When Heathcliff ends his directions for his own funeral by declaring, "I tell you, I have nearly attained *my* heaven; and that of others is altogether unvalued and uncoveted by me!" we witness the extent to which his craving for continued communion with Catherine has pushed aside any desire for communion with a recognizably Christian God. Many of Brontë's notions of sin and redemption are certainly singular, but in illuminating some of them J. Hillis Miller could as easily be talking of Greene: "Death is the true goal of life, and death is most quickly reached by those who exhaust themselves in the futile attempt to deny the law of separateness imposed by God. . . . [T]he two kinds of action which lead most directly to death are illicit love and physical violence. Though sadistic cruelty or illicit union with another person are not the same things as death and the union with God which follows death, they are more

8. Ibid., 101, 139.
9. John Spurling, *Graham Greene,* 28.

like them than patient endurance of separateness. They break down the tough envelope of the self and prepare it for its dissolution into the boundless sympathy and love of heaven."[10] Indeed, it will become clear that Heathcliff's preceding remark about enjoying a unique and personalized heaven could easily stand as an epigram for Greene's own idiosyncratic religious vision.

It is always possible to argue, of course, that *Wuthering Heights* eventually takes back much of what it gives. True, by the end of the book, horticulture and literacy have returned to the Heights, and watered-down versions of Cathy and Heathcliff are in possession. However, most of us leave the book feeling somewhat the way we do about Shakespeare's problem plays—that the tragic elements we have encountered cannot be adequately assimilated to the ostensibly comic structure of the work. As Robert Polhemus reminds us, there can be little dispute concerning what side of the mediated/absolutistic divide Brontë's novel finally resides on: "One strain in Brontë is a hope that the novel can teach proper love, as, say *Pride and Prejudice* does. But *Wuthering Heights* is much better at starting erotic ghosts than at containing them. Conflict exists between the mediation of love through literacy and books—reading and writing—and the drive, erotic in itself, for unmediated love."[11] At book's end, the world may be safe for those immanent if not eminent Victorians, Nelly Dean and Mr. Lockwood, but most readers would agree that a glory has passed away from the earth.

When we turn to Conrad, we find that the great gulf fixed between the mediated and the absolute, which in Brontë was geographical (or perhaps a matter of altitude), has now become centered on gender and occupation. One can still perhaps conceive of the split as having something to do with location, with absolutistic sailors battling human darkness and elemental indifference on the world's uncivilized peripheries and there garnering knowledge unavailable to those who sit safely by firesides in Europe, but this is as much as to say with Marlow in *Heart of Darkness* that "they—the women I mean—are out of it—should be out of it." As he has explained previously, the world

10. Brontë, *Wuthering Heights,* 263 (Brontë's italics); Miller, *Disappearance of God,* 203–4.
11. Robert Polhemus, *Erotic Faith: Being in Love from Jane Austen to D. H. Lawrence,* 101.

women inhabit is "out of touch with truth" and "too beautiful altogether," a fragile objet d'art that would shatter at the touch of "some
confounded fact we men have been living contentedly with ever
since the day of creation." True, Marlow attempts at times to make
the male and female spheres appear as two interdependent halves of
a necessary dyad, asserting that "we must help them to stay in that
beautiful world of their own, lest ours gets worse," but such efforts
are less than convincing. In the end, gnosis always trumps safety—
no one comes away from the novel willing to value the Intended's
ignorance above Marlow's insight. The pervasive tone of Conrad's
fictions insists, in spite of Marlow's dire reckoning of the psychic
costs of absolutistic vision and in spite of the high toll in suicides
among Conradian initiates into the dark truths, that it is a finer thing
by far to be one who has dangerously peered than one whose eyes
have been dimmed by gender or occupation or circumstance. To
illustrate this, we need only compare two telling passages. In *Heart
of Darkness,* the Little Russian's ambiguous involvement with Kurtz's
atrocities puts him in, to put it mildly, a dubious moral position vis-
à-vis the intermittently scandalized Marlow. But even this figure is
partially redeemed by his total immersion in the realm of absolutes—
that is to say, by his life of chronic danger. Marlow even confesses
himself to be "seduced into something like admiration—like envy.
Glamour urged him on, glamour kept him unscathed. He surely
wanted nothing from the wilderness but space to breathe in and
to push on through. His need was to exist, and to move onwards at
the greatest possible risk, and with a maximum of privation. If the
absolutely pure, uncalculating, unpractical spirit of adventure had
ever ruled a human being, it ruled this be-patched youth. I almost
envied him the possession of his modest and clear flame."[12] Contrast
this with the klaxon-blast of scorn that the Marlow of *Lord Jim* directs
at travelers in somewhat more comfortable circumstances:

> An outward-bound mail-boat had come in that afternoon, and the
> big dining-room of the hotel was more than half full of people
> with a-hundred-pounds-round-the-world tickets in their pockets.
> There were married couples looking domesticated and bored with
> each other in the midst of their travels; there were small parties

12. Joseph Conrad, *Heart of Darkness,* 84, 39, 84, 93.

and large parties, and lone individuals dining solemnly or feasting boisterously, but all thinking, conversing, joking, or scowling as was their wont at home; and just as intelligently receptive of new impressions as their trunks upstairs. Henceforth they would be labeled as having passed through this and that place, and so would be their luggage. They would cherish this distinction of their persons, and preserve the gummed tickets on their portmanteaus as documentary evidence, as the only permanent trace of their improving enterprise. . . . [N]ow and then a girl's laugh would be heard, as innocent and empty as her mind.[13]

Clearly, in Conrad's nautical world, passengers are all honorary women, and as such shut away below decks from that dangerous but invaluable illumination that the sea sometimes deigns to bestow upon those who inhabit the bridge.

The most interesting specific parallels between Conrad's handling of our theme and Greene's is in the irrevocable nature of the absolutistic vocation. In *Wuthering Heights,* Catherine and Heathcliff always seem to be keeping a suspicious eye on each another, fearful that one or the other will decide that their deadly serious game is not worth its scorching candle and defect to the creature comforts and psychic relief of the Grange. Indeed, Heathcliff's self-imposed exile from the Heights is precipitated by his mistaken belief that Catherine has in fact gone over to the other side. In Conrad's novels, however, no such danger exists. What Marlow quickly discovers when he returns from Kurtz's Inner Station to the mediated civilization of Brussels is that you can't go home again:

I found myself back in the sepulchral city resenting the sight of people hurrying through the streets to filch a little money from each other, to devour their infamous cookery, to gulp their unwholesome beer, to dream their insignificant and silly dreams. They trespassed upon my thoughts. They were intruders whose knowledge of life was to me an irritating pretense, because I felt so sure they could not possibly know the things I knew. Their bearing, which was simply the bearing of commonplace individuals going about their business in the assurance of perfect safety, was offensive to me like the outrageous flauntings of folly in the face of a danger it is unable

13. Joseph Conrad, *Lord Jim,* 99–100.

> to comprehend. I had no particular desire to enlighten them, but
> I had some difficulty in restraining myself from laughing in their
> faces, so full of stupid importance.[14]

This notion that all travel into the realm of the absolute is by one-way-
ticket is insisted upon by Greene. Whether it is Raven's introduction
into terror by means of his mother's suicide, Pinkie's by witnessing
his parents' primal scene, the whisky priest's by pursuit, or even
Querry's by searing self-scrutiny, the initiate into gnosis is forever
unfitted to join or rejoin the mediated mainstream and can only
claim membership in communities that exist, whether permanently
or evanescently, on the dangerous margins of society. The whisky
priest, after all, has a chance to return to something like his old
routine of altar guilds and communion suppers, but, having been
rebaptized in the acid bath of the absolute, he chooses instead to
return to a more arduous duty and an almost certain death. As with
Conrad's sailors and, later, La Carré's spies, with Greene there is no
coming in from the heat.

It is possible, I think, to consider our theme's manifestation in
D. H. Lawrence without at once going into the vexed question of
Greene's relationship with, or participation in, or rejection of, high
Modernism. It is enough for our current purposes that references
in *Stamboul Train* and *The Lawless Roads* make it clear that he was
familiar with Lawrence's work and saw fit to mention it alongside
Joyce's. If he later in life voiced skepticism about "the grand designs
of Lawrence and the myth of his plumed serpent,"[15] this merely
marks him as a typical postwar reader of those fictions and does
not preclude us from seeing parallels between Lawrence's critique
of mediated society and Greene's own. Lawrence brings our theme
firmly into the twentieth century in part by erasing the hierarchies of
gender that Conrad had yoked to it. This is especially evident in the
short novel *St. Mawr* (1925), where it is the female protagonist, Lou
Witt, and her mother who yearn for and (in Lou's case) eventually
achieve a life in touch with absolutistic energies. Stuck in a sexless
marriage and surrounded by fashionable dullards, Lou voices discon-
tent with "our whole eunuch civilization, nasty-minded as eunuchs

---

14. Conrad, *Heart of Darkness,* 113–14.
15. Cassis, *Man of Paradox,* 136.

are, with their kind of sneaking, sterilizing cruelty," and sums up even her possible lovers as "unrealities" and "nonentit[ies]." Her dissatisfaction with the soul-narrowing restraints of her materially privileged milieu are brought to a head by her meeting with the mysterious and violent stallion St. Mawr, whom Lawrence insists is a kind of animistic emanation from an earlier heroic age and whom Lou instinctively understands to be both catalyst and conduit for powerful primal energies that have long lain dormant within her. The problem with St. Mawr from the perspective of Lou's husband and acquaintances—who are "horsey" in a quite conventional sense— is that he is a killer, having already been the cause of two deaths. It is Lou, in a conversation with the local Dean, who begins to identify danger as the necessary price of a life imbued with redemptive intensities:

> "A vicious horse is worse than a vicious man—except that you are free to put him six feet underground, and end his vice finally, by your own act."
> "Do you think St. Mawr is vicious?" said Lou.
> "Well, of course—if we're driven to definitions!—I know he's dangerous."
> "And do you think we ought to shoot everything that is dangerous?" asked Lou, her color rising.[16]

The local majority's answer to this question being a resounding "yes," Lou is driven "almost . . . to hatred" against "these awful, house-bred, house-inbred human beings." Lou's mother is in general agreement with her, and strikes a Brontë-esque note by stating that she herself needs "something to stand up against, no matter whether it's great heat or great cold. This climate, like the food and the people, is most always lukewarm or tepid, one or the other. And the tepid and the lukewarm are not really my line." Her—to the mediated mind's—topsy-turvy view of death shows that she herself is already on the road to a loftier and stonier psychic landscape: "And you know, Louise, I've come to the conclusion that hardly anybody in the world really lives, and so hardly anybody really dies. They may well say: *O Death, where is thy sting-a-ling-a-ling?* Even Death can't sting those

16. D. H. Lawrence, *St. Mawr,* 90, 27, 80.

that have never really lived. . . . I want death to be real to me. . . . I *want* it to hurt me, Louise. If it hurts me enough, I shall know I was alive."[17]

The only solution turns out to be immigration to the American west, where, amid the mountainous desert of New Mexico, Lou lays claim to a ranch whose "pure beauty, *absolute* beauty" wrought powerful changes within the soul of a pioneer woman from New England in the previous century. Fighting continually against the landscape's almost purposeful antipathy to human occupation, this precursor of Lou's felt herself penetrated by a "curious, frenzied energy" that "enter[ed] her like a sort of sex passion, intensifying her ego, making her full of violence and of blind female energy. The energy, and the blindness of it! A strange blind frenzy, like an intoxication while it lasted." Lou, proclaiming that she has finally found what might be termed the objective correlative of her now fully emergent absolutistic yearnings—*"this is the place"*—determines to give herself over in a kind of mystic marriage to the autochthonous genius of the place:

> "There's something . . . that loves me and wants me. I can't tell you what it is. It's a spirit. And it's here, on this ranch. It's here, in this landscape. It's something more real to me than men are, and it soothes me, and it holds me up. I don't know what it is, definitely. It's something wild, that will hurt me sometimes and will wear me down sometimes. I know it. But it's something big, bigger than men, bigger than people, bigger than religion. It's something to do with wild America. And it's something to do with me. It's a mission, if you like."[18]

Although there is an air of breathless vagueness about Lawrence's vision that seems worlds away from the seedy specificities of Greeneland, the kinds of places that Lawrence's protagonists come to inhabit have many affinities with the psychological environments of Greene's more darkly hued heroes. They are both places of great power and danger, where intensity is purchased at the price of mortal risk and deeper human empathy always arrives encumbered with profound loneliness—and they are both sharply lit, sharply

17. Lawrence, *St. Mawr,* 80, 81, 85–86.
18. Lawrence, *St. Mawr,* 147, 145, 141, 158.

shadowed summits, where an existential freedom redeems life from the soul-straitening daily routines of the good, gray, bourgeois world below.

One of the implications of situating Graham Greene within the foregoing strain of the English novel's social critique has to do with motive. Once we see the tradition that stands behind some of the absolutistic protagonists such as *Brighton Rock*'s Pinkie and Rose, we can begin to see their exceptionalism as something more than an advertisement for the moral frissons of Catholicism. Now Greene may indeed be making the point that Catholics tend to live more absolutistic lives than other sorts of people, but it is my contention that in dealing with characters like Pinkie and Rose our focus should more properly be on the author's conception of what it means to live in a mediated or an absolutistic fashion *in a general sense,* and not on Catholicism in particular. There are other gateways to the absolute in Greene's fictional world than Catholicism: political commitment is one, criminality is another, sheer chance is a third, and still more could be listed. In what follows, I will attempt to illustrate how Greene carries on and lends his own peculiar stamp to the theme we have heretofore traced through Brontë, Conrad, and Lawrence. It is my belief that such a discussion will throw light not so much upon Greene the religious apologist as upon Greene the scourge of middle-class compromise.

II

If, like *Heart of Darkness, Brighton Rock* posits the existence of a dark but mind-expanding gnosis, Ida Arnold, like Conrad's Intended, is "out of it—completely."[19] At several points in the novel, her lack of some essential knowledge is insisted upon. Rose, for instance, declaring her loyalty to Pinkie, asserts that she would rather "burn with [him] than be like Her. . . . She's ignorant" (*BR,* 114). And when Ida herself confronts the girl and contends that her meddling is just an attempt to insure that the innocent don't suffer, Rose replies: "As if you knew . . . who was innocent" (121–22). For her part, of course, Ida is always ready to brag about the extent of her worldly knowledge—how long she's knocked about—but in this novel, *worldly* is a synonym for *mediated,* and there is a higher knowingness that

19. Conrad, *Heart of Darkness,* 84.

is a matter of intensity rather than duration.[20] In a necessarily con-
voluted passage, Greene manages to evoke both Rose's naïveté and
her participation in absolutistic gnosis simultaneously:

> "You're young. That's what it is," Ida said, "romantic. I was like
> you once. You'll grow out of it. All you need is a bit of experience."
> The Nelson Place eyes stared back at her without understanding.
> Driven to her hole the small animal peered out at the bright and
> breezy world; in the hole were murder, copulation, extreme poverty,
> fidelity and the love and fear of God, but the small animal had not
> the knowledge to deny that only in the glare and open world outside
> was something which people called experience. (123)

As for Pinkie, his unworldly or otherworldly experience is written
upon his features. If eyes are in fact the mirror of the soul, the boy
has apparently lived a lifetime and more in his seventeen years,
for "his gray eyes had an effect of heartlessness like an old man's
in which human feeling has died" (8) and are "touched with the
annihilating eternity from which he had come and to which he went"
(21)—indeed, they "had never been young" (49). It is entirely to
the point that Pinkie's age is so frequently mentioned—that he is
so often referred to as "the Boy"—for the juxtaposition of his moral
extremity and his lack of years is continual evidence that in *Brighton
Rock* worldly knowledge is shadowed by a competitor.

But what exactly is Ida ignorant *of?* One answer assuredly is
Catholic doctrine—"a zenithal paradise, a nadiral hell," to borrow
from Thomas Hardy[21]—for that is unquestionably one avenue into
the absolute, but the novel also makes it clear that her lack of
knowledge embraces attitudes toward life that are not themselves
coextensive with Catholic orthodoxy. For one thing, she lacks any
notion of the relentless entropy shadowing human existence—an
understanding that the overall trajectory of the sensual and emotional life is necessarily a downward one. For Ida, "life [is] sunlight
on brass bedposts, Ruby port, the leap of the heart when the outsider you have backed passes the post and the colours go bobbing
up. Life [is] poor Fred's mouth pressed down on hers in the taxi,
vibrating with the engine along the parade. . . . There was something

20. See David L. Kubal, "Graham Greene's *Brighton Rock:* The Political
Theme," 50.
21. Thomas Hardy, *Tess of the d'Urbervilles,* 218.

dangerous and remorseless in her optimism" (36). When it comes
to Ida's vision of final things we find only an absence, a spiral of
truncated notions that endlessly doubles back upon itself under the
impetus of panicked denial: "Nothing could ever make her believe
that one day she too, like Fred, would be where the worms . . . Her
mind couldn't take that track; she could go only a short way before
the points automatically shifted and set her vibrating down the accustomed line, the season ticket line marked by desirable residence
and advertisements of cruises and small fenced boskages for rural
love" (144, Greene's ellipses). By contrast, Pinkie's overview of the
human condition is both far-reaching and radically entropic: "I'll tell
you what [life] is. It's gaol, it's not knowing where to get some money.
Worms and cataract, cancer. You hear 'em shrieking from the upper
windows—children being born. It's dying slowly" (226). This might
be mistaken for an orthodox "contempt for the world" were it not for
the fact that while Pinkie can enthusiastically affirm hell—"of course
there's Hell[, f]lames and damnation . . . torments"—the possibility
of heaven only rates an apathetic "Oh, maybe . . . maybe" (52). In
Pinkie's view, life arcs downward, endlessly.

Which of these two descriptions of the human condition is en-
dorsed by the novel as a whole, every reader feels. Whereas Pinkie
may be half-wrong (at least) about any supposed afterlife, Ida is
wholly mistaken about the tenor of this one. In this regard, the text's
details are eloquent: a raped and murdered child in the newspaper,
a blind band marching through the gutter, the porcine sunbathers,
the municipal building resembling a vast public lavatory with its
disinfected corridors leading off to birth, death, and taxes. All through
the book the fortissimo horrors of the main action are interspersed
with grace notes of entropic futility: "One leg was gammy, he moved
it with a mechanism worked from his pocket, lurching with an air of
enormous strain to pocket sixpence, to say 'It's a fine night'; he looked
worn with the awful labour of the trivial act" (236). As Mr. Prewett
insists, "This is Hell nor are we out of it" (211). Thus we can say
that Ida's worldly wisdom is foolishness in the eyes of the novel,
for it refuses to acknowledge the facts of existence as *Brighton Rock*
defines them: "Ida knows nothing," says Gwenn Boardman, "of either
the 'purer' terror or the 'deeper' pleasures of primitive darkness and
religious power."[22] Whatever Pinkie and (perhaps to a lesser extent)

22. Gwenn R. Boardman, *Graham Greene: The Aesthetics of Exploration*, 45.

Rose know counts as gnosis rather than mere delusion or the effects of a sectarian upbringing. But if all we have to choose between is a gnosis that wields a razor and a blindness that at worst doesn't mind its own business, perhaps we are back in a familiar Conradian territory where clarity of knowledge about the world is inversely proportional to civilized restraint in dealing with it. Marlow sees to the awful bottom of things, but unlike Kurtz and Pinkie, he has a steady and demanding job to redemptively distract him from going ashore for a howl and a dance. The pressing question is, what, if anything, redeems Pinkie's vision of hell followed by Hell? Greene's surprising answer—one that sounds strikingly Brontëan and Lawrencian—is that only those who in some measure participate in it are capable of genuinely redemptive love.

Ida is ignorant, then, of the harrowing realities of life; she averts her eyes from the horror—and it is *Brighton Rock*'s contention that precisely *because* she averts her eyes she is loveless. In Greene's world, through a process similar to that by which only catastrophic pressure can transform coal into diamonds, only the harrowed soul can adequately love. As Frederick Karl surmises, "the violence of many of Greene's novels is perhaps predicated on this belief: that only violence or stress or chaotic conditions can upset a man's complacency and create out of his former indifference the kind of belief necessary for his salvation." Before going farther in this direction, however, it is necessary to point out that it is not only Ida herself who is thus found fatally lukewarm—rather, she is a representative figure, a "symbol of secularized middle-class society," an emblem of the kind of citizen produced by an unselfconscious liberal reformism, the middle-of-the road mediated orthodoxy of our century. We shall find that, as Neil Nehring insists, there is strong reason to suspect that Ida Arnold is in fact "the namesake of Matthew Arnold."[23]

Throughout his canon, Greene portrays liberalism in two modes, the hopelessly feckless and the fitfully militant. This first mode is best represented by the Entrenationo international language academy in *The Confidential Agent,* which, in its offices above those of a magazine entitled *Mental Health,* contains underpaid idealists "in an

---

23. Frederick R. Karl, "Graham Greene's Demonical Heroes," 63; Sharrock, *Saints,* 95; Neil Nehring, "Revolt into Style: Graham Greene Meets the Sex Pistols," 229.

ivory tower, waiting for miracles" (*CA*, 132). Dr. Bellows, its visionary founder, has decreed that "the first words of the Entrenationo
Language must always be one of welcome" (42), for his goal is to
pacify the world: "All this hate, . . . these wars we read about in the
newspapers, they are all due to misunderstanding. If we all spoke
the same language . . ." (43). Of course Greene's cruelly funny joke
is that the academy is already infected with the murderous passions
of the foreign civil war that D. and his untrustworthy contacts—using
the school as a cover—have imported from their homeland, and that
even as D.'s false offer to open an Entrenationo center in his bomb-
ravaged country brings tears to Dr. Bellow's "old liberal eyes" (132),
the front line of battle is running directly through the earnest man's
noble but hopeless enterprise.

Ida, however, represents secular liberalism in a more dangerous
phase. Time and again, she is described in a way that reminds us
that she symbolically carries with her the shadowy imprimatur of
the state. "She rose formidably and moved across the restaurant, like
a warship going into action, a warship on the right side in a war to
end wars, the signal flags proclaiming that every man would do his
duty" (*BR*, 120–21). Later, we are told that "she was like a chariot in a
triumph—behind her were all the big battalions" (221), and that she
resembles "a figurehead of Victory" (244). It is worth noting in this
regard how closely Greene seems to prefigure Foucault's descriptions of bourgeois society's techniques for enforcing consensus.[24]
After all, the police in Brighton are not very effective—they lack
zeal—and by making the private citizen Ida Arnold the implementor
of justice, Greene seems to be making a self-conscious comment
about the extent to which his culture's disciplinary energies have
enjoyed a widespread dispersion without any accompanying decline
in efficiency.[25]

In a passage whose final phrase is obviously meant to shock—to
retroactively convert its own preceding catalog of casual virtues into
a checklist of shallowness—Greene makes Ida's emblematic status
explicit.

---

24. See Michel Foucault, *Discipline and Punish: The Birth of the Prison*.
25. Trevor L. Williams, "History over Theology: The Case for Pinkie in
Greene's *Brighton Rock*," 72–73; Elliott Malamet, "Graham Greene and the
Hounds of *Brighton Rock*."

Her friends—they were everywhere under the bright glittering Brighton air. They followed their wives obediently into fishmongers, they carried the children's buckets to the beach, they lingered round the bars waiting for opening time, they took a penny peep on the pier at "A Night of Love." She had only to appeal to any of them, for Ida Arnold was on the right side. . . . [S]he was honest, she was kindly, she belonged to the great middle law-abiding class, her amusements were their amusements, her superstitions their superstitions (the planchette scratching the French polish on the occasional table, and the salt over the shoulder), she had no more love for anyone than they had. (80)

Cut off from any tragic, entropic vision of life by cheery visions of material comfort, faith in incremental improvement, and dabblings in spiritualist parlour-games, Ida and the polity she represents cannot respond to the human predicament with anything resembling redemptive love. Greene insists upon the connection between Ida's personal lack of *caritas* and that of the culture's at large by repeatedly mixing Old Testament language with popular clichés as he ticks off the contents of her mind: "The world was a good place if you didn't weaken . . . right's right, an eye for an eye, when you want to do a thing well, do it yourself" (221). Her practical philosophy of life, like that of all her numberless "friends," entails an arid mélange of revenge, recreation, respectability, and rationality: "an eye for an eye, law and order, capital punishment, a bit of fun now and then, nothing nasty, nothing shady, nothing you'd be ashamed to own, nothing mysterious" (77). As the multiplying negatives attest, the novel defines this careful treading around the edges of transgression as essentially an act of denial, of willful blindness.

Greene's assertion that Pinkie's participation in the homicidal realm of absolutes places him in proximity to a wholly adequate love from which Ida's good citizenship utterly banishes her is articulated on several levels. While Ida possesses "no pity for something she d[oes]n't understand" (72) and is "prepared to cause any amount of unhappiness to anyone in order to defend the only thing she believe[s] in" (36), Pinkie several times bewails the necessity of his multiplying crimes: "have I got to have that massacre?" (201); "Christ! he thought, had he got to massacre a world?" (175). Of course here the Boy is primarily worried about the risk to himself, but there are indications throughout the book that Pinkie is forever trembling on the brink of a comprehensive change of heart while it is clear that Ida's carapace of mediated self-satisfaction will never show a crack.

> "People change," [Rose] said.
> "Oh, no they don't. Look at me. I've never changed. It's like those sticks of rock: bite it all the way down, you'll still read Brighton. That's human nature." She breathed mournfully over Rose's face—a sweet and winey breath.
> "Confession . . . repentance," Rose whispered.
> "That's just religion," the woman said. "Believe me, it's the world we got to deal with." (198)

Pinkie's heart, by contrast, is forever under siege, forever accosted by feelings of connection with Rose and with divine grace that he attempts, not wholly successfully, to quash. When Cubitt denigrates Rose, for example, "an extraordinary indignation jerked in the Boy's brain and fingers. It was almost as if someone he loved had been insulted" (149). On the way to their squalid wedding, he "touches her arm with next to tenderness. As once before he had the sense of needing her" (167), and after their consummation "a faint feeling of tenderness woke for his partner in the act" (181). Whereas we know that every unadventurous erotic encounter of Ida's will end in the same postcoital depression, there is a sense that each new phase of Rose and Pinkie's courtship and marriage carries with it an explosive charge potentially powerful enough to rip the Boy away from his loverlike embrace of hatred: "she took deception with such hopeless ease that he could feel a sort of tenderness for her stupidity and a companionship in her goodness" (220). Redemption stalks Pinkie, sometimes taking the traditionally Christian form of the descending dove, as it does during his final drive with Rose toward the cliffs.

> "Last night . . . the night before . . . you didn't hate me, did you, for what we did?"
> He said, "No, I didn't hate you."
> "Even though it was a mortal sin."
> It was quite true—he hadn't hated her; he hadn't even hated the act. There had been a kind of pleasure, a kind of pride, a kind of—something else. The car lurched back on to the main road; he turned the bonnet to Brighton. An enormous emotion beat on him;

it was like something trying to get in; the pressure of gigantic wings against the glass. Dona nobis pacem. (239)

Sometimes, though, even the most determinedly secular offering of Brighton's Vanity Fair can threaten to touch off a benign cache of powder within Pinkie, as happens when the couple watches the "romantic film" full of "esoteric beds shaped like winged coracles" and "a song under a window":

> The actor with a lick of black hair across a white waste of face said "you're mine. All mine." He sang again under the restless stars in a wash of incredible moonshine, and suddenly, inexplicably, the Boy began to weep. He shut his eyes to hold in his tears, but the music went on—it was like a vision of release to an imprisoned man. He felt constriction and saw—hopelessly out of reach—a limitless freedom: no fear, no hatred, no envy. It was as if he were dead and were remembering the effect of a good confession, the words of absolution. (179)

As has been often pointed out, and as the above passages amply suggest, in Greene sex can be a gateway to genuine *eros*, and *eros* a gateway to *caritas*, even *agape*.[26] But Ida engages in a lot of sex and Ida will never love. Pinkie responds to a hateful world of privation and entropy with hatred, but the novel insists that it is only by the sheer principled intensity of that hatred that the Boy can earn his passport through the thresholds of better emotions. "Gushing up from elemental sources, passion, however destructive, always surpasses tepid good conduct."[27]

I say "better emotions," but such an attempt to draw a clear moral distinction between great hate and great love is itself a strategy of the mediated world, and therefore largely beside the point in Greene's preferred realm of the absolute. *Brighton Rock*, like *Wuthering Heights*, attempts to argue that when it comes to an emotion, its intensity is far more important that its kind. In a safely conventional and orthodox sense, Rose embodies love and Pinkie hate, her angelic charity throwing his satanic egoism into bold relief. But the novel

26. Carola Kaplan, "Graham Greene's Pinkie Brown and Flannery O'Connor's Misfit: The Psychopathic Killer and the Mystery of God's Grace," 122.
27. Wolfe, *Graham Greene the Entertainer*, 28.

attempts a refutation of this way of thinking, insisting that because they feel their respective emotions to the height of human capacity, they inhabit virtually the same moral space, and that a valorized one. At several points, we are told that far from being opposites in any meaningful sense, Pinkie and Rose are in fact two sides of the same precious coin: "he was aware that . . . she was something which completed him. . . . What was most evil in him needed her: it couldn't get along without goodness. . . . She was good, he'd discovered that, and he was damned: they were made for each other" (126). Later, when Pinkie discovers that Rose guessed all along that he murdered Hale, he exclaims "with a kind of respect, 'There's not a pin to choose between us'" (185), a point of view the text goes on to repeatedly confirm: "*she* stood now where Pinkie had stood—outside, looking in. This was what the priests meant by one flesh" (194). It is at those moments when Rose testifies to the almost nihilistic power of her devotion to Pinkie that we see that the lovers inhabit the same high rung on a ladder that leads from Greene's banal suburbans to his absolutistic elites. Looking out from her seedy bridal chamber at the faithful walking home from mass, Rose affirms that "she didn't envy them and she didn't despise them: they had their salvation and she had Pinkie and damnation" (194). And it is here too that Greene's conception of gnosis clearly leaves the confines of Catholic orthodoxy and takes its place within the literary tradition we have outlined above, for both Ida and orthodoxy must disapprove of Rose's determination to be damned for love, and the determination of Greene's novel to applaud the courage of her choice: "He was going to damn himself, but she was going to show them that they couldn't damn him without damning her too. There was nothing he could do, she wouldn't do: she felt capable of sharing any murder. . . . She felt responsibility move in her breasts; she wouldn't let him go into that darkness alone" (228). Like Heathcliff, Rose has nearly attained *her* heaven; and that of others is altogether unvalued and uncoveted by her—or, for that matter, by *Brighton Rock*.

If one searches the pages of Greene's fiction for an answer to the question of *why* participation in the frequently violent and despairing life of the absolute is necessary to awaken the heart—of why the cure for lovelessness has always to be so extreme—the answer turns out to be the sheer pervasiveness in Greeneland of entropy's workaday brother, habit. As the author's much-admired Péguy states, "what is most contrary to salvation is not sin but habit,"[28] and indeed in Greene's hands habit is presented as the soul-deadening default setting of the human race, a sort of lotus-eating Circe that continually urges us to abandon the rocky slopes of intensity for the sleepy hollow of ease. Perhaps *Brighton Rock*'s funniest ongoing gag at Pinkie's expense is the way that the members of his supposedly vicious gang keep deserting him to take up the lives of bourgeois respectability they've always secretly longed to inhabit. First Spicer opts out in order to become a publican; then we find that Cubitt, like Ida, has conversed with his dear departed at séances, and so it is no surprise that he takes to Ida as a "fellow countryman" (160) when they finally meet. And last, Dallow—whose mediated "creed" is "the world's all right if you don't go too far" (165)—discovers in himself "a sudden sentimental desire which Judy couldn't satisfy: for a paper with your breakfast and warm fires" (235). Pinkie eventually finds it very lonely at the top, but he is not without understanding of how, at our weakest moments, the mediated seduces us into the living death of habit.

> "An' you got a girl," Dallow said with hollow cheeriness. "You're growing up, Pinkie—like your father."
> Like my father . . . The Boy was shaken again with his nocturnal Saturday disgust. He couldn't blame his father now . . . it was what you came to . . . you got mixed up, and then, he supposed, the habit grew . . . you gave yourself away weakly. You couldn't even blame the girl. It was life getting at you . . . there were the blind seconds when you thought it fine. (220, Greene's ellipses)

It is this understanding of how entropy so often rules the spirit as well as the body that prompts Pinkie to, in a manner of speaking, renew his faith with acts of absolutistic cruelty.

Pinkie may seem bound for the hell of Catholicism because of his murders, but there is an alternate underworld in *Brighton Rock*—a place of torment that revolves around mediated domestic routine—which, ironically, even the Boy's victories may lead him into: "They'd won out—finally. He had—Dallow was right again—sixty years ahead. His thoughts came to pieces in his hand: Saturday nights: and then the birth, the child, habit and hate. He

28. Charles Péguy, *Basic Verities: Prose and Poetry,* 183.

looked across the tables; [Ida's] laughter was like defeat" (224). It is in connection with this suburban version of Tophet that I believe we can see the gang's visit to Mr. Prewitt's house in its true light—as a voyage into the only kind of torment-filled underworld in which Greene could actually believe. The lawyer's abode has, in fact, many Plutonic associations, for it is "shaken by shunting engines" as "the soot settle[s] continuously on the glass and the brass plate. From the basement window a woman with tousled hair"— Prewitt's wife—"stare[s] suspiciously up at" Pinkie while the door is opened by "a girl with underground skin" (207). Ensconced in the hallway, Pinkie senses that "under his feet in the basement someone was moving the furniture about—the spouse, he thought. A train hooted and a smother of smoke fell into the street" (208). Prewett, who has been "twenty-five years at the [marriage] game" and is consequently tortured by an ulcer, refers to his wife as the "old mole" and insists that he has "married beneath [him]self" (207–8). The lawyer, we find, fiercely envies Pinkie's celibate freedom, no matter what dangers attend it: " 'Has it ever occurred to you,' Mr. Prewitt said, 'that you're lucky? The worst that can happen to you is you'll hang. But I can rot' " (209). To hang or rot—such may be a concise summation of how Greene views the choices offered by his fictional Brighton—if so, it is clear that Prewitt has not chosen the better option. Indeed, he is a man who longs for some sort of absolutistic breakout from his prison, but who hasn't quite the courage or imagination to mount one. As he confesses his torments to Pinkie he begins to resemble "a man determined to live before he died" (210), but his transgressions remain imaginary: "I watch the little typists go by carrying their cases. I'm quite harmless. A man may watch. . . . I could embrace their little portable machines" (209, 211). As Pinkie departs, Mrs. Prewitt "watche[s] him like a bitter enemy from her cave, under the foundations" (212). Yes, this is hell nor is Prewitt out of it—but Pinkie *is* out of it, whatever else one can say against him.

Brighton Rock's positing of domestic routine as hell, which will be discussed again in subsequent chapters, has implications when we consider Pinkie's one posthumous act of cruelty—the recording he leaves for Rose. This record—which the narrator famously calls "the worst horror of all" (247)—seems to some readers to be a final, gratuitous reminder on the author's part that Pinkie is damned. This is not the time to explore the well-worn topic of Pinkie's eternal destination, which will also be covered in due course—but the recording, when looked at in light of the novel's concern with the mediated and the absolute, takes on an interesting coloring. Its command— "God damn you, you little bitch, why can't you go back home for ever and let me be?" (177)—is quite impossible to comply with, since Pinkie and Rose's homes, Paradise Piece and Nelson Place, respectively, are the equally impoverished and emotionally arid environments that, Greene is careful to insist upon, had most if not everything to do with absolutizing both of them.[29] Thus while the vile recording, recalled to our minds by the narrator amidst Rose's returning desire to live, serves to differentiate once more between the Boy's evil and his wife's goodness, it also, by virtue of both its explicit meaning and the virulence of its emotion, points up their equivalence and their inseparability. They came from the same place and ended up there, too; they are nearly identical and thus *can't* leave each other alone—the message is a fitting memorial to their enduring cohabitation in the realm of the absolute.

More than this, the recording is a guarantee that Rose's emotions concerning Pinkie will not be channeled into the approved and mediated culverts where the priest Rose consults at the book's end wants to send them. When she enters the confessional, Rose regrets not staying the satanic course: " 'I wish I'd killed myself. I ought to 'ave killed myself.' The old man began to say something, but she interrupted him. 'I'm not asking for absolution. I don't want absolution. I want to be like him—damned' " (245). For his part, the priest is full of attractive Greenean reflections on the unlikelihood of anyone's damnation, but he also tells Rose that she can reconvert her time with and feelings for Pinkie into an acceptable narrative by "mak[ing] her unborn son] a saint—to pray for his father." This prompts Rose to begin thinking in a manner that, while conventionally hopeful, also carries with it—according to the novel's terms of argument—the taint of mediated routine. "A sudden feeling of immense gratitude broke through the pain—it was as if she had been given the sight a long way off of life going on again" (247). Life going on again—and on and on and on. In Greene's unredeemed Brighton of kitsch and cancer, this is the banishment into darkness that counts: " 'Sixty-odd years,' the

29. Nehring, "Revolt," 229–30.

Boy said, 'it's a long time.' . . . Sixty years: it was like a prophecy—a certain future: a horror without end" (224). As one critic reminds us, "Pinkie revolts, not because, paradoxically, the society is evil, but because it offers nothing so definite or real as evil." Rose herself has already acknowledged the power of sheer duration to wear down glorious apostates into mere citizens: "To go on living for years . . . you couldn't tell what life would do to you in making you meek, good, repentant. . . . You could win to the evil side suddenly, in a moment of despair or passion, but through a long life the guardian good drove you remorselessly toward the [Christmas] crib, the 'good death' " (241). The Boy's vulcanite missive, whatever else it means or does, insures that Pinkie and Rose's bond will continue to escape the clutches of both Catholic orthodoxy and bourgeois normality. It is almost as if Pinkie is performing what Heathcliff begged of his dead Catherine: "Be with me always—take any form—drive me mad! only *do* not leave me in this abyss, where I cannot find you."[30]

Before going on to discuss the ways in which this tension between the mediated and the absolute is played out in some of Greene's other novels, we need to look at one more passage in *Brighton Rock,* because it clearly illustrates how this theme—which we have so far seen frequently enmeshed within a specifically Catholic context— can exist even in this text as a freestanding concern. After Pinkie narrowly escapes death at the hands of Colleoni's razor gang, he flees the racetrack and finds himself hiding in a garage located on a "neat barren bourgeois road" (108). Pinkie, bearing what might be called the Brighton stigmata (he is "bleeding down his face and from both hands" [107]), surveys the contents of the place, which, significantly, includes "a pile of ancient records—'Alexander's Rag Time Band,' 'Pack Up Your Troubles,' 'If You Were the Only Girl' "— evocative of the shallow, recreational atmosphere of Brighton. The other items on display seem to paint a clear picture of their owner as one who has led a thoroughly mediated, suburban existence and who is now preparing to die in mediocre obscurity.

> Whoever the owner was, he had come a long way to land up here. The pram-wheelbarrow was covered with labels—the marks of innumerable train journeys—Doncaster, Lichfield, Clacton (that

30. Kubal, "Political Theme," 51; Brontë, *Wuthering Heights,* 139.

must have been a summer holiday), Ipswich, Northhampton—
roughly torn off for the next journey they left, in the litter which
remained, an unmistakable trail. And this, the small villa under the
racecourse, was the best finish he could manage. You couldn't have
any doubt that this was the end, the mortgaged home in the bottom;
like the untidy tidemark on a beach, the junk was piled up here and
would never go farther. (108)

Pinkie's reaction to this absent owner of his temporary hideout is
extreme—and a bit puzzling unless one has been attentive to the
theme we are tracing: "And the Boy hated him. He was nameless,
faceless, but the Boy hated him, the doll, the pram, the broken rock-
ing horse. The small pricked-out plants irritated him like ignorance"
(108). Like ignorance—just as Marlow dismissed the labels of the
round-the-world passengers or the mediated citizens of Brussels who
"could not possibly know the things [he] knew," so Pinkie aims his
venom at those lesser breeds within the law. Once initiated into the
dangerous gnosis of a life lived amidst the absolutes, all denizens of
the mediated world cannot help but appear as so many fools, and,
for Pinkie at least, it is difficult to suffer them with patience.

Here, finally, it might behoove us to admit at least one objection
from the realm of everyday common sense: "If God likes outlaws
better than solid citizens, if Ida is damned and Pinkie saved, what
is the status of man's law?"[31] Is Greene really urging us to wink at
murder because the murdering life offers its participant a golden
opportunity to experience existential intensities? I would answer
that what is asked of us is more a matter of understanding and
self-evaluation than approval. Anne Salvatore, who likens Greene's
overall project to that of Kierkegaard, agrees that what *Brighton Rock*
really attempts to do is "to trick us out of our complacent way of
thinking and into an existential crisis." By reading the novel on its
own disturbing terms, she continues, we "become free to imagine
other existence possibilities—not only for the characters, but also for
[our]selves." Or, as Trevor Williams would have it,

> given that this Brighton, this England, this world even, is utterly
> "fallen" . . . do we have to recognize that fact and *change* it, as

31. Karl, "Demonical Heroes," 57.

Marx urged, or do we go along with Ida and raise our glasses to this imperfect world which nonetheless allows us a modicum of happiness as we float by? It is at this deeper structural level that one makes a case for admiring Pinkie and Rose as against Ida, Prewitt, Colleoni and all the other corrupt and fallen characters. However minimally, Pinkie and Rose make a choice, an act of resistance, and briefly step on to firm ground out of a sea of false consciousness.[32]

In *Brighton Rock,* then, Greene is attempting nothing less than to overturn our comfortable feelings about comfort—material, emotional, moral, spiritual. If his demonstration here is too fraught with violence and destruction to quite convince us that a leap into Pinkie's world of mortal extremities is worth the attendant costs, we must remember that this novel is only one assay among several in this vein that Greene undertakes. As a subsequent chapter will show, we need only turn to *The Power and the Glory* in order to encounter a protagonist whose immersion in the realm of the absolute issues in different results altogether.

III

Throughout Greene's next novel, *The Confidential Agent,* a good deal of situational irony is generated by the juxtaposition of D., that emissary from a land of total war, with the sleepy, peaceful, and oblivious inhabitants and locales of England. From the book's opening page, D. feels that between those who live amidst the mediated and those who traffic in absolutes, there is a great moral chasm that makes their physical proximity disorienting or even ludicrous. "He was filled with a sense of amazement at these people; you could never have told from their smoky good fellowship that there was a war on—not merely a war in the country from which he had come, but a war here, half a mile outside Dover breakwater. He carried the war with him. Wherever D. was, there was a war. He could never understand that people were unaware of it" (*CA,* 9). The metaphor Greene insists upon throughout the novel is that of disease, with D. playing the role of an absolutistic contagion's unwilling carrier:

---

32. Anne T. Salvatore, *Greene and Kierkegaard: The Discourse of Belief,* 34–35; Williams, "History over Theology," 75.

There was a sharp report, the car swerved and he flung his arms up over his face. The car came to a stop. She said, "They've given us a dud tyre." He put his arms down. "I'm sorry," he said. "I do still feel that." His hands were trembling. "Fear."

"There's nothing to be afraid of here," she said.

"I'm not sure." He carried the war in his heart: give me time, he thought, and I shall infect anything—even this. I ought to wear a bell like the old lepers. (19)

D.'s secret activities on behalf of his besieged government do in fact cause the deaths of both innocent and guilty parties in England's gray and pleasant land, but, as *Brighton Rock* might have led us to expect, there is a revaluation of conventional values at work within Greene's trope of health and disease. As it turns out, the dose of absolutistic mayhem that D. imports proves therapeutic for a country that has too long suffered from a lack of spiritual stimulus. As on the streets of Brighton, so in London there are worse things than dying or slaying—things such as safety and habit—which make D. nostalgic for the killing fields of home. "Oh, to be home. . . . An east wind blew from the City: it had the stone-cold of big business blocks and banks. You thought of long passages and glass doors and a spiritless routine. It was a wind to take the heart out of a man" (56).

Just as Greene makes no attempt in *Brighton Rock* to soft-pedal the terrible cruelty of Pinkie's murders, so there is no tendency in *The Confidential Agent* to diminish the horrors of war. But just as Pinkie is immune from the mediated moral infection spread by all of Brighton's hollow amusements and glittery junk, so in this novel are those who wage war immune to the myriad small vices that drag life down below the dignified threshold of tragedy, as is evidenced by D.'s strong reaction to a popular song:

People set down their wine and listened as if it were poetry. Even the girl stopped eating for a while. The self-pity of it irritated him; it was a vice nobody in his country on either side of the line had an opportunity of indulging.

"I don't say you lie: it's just the modern way
I don't intend to die: in the old Victorian
   way."

> He supposed it represented the "spirit of the age," whatever that meant; he almost preferred the prison cell, the law of flight, the bombed house, his enemy by the door. (26)

It is said of Pinkie and Rose that "they faced each other as it were from opposing territories, but like troops at Christmas time they fraternized" (*BR*, 139). In Greeneland there is apparently always a fellowship of combatants that binds one's heart more closely to a foe's than to that of any mere civilian.

The England that D. encounters is, on the one hand, a bleak industrial desert whose inhabitants have been demoralized and hardened by economic depression. At the same time, however, Greene contrasts it with D.'s Guernica-like homeland by depicting it as a realm where Victorian gentility lives on. Customs agents are trusting and apologetic, the police interrogate D. with the aid of tea and biscuits, and a rural stationmaster is full of deferential memories of gentry upon the platform. The closest thing to a martial character that England can produce bears the Gilbert-and-Sullivanesque name of Colonel Currie and menaces D. with appropriately comic inefficiency. Else, the young hotel maid who instantly befriends D. and becomes his enthusiastic accomplice, seems the familiar Dickensian urchin whose heart of gold is untouched by dubious companions. All the sentimental associations surrounding Else fall away, however, as soon as she is fatally enmeshed in the absolutistic forces D.'s presence unleashes.

> He thought of the child screaming at the window, scratching with her nails at the paint, breaking through the fog, smashed on the pavement: she was one of thousands. It was as if by the act of death she had become naturalized to his own land—a countrywoman. His territory was death: he could love the dead and the dying better than the living. Dr. Bellows, Miss Carpenter—they were robbed of reality by their complacent safety. They must die before he could take them seriously. (128)

This notion of the proximity of death as the only thing capable of conferring ontological respectability is echoed by Pinkie's dismissal of Ida: "'She?' The Boy laughed. 'She's just nothing'" (*BR*, 127). And as with the characters within a novel, so perhaps with novels themselves, for one can see Greene attempting to counteract the inevitable fall into mediated happiness required by his entertainment's standard happy ending—an ending that features D. and Rose Cullen united in love by figuring it under the shadow of imminent death.

> She looked older than he had ever seen her yet—plain. It was as if she were assuring him that glamour didn't enter into this business. She said, "When you are dead, she [D.'s late wife] can have you. I can't compete then, and we'll all be dead a long, long time."
>
> The light went by astern: ahead there was only the splash, the long withdrawal, and the dark. She said, "You'll be dead very soon: you needn't tell me that, but *now* . . ." (206)

But of course "glamour" *does* enter into it, as Marlow's envious use of that selfsame term to describe the Little Russian's hyperprecarious life attests. There is an undeniable glamour about being fully alive, and it is Greene's argument that it is most likely to manifest itself under the shadow of immanent and violent death.

It is this same luminous and illuminating shadow of death that, in *The Quiet American,* moves the cynical narrator, Fowler, to fall in love with a country over which it hangs. Indeed, it is seemingly impossible for him to describe the captivating beauties of Vietnam without including some sign of violence, some reminder of the dangerous absolutes that threaten (or rather, promise) to intrude into the otherwise regular rhythms of his journalistic life. Devoid of such intrusions, his previous existence in a mediated London has lost its attraction:

> When I first came I counted the days of my assignment, like a schoolboy marking off the days of term; I thought I was tied to what was left of a Bloomsbury square and the 73 bus passing the portico of Euston and springtime in the local in Torrington Place. Now the bulbs would be out in the square garden, and I didn't care a damn. I wanted a day punctuated by those quick reports that might be car-exhausts or might be grenades, I wanted to keep the sight of those silk-trousered figures moving with grace through the humid noon, I wanted Phuong, and my home had shifted its ground eight thousand miles. (QA, 25)

Fowler's descriptive catalogs of Vietnam are couched in such a way as to depict wartime violence as simply another aspect of the scenery, and that invariably the best part: "it seemed impossible to me that I could ever have a life again, away from the rue Gambetta and the rue Catinat, the flat taste of vermouth cassis, the homely click of dice, and the gunfire traveling like a clock-hand around the horizon" (68). We have heard D. speaking of his true home as the "territory of death," and here too it becomes clear that the geography that matters is not one of latitude and longitude, but one of elevation above the dull plains of a mediated, bourgeois existence.

The flip side of Fowler's love affair with a country at risk is, I would argue, his notorious anti-Americanism, and I think we can now see clearly how the novel's U.S.-bashing is an almost inevitable result of Greene's long-term occupation with the theme we have been tracing. Throughout *The Quiet American,* the United States is portrayed as a civilization almost single-mindedly devoted to creating a world safe from all contact with the realm of the absolutes. Whenever American life is imagined, the vision is of an endless and impregnable middle-class routine. Fowler, for instance, insists that Pyle would be better off with "a standardized American girl who subscribed to the book club" (32), and wonders if Phuong will "like those bright clean little New England grocery stores where even the celery was wrapped in cellophane" (156). Greene elsewhere wittily refers to Americans as living behind the "cellophane curtain,"[33] but it is another piece of U.S. technology that prevents Fowler from experiencing—or at least properly expressing—his strongest emotions. "There was a door opposite me marked Men. I went in and locked the door and sitting with my head against the cold wall I cried. I hadn't cried until now. Even their lavatories were air-conditioned, and presently the temperate tempered air dried my tears as it dries the spit in your mouth and the seed in your body" (147). This idea of the perfectly mediated life being one lived at the greatest possible distance from both the demands of the body and the convulsions of the spirit is followed up when Fowler sees the two American girls in the Pavilion and finds it "impossible to conceive either of them a prey to untidy passion: they did not belong to rumpled sheets and the sweat of sex. Did they take deodorants to bed with them? I found myself for a moment envying them their sterilized world, so different from this world that I inhabited" (159–60). *Sterile*—if there is a single word

33. Cassis, *Man of Paradox,* 110.

that well describes the despised realm of the Grange in Brontë, of passengers in Conrad,[34] and of modern "eunuch" civilization in Lawrence, this one will surely serve.

There are other instances of this theme in Greene's later fiction, but they do not greatly augment what has already been said about it. In both *A Burnt-Out Case* and *The Honorary Consul,* an acquaintance with the absolute is seen as an efficacious method of transcending an old and unwanted identity. In the former novel, Querry retraces Marlow's route up the Congo, hoping that "perhaps out here there would be enough pain and enough fear to distract" him from the burdens of a public persona that he can no longer square with his own estimate of himself (*BC,* 111). In the latter, the alcoholic Charley Fortnum, mistakenly kidnapped and menaced with death, unexpectedly finds himself "beginning to live in the region of truth" (*HC,* 122). It is, however, the comic *Travels with My Aunt* that points up one final benefit that accrues to those who, by choice or chance, wind up living on the dangerous edge of things. Recall that Pinkie saw the perils he courts as preferable to facing directly the—for him— hellish prospect of sixty more years of married life, reproduction, and creeping habit. Here, though, Henry Pulling's aunt (or rather, mother) Augusta has a different take on the distractive possibilities of the absolute. She lectures Henry that if he stays in his suburban world of dahlias and solitary domestic routine he "will think how every day [he is] getting a little closer to death. It will stand there as close as the bedroom wall. And [he will] become more and more afraid of the wall because nothing can prevent [him] coming nearer and nearer to it every night while [he tries] to sleep." If, on the other hand, he joins her in her high-risk smuggling operation in Paraguay, his dealings with mortality will be quite different.

> Tomorrow you may be shot in the street by a policeman because you haven't understood Guaraní, or a man may knife you in a *cantina* because you can't speak Spanish and he thinks you are acting in a superior way. Next week, when we have our Dakota, perhaps it will crash with you over Argentina. . . . My dear Henry, if you live with us, you won't be edging day by day across to any last wall. The wall will find you of its own accord without your help, and every day

34. See Pendleton, *Conradian Masterplot,* 122–23.

you live will seem to you a kind of victory. "I was too sharp for it that time," you will say, when night comes, and afterwards you'll sleep well. (*TA*, 225)

There is something poignant about the restless and inveterate traveler Graham Greene imagining death as a wall, as a final obstacle to further journeying. But after all, isn't it finally a kind of *movement* that a life lived amidst the absolutes really promises—a perpetual movement of spirit that forever outdistances the snares of habit and appears at least to deny the inevitable triumph of entropy? For Greene, bodies at rest tend to stay at rest—bodies in motion tend to end up in places where a libidinal, intellectual, and empathic gnosis expands the self to proportions unknown in the safer realms of middle-class normality. As Greene stated in an interview, "One thing I feel sure, if there is such a thing as life after death it won't be a static state. I think it will be a state of movement and activity. I can't believe in an ultimate happiness which doesn't include a form of development."[35] Travel is risky, but for those who climb on board or are just luckily swept up, it has its rewards.

IV

There is—unsurprisingly for Greene—a countercurrent to the theme we have been tracing above, an exception to our author's championing of absolutistic transgressors against middle-class safety and security. Whereas outright criminals such as Pinkie and flaunters of bourgeois pieties such as Fowler and Aunt Augusta are consistently painted as the moral superiors of good citizens, spies are not. Several critics have, for instance, remarked upon the extent to which Greene's late espionage novel, *The Human Factor,* seems to retract his earlier skepticism concerning the possibilities of domestic happiness.[36] In actuality, though, a first hint of this alternative conception can be found in Greene's wartime novel of spy and counterspy, *The Ministry of Fear.* Arthur Rowe, the protagonist whose involvement in a mercy killing and confinement in a sanitarium have already established his credentials as an uneasy resident within the bourgeois fold, finds himself caught up in a life-and-death struggle

35. Cassis, *Man of Paradox,* 252.
36. Smith, *Achievement,* 186–92.

to prevent Nazi spies from smuggling vital military secrets out of England. At the height of the chase's excitement, however, he is struck by a surprising nostalgia for the normalcy he believed he had forever resigned. Hurtling away from London in a police car, he looks out over a blacked-out nation that is still enjoying, even in wartime, all the ordinary occurrences of birth, love, and natural death, and suddenly discovers within himself an impatience for

> this violent superficial chase, this cardboard adventure hurtling at seventy miles an hour along the edge of the profound natural common experiences of men. Rowe felt a longing to get back into that world: into the world of homes and children and quiet love and the ordinary unspecified fears and anxieties the neighbour shared; he carried the thought of Anna like a concealed letter promising just that: the longing was like the first stirring of maturity when the rare experience suddenly ceases to be desirable. (*MF,* 178–79)

The use of the word "maturity" in this connection is interesting. In *The Ministry of Fear* itself there is an extended exploration of the fitness or unfitness of childhood and childhood memories as places of refuge from the modern world, but more to our immediate purpose is the way in which Greene's next fiction of espionage, *Our Man in Havana,* insists upon painting the intelligence game as adolescent or even infantile. Hawthorne, who is Wormold's gullible contact with MI6, is described as belonging to "the cruel and inexplicable world of childhood" (44), and the protagonist likens this spymaster's credulous nature to that of his pious daughter's, except that instead of virgin births "what [he] swallowed were nightmares, grotesque stories out of science fiction" (*OM,* 72). Furthermore, when Hasselbacher's room is searched it "looks as though a malevolent child ha[s] been at work" while Beatrice likens spying to "a *Boy's Own Paper* game" (109). That the adolescent Pinkie's adventures in the realm of the absolute should have a wizened or even ageless quality about them while those of Hawthorne and Wormold are likened to a nursery pastime confirms the fact that Greene sees criminality as a somehow more authentic or uncompromised conduit into the mysteries of the absolute than espionage.

This contrary stream in the midst of Greene's own contrarian discourse rises again in *The Human Factor,* where the risks run by the double agent Castle are a good deal more serious than those courted by Wormold in his comic entertainment. Here, Castle's home is his castle, but the problem is not, as we might expect from the body of Greene's canon, that he is chained within it to a demonic domestic partner, but rather that his genuinely redemptive refuge there is fatally menaced by outside forces. His working life consisting largely of a secretive treachery within the secret service, it is at home with his wife and son that Castle most closely approaches that longed-for "city where he could be accepted as a citizen, as a citizen without any pledge of faith, not the City of God or Marx, but the city called Peace of Mind" (*HF,* 141). In a passage familiar in kind but unique in tone for Greene, Castle catches a glimpse of a suburban family while desperately trying to make contact with his Soviet handler from a callbox:

> At a house across the road he could see through the uncurtained window a family sitting down to a high tea or an early dinner: a father and two teenage children, a boy and a girl, took their seats, the mother entered carrying a dish, and the father seemed to be saying grace, for the children bowed their heads.
> . . . . The father made a joke and the mother smiled her approval and the girl winked at the boy, as much as to say "The old boy's at it again." Castle went on down the road toward the station—nobody followed him, no one looked at him through a window as he went by, nobody passed him. He felt invisible, set down in a strange world where there were no other human beings to recognize him as one of themselves. (239–40)

One must perhaps read a few Greene novels in succession to properly appreciate what does *not* happen in this passage. Yes, the denizen of the absolute is once more profoundly isolated from the residents of the mediated sphere, but here there is not a single word suggesting the former's gnostic superiority and not the faintest breath of criticism directed at the safety and security of the latter. In the context of Greene's canon as a whole, this silence is startling. As William Chace says, in *The Human Factor,* Greene "returns, by way of an admirably cogent reprise, to themes that had perplexed and driven him since *The Confidential Agent* . . . but it is a reprise in which the glamour of all these familiar themes has been erased."[37]

37. William M. Chace, "Spies and God's Spies: Greene's Espionage Fiction," 171.

Why, then, is espionage disqualified as the pathway to a life of redemptive absolutes? After all, Pinkie's criminality is no less secretive. Surely it must have to do with spying's involvement with state interests, with its status as a tool of the powers that be. (The valorized D. is a "confidential agent," but then again his business is not espionage and he is pointedly distrusted by his own government," and thus operates essentially on his own.) But this notion that *any* commitment to or involvement with an "official" ideology (such as spies often evidence) strips the renegade of absolutistic glamour leads us into a potentially damaging criticism of Greene's entire investment in our theme, for consider what cause Castle believes himself to be working for: He is feeding information to the Soviets strictly limited to those items that might be helpful to black South Africans' struggle against the apartheid regime and its imperialistic American backers. As he tells his handler, "I'll never be a Communist. . . . I'll fight beside you in Africa, Boris—not in Europe" (*HF,* 160). From all we know about Greene's real-world political commitments, Castle's position is so politically correct as to approach the immaculate, and yet his risk taking garners none of the glamour we have earlier spoken of. If it is in fact the case that Greene refuses to champion any transgressors who, like Castle, even tangentially serve some official center of power *regardless of the regime involved,* then is not his valorization of daring outsiders too generic to be politically serious, too monolithic to discriminate between left and right, progressive and imperialist? Consider in this regard the strangely generic quality of Dr. Magiot's final letter to Brown in *The Comedians,* urging the protagonist to action: "Catholics and Communists have committed great crimes, but at least they have not stood aside, like an established society, and been indifferent" (*TC,* 286). "An established society"—this phrase covers a great deal of historical and political ground and suggests that all of it is pretty much of a piece.

To what extent, then, does this failure to differentiate among denigrated regimes or their glamorized renegades blunt the political efficacy of Greene's critique of the bourgeois imagination? Does it go so far as to render it nonpolitical altogether? Isn't it just the case that he hates the *look* of a winner or a boss or an "established society," no matter what his or its political coloring? It must be admitted that Gwenn Boardman is correct when she asserts that Greene's anti-Americanism is "largely aesthetic," and, given his Marxist convictions, one cannot blame Terry Eagleton for complaining that *The Quiet American* raises "less an objection to what the Americans *do* . . . than a criticism of what they *are,* an almost physical disgust for the trivia of hairstyle and manner. Fowler's anti-Americanism is closer to a vulgar snobbery than a shrewd analysis of the brutalities of U.S. imperialism."[38] One can always reply, of course, that since novels are themselves aesthetic endeavors, they are simply more adept at addressing truth to power in aesthetic rather than more finely reasoned modes, but I don't see any way to avoid admitting that Greene feels an instinctive antipathy to all insiders and an equally automatic sympathy with every outcast. As Castle himself muses, "Why are some of us . . . unable to love success or power or great beauty? Because we feel unworthy of them, because we feel more at home with failure? He didn't believe that was the reason. Perhaps one wanted the right balance, just as Christ had, that legendary figure whom he would have liked to believe in" (*HF,* 194). As this passage suggests, though, the motive behind such instinctive reactions may be an even deeper seated longing for justice, and in that sense quite definitely political. Certainly Greene himself believes that celebrating the violent aesthetic integrity of such "irredeemable" social outcasts as Pinkie ultimately serves a valuable political purpose:

> It has always been in the interests of the State to poison the psychological wells, to encourage cat-calls, to restrict human sympathy. It makes government easier when the people shout Galilean, Papist, Fascist, Communist. Isn't it the story-teller's task to act as the devil's advocate, to elicit sympathy and a measure of understanding for those who lie outside the boundaries of State approval? The writer is driven by his own vocation to be a Protestant in a Catholic society, a Catholic in a Protestant one, to see the virtues of the Capitalist in a Communist society, of the Communist in the Capitalist state. Thomas Paine wrote, "We must guard even our enemies against injustice."
>
> . . . If we enlarge the bounds of sympathy in our readers we succeed in making the work of the State a degree more difficult. That is a genuine duty we owe society, to be a piece of grit in the State machinery. (*RE,* 268–69)

38. Boardman, *Aesthetics of Exploration,* 102; Terry Eagleton, "Reluctant Heroes: The Novels of Graham Greene," 112.

Thus instead of concluding that Greene's critique of middle-class habits of mind is insufficiently political, we might instead agree that it is merely part of a larger political argument that is simply too wide-ranging and flexible for sectarian comfort. After all, his insistence that the writer "stands for the victims, and the victims change" (*R*, 269) is unlikely to make partisans of any particular persuasion feel secure, even libertarians. I am not suggesting that we can or should abandon our own hard-fought partisan positions— only that we should not denigrate Greene's argument by mislabeling it simply because it can potentially be turned back upon us in our moment of victory. His critique is in fact thoroughly political in that, by continually threatening to invert the moral hierarchies attached to the figures of "insider" and "outsider," it continually addresses the distribution of power within society. The truth is that "the mediated" and "the absolute" are, like so many things, culturally determined— and Greene understands that given a change of regime, today's stifling routine could become tomorrow's "monstrous" transgression. The devil's advocate, like the devil himself, never sleeps.

2 Waning Power and Faded Glory

Greene's Conception of God

I

The Power and the Glory has been called the greatest Catholic novel ever written. While I would not quarrel with this assessment, I would also contend that it is also perhaps the greatest anti-Catholic novel ever written. This second, countervailing accolade owes nothing to the protagonist's many lapses from his priestly vows—rather, it is the consequence of Greene's continuing elaboration of the theme we have already traced throughout *Brighton Rock*. In this novel, too, the spiritual atmosphere of the mediated world is weighed against that found in the dangerous precincts of the absolute and judged wanting. The result in Greene's Mexican epic is a radical critique of a Catholic Church—and, by implication, any other institutionalized religion—which, in its unavoidable desire to embrace all people and perpetuate its temporal existence, must necessarily foster a set of lulling rituals and rote moral gestures that shield its members from direct, harrowing—and (in our novelist's view) genuinely redemptive—encounters with God and final things.

The discussion of this theme, however, will only stand as prologue to the present chapter's main business, which will be to discern the lineaments of God as Greene conceives them. In doing so we shall discover a surprising fact: the Deity of Greeneland, who can only be grappled with in places above and beyond the bourgeois pale, possesses neither the immanence nor the omnipotence that Catholic and bourgeois orthodoxies ascribe to Him. If Christ is traditionally thought of as the human face of God, in *The Power and the Glory* and subsequent novels, the first person of the trinity also takes on a peculiarly human cast.

As in *Brighton Rock,* Greene's desire to champion the absolutistic life in *The Power and the Glory* involves the overturning of much conventional wisdom. Take, for instance, the obvious question of the whisky priest's fitness to act as God's representative in Tabasco. The protagonist's present-tense existence is scandalous in a conventional sense in part because it is lived continually in extremis: Hounded by the zealous lieutenant, he has little or no time for the niceties of church doctrine, the accoutrements of the mass, or the regulations of clerical life. "On paper," if you will, the whisky priest's frightened immersion in the realm of the absolutes renders him a sorry shepherd of souls. And yet Greene makes it unmistakably clear that it is precisely this daily acquaintance with acute suffering and death that allows him to save his own soul and to dispense aid and comfort to the souls of others. But there is more to it than this, for the priest is intermittently haunted by a past in which, amidst the safety of a mediated vocation, he played strictly by the rules. Unfortunately, it also appears that when he was a "normal" priest his spiritual influence upon his parishioners was almost nil, and that his days consisted of a soul-deadening routine that had little if anything to do with God: "The good things of life had come to him too early—the respect of his contemporaries, a safe livelihood. The trite religious word upon the tongue, the joke to ease the way, the ready acceptance of other people's homage . . . a happy man" (*PG*, 22). These thoughts occur to the anticlerical lieutenant as he gazes at the priest's photo upon the police-station wall, but when the priest himself sees the same photo his own reconstruction of the scene merely confirms how embedded was his old existence in mediated trivialities:

> Montez had talked at some length. He had reported the progress of the Altar Society in the last year—they had a balance in hand of twenty-two pesos. He had noted it down for comment—there it was, A. S. 22. Montez had been very anxious to start a branch of the Society of St. Vincent de Paul, and some woman had complained that bad books were being sold in Concepción, fetched in from the capital by mule: her child had got hold of one called *A Husband for a Night.* In his speech he said he would write to the Governor on the subject. (92–93)

As if to underscore that his earlier career brought him into closer proximity with Caesar than with Christ, we are informed that the photographer's flash had caught "the fat youngish priest who stood with one plump hand splayed authoritatively out while the tongue played pleasantly with the word 'Governor' " (93).

This notion that easy postings call forth no needful fire from the clergy who occupy them is revisited in later novels. Father Rank, for instance, tells Scobie that he once served a parish in Northampton with a generous flock who "used to ask [him] out to tea" and "talk of the Children of Mary and repairs to the church roof." According to Rank, however, it was also the case that in such a venue he "wasn't of any use to a single living soul" (*HM,* 183). In a similar vein, Querry stops off at a seminary on his way upriver and, after a few hours in the company of priests who live in "the innocence and immaturity of isolation" decides that "those who marry God . . . can become domesticated too—it's just as hum-drum a marriage as all the others" (*BC,* 14). This impatience was experienced by Greene himself, for when he returned to London from the convulsions of Mexico he discovered a lack of authenticity about worshipping in mediated circumstances and seemed to be groping toward a paradox that would find fuller expression in his novels—that the Prince of Peace can only be genuinely worshipped under the shadow of menace: "Mass in Chelsea seemed curiously fictitious; no peon knelt with his arms out in the attitude of the cross, no woman dragged herself up the aisle on her knees. It would have seemed shocking, like the Agony itself. We do not mortify ourselves. Perhaps we are in need of violence" (*LR,* 224). Some such idea was certainly behind his pronouncement—baffling to many ears—that the Church would be better off under Soviet repression than American indifference (*YE,* 138), since for Greene duress seems to strengthen the soul as exercise does the muscles, while to his mind success is always too near a neighbor to complacency when it comes to spiritual matters. As Sarah Miles tells God in her diary, "I am kissing pain and pain belongs to You as happiness never does" (*EA,* 122).

Certainly the impatience that we saw Pinkie manifest toward all citizens of the mediated world also infects the whisky priest, though of course in a less dangerous form. After years on the run and the commission of mortal sin, the minor infractions incidental to workaday religious life bore and depress the priest, as the following passage attests. Note too that as in *Brighton Rock* the hallmark of a mediated life is lovelessness, a fact the priest understands and articulates in a manner impossible for Pinkie:

He interrupted the woman savagely, "Why don't you confess properly to me? I'm not interested in your fish supply or in how sleepy you are at night . . . remember your real sins."

"But I'm a good woman, father," she squeaked at him with astonishment.

"Then what are you doing here, keeping away the bad people?" He said, "Have you any love for anyone but yourself?"

"I love God, father," she said haughtily. He took a quick look at her in the light of the candle burning on the floor—the hard old raisin eyes under the black shawl—another of the pious—like himself.

"How do you know? Loving God isn't any different from loving a man—or a child. It's wanting to be with Him, to be near Him." He made a hopeless gesture with his hands. "It's wanting to protect Him from yourself." (172–73)

Contrasting sharply with this scene is the confession—if that is the right word—of the American bank robber Calver. The text makes it clear that despite the surface contrast of their occupations, the murderer and the priest share that all-important quality which puts the latter at such a moral distance from his pious parishioners— an absolutistic career. Recall that Calver's mug shot was pinned up next to the priest's, for here, in words that could equally apply to the protagonist, we are told that the felon "was hardly recognizable from the news picture on the police station wall; that was tougher, arrogant, a man who had made good. This was just a tramp's face" (187). Now we find that just as Calver's life has flown in the face of bourgeois morality, so will his salvation, for the priest tells him that he may gain forgiveness "at the last moment[. . . l]ike a thief," a phrase that has relevance for the hero's own spiritual destiny as well. Finally, in contrast to the peasants who ignore the priest's predicament in their hunger for absolution, Calver repeatedly tells the priest to "beat it"—"You look after yourself. You take my knife . . ." (189). Greene's protagonist may be able to offer the bank robber only conditional absolution because his last act was "at the best . . . only one criminal trying to aid the escape of another," but the fact is that in Greeneland such an act is more salvational than most of what goes on in churches. This the priest unintentionally acknowledges when, likening himself to Calver, he concludes that "whichever way you looked, there wasn't much merit in either of them" (189–90).

Greene's inversion of Catholic orthodoxy—which echoes Péguy's[1]—
can be summed up by the priest's musings amid the relative safety of
the Lehrs' homestead that while "God might forgive cowardice and
passion . . . was it possible to forgive the habit of piety?" (169).

What is significant about the way religious belief and devotion are
portrayed in these and other passages is that no acceptable, stable
middle ground is depicted as existing between the selfish, mechanical pseudofaith of the conventionally pious and the priest's own
lacerating spiritual ordeal. Throughout the novel, the hard-hearted,
complacent women whom the priest encounters are represented
as so many living embodiments of the tenor of his entire previous
vocation. Amidst the cursing and copulating prisoners in the fetid
cell, for instance, he feels "a sense of companionship which he had
never experienced in the old days when pious people came kissing
his black cotton glove" (128). Confronted nevertheless in this very
cell with just such a self-satisfied apparition from his past, he claims
that "he would have known what to say to her in the old days, feeling
no pity at all, speaking with half a mind a platitude or two. Now he
felt useless. He was a criminal and ought only to talk to criminals"
(132). This is not to deny, of course, that many of the peasants in
The Power and the Glory are depicted as people of sympathy, dignity,
and genuine faith. But here again, all the peasants that the priest
meets in Tabasco are members of a religious community under
mortal threat—it is the city-dwelling pious women, hoarding their
holy pictures, hagiographic books, and certainty of spiritual election
who, by default, stand as the synoptic embodiment of Catholicism
under ordinary—which is to say mediated—circumstances.

In fact, if one prayer could be distilled from the narrative of
The Power and the Glory, it might well read "God save us from
ordinary life," for here, as in *Brighton Rock,* habit and safety are
sirens against which the absolutistic quester in search of Beulah
must block his ears. In Greene's view, being a good citizen of the
established Church is seemingly no better than going straight in
Brighton. Once the priest's bodily dangers are passed and he is
safe in the neighboring province, for instance, the spiritual dangers
associated with performing a religious office in a comfortable setting
waste no time in returning: "He felt respect all the way up the street:

---

1. Péguy, *Basic Verities,* 183.

men took off their hats as he passed: it was as if he had got back to the days before the persecution. He could feel the old life hardening around him like a habit, a stony cast which held his head high and dictated the way he walked, and even formed his words" (167–68). The protagonist catches himself in time, though, for, as stated previously, in Greene as in Conrad there is no return ticket from the absolute. Feeling that his new shoes—standard issue in his old life—are now "the badge of a deserter" (163), the priest experiences positive relief when the mestizo reappears to lure him back across the border to martyrdom.

Look where you will, there is no instance in *The Power and the Glory* where an unpersecuted church is depicted to be, or re-membered to have been, spiritually adequate—no occasion upon which a Catholic community at peace attains or attained anything approaching an acceptable *imitatio Christi*. Padre José was a bet-ter priest—or at least a better believer—than Greene's hero during the good times, but Padre José has buckled rather than run the risk of defying, or even eluding, the new regime. The choice that this novel offers, then, is truly one of either/or. As Unamuno, one of Greene's favorite authors, puts it, "Whosoever believes in God, but believes without passion, without anguish, without uncertainty, without doubt, without despair-in-consolation, believes only in the God-Idea, not in God Himself."[2] This can be cited as a pardon for the protagonist's backsliding from the conventional priestly ideal, but it also lays an indictment against all the other modes of religious life depicted in the novel, "everyday" Catholicism included. The priest, we are compelled to understand, is acceptable to God, but it seems to be his very *isolation* from the body of his church that is the making of his worth in the eyes of Divinity, for in Greene, "God, like the devil, operates inexplicably apart, if necessary, from the Church's body of dogma."[3] Leaving the safety of Chiapas, for instance, he passes "the whitewashed church—that too belonged to a dream. Life didn't contain churches" (181). And indeed when the priest finally does enter a sanctuary under the dispensation of sleep, he is once again strangely—and fortunately—isolated. In the "curious dream" that he has on the eve of his execution, and that seems so clearly

2. Miguel de Unamuno, *The Tragic Sense of Life in Men and Nations*, 211.
3. Karl, "Demonical Heroes," 53.

prophetic of his salvation, a mass is taking place. "But *he* sat on, just waiting, paying no attention to the God over the altar, as though that were a God for other people and not for him. Then the glass by his plate began to fill with wine" (209). The only communication he has with the dream's shadowy congregation comes through the secretive language of Morse code, for finally in that cipher "a whole invisible congregation tapped along the aisles" (210). In practice the priest appears not so much a Catholic saint as he does the founder, martyr, and last adherent of an arduous and exclusive faith that is strictly a matter between himself and God.

In fact, if one were in a mischievous mood, one could make the argument that *The Power and the Glory* is one of the century's great Protestant documents. After all, when the priest was loaded down with his full regalia he was corpulent and spiritually ineffectual. It is only after his hierarchy is swept away, his priestly gear discarded, and his liturgical calendar forgotten that he begins to grow into a genuine spiritual office:[4] "feast days and fast days and days of abstinence had been the first to go: then he had ceased to trouble more than occasionally about his breviary—and finally he had left it behind altogether at the port in one of his periodic attempts to escape. Then the altar stone went—too dangerous to carry with him. . . . [H]e was probably liable to suspension, but penalties of the ecclesiastical kind began to seem unreal in a state where the only penalty was the civil one of death" (60). He makes a game effort to procure wine for a mass, but the Jefe guzzles it down. Then, just before his night in the prison, he prudently drops the last of his "credentials" and we are told "it was like the final surrender of a whole past" (118)—even though, it can be argued, the highest peaks of his religious witness lie in the hours ahead. Finally, there is the matter of the novel's title, which is a phrase from the Lord's Prayer that is spoken during Protestant services but routinely dropped from the Catholic mass. Graham Greene has been labeled both a Catholic novelist and a spy novelist—was he then some kind of Protestant mole?

What keeps this line of argument a mere fancy, and what supports our main contention, is the harsh treatment that the Lehrs' Protestantism comes under for being entirely too comfortable. In

---

4. See Heyward D. Brock and James M. Welsh, "Graham Greene and the Structure of Salvation," 39.

what must, for instance, stand as a deliberate parody of the whisky priest's attainment of gnosis through suffering, Mrs. Lehr recounts her horrific encounter with the absolute in Pittsburgh: "But when I opened it—it was called something like *Police News.* I never knew such dreadful things were printed. Of course, I didn't read more than a few lines. I think it was the most dreadful thing that's ever happened to me. It . . . well, it opened my eyes" (171). This willful turning away from encounters with evil is symbolically extended to encompass Mr. Lehr as well, for in answer to the priest's question of whether there are any snakes on the "German-American homestead," Mr. Lehr "grunt[s] contemptuously that if there were any snakes they'd pretty soon get out of the way" (163). Though the priest generously concedes that the sanitized compound the brother and sister have built is, "in its way, an admirable mode of life" (163), the Gideon Bible that he discovers in his room underscores its fatally mediated character. This volume, with its "ugly type and . . . over-simple explanations" ("If you are in trouble read Psalm 34. . . . If you are lonesome and discouraged[,] Psalms 23 and 27") is designed to "Wi[n] Commercial Men for Christ," and surely represents a formu-laic, materialistic, and altogether too sanguine religious conception that places it at the farthest possible distance from the whisky priest's needfully tortuous wrestlings with his soul and its Creator. Finally, to drive home the fact that what really separates Mr. Lehr's religion from that of the hero's is not that one is Protestant and the other Catholic, we are informed that "Mr. Lehr slept on undisturbed upon his back with the thin rectitude of a bishop upon a tomb" (174). In Greeneland it is not the content of the religious doctrine one espouses that matters so much as the tones of complacent smugness or trembling self-doubt with which it is enunciated.

That location which exists at the spiritual antipodes of the Lehrs' ranch is, in a manner of speaking, a church, but of a most unorthodox and absolutistic cast. Fittingly, it is a holy site that the protagonist attains only when he is exhausted, feverish, and starving: "At sunset on the second day they came out on to a wide plateau covered with short grass. A grove of crosses stood up blackly against the sky, leaning at different angles—some as high as twenty feet, some not much more than eight. They were like trees that had been left to seed. The priest stopped and looked at them. They were the first Christian symbols he had seen for more than five years publicly exposed—if

you could call this empty plateau in the mountains a public place"
(154). Here God seems almost to be a ground-dwelling power, and
one is put in mind of the spirit described in Lawrence's *St. Mawr*,
whose seat is also within the mountains. Certainly the Christianity
they testify to is an unorthodox or even an heretical one, for "no priest
could have been concerned in the strange rough group; it was the
work of Indians and had nothing in common with the tidy vestments
of the Mass and the elaborately worked out symbols of the liturgy."
Further, when the Indian woman who is traveling with the priest
kneels before them, she "crosse[s] herself, not as ordinary Catholics
do, but in a curious and complicated pattern which included the
nose and ears." (Recall the priest's refusal in prison to conventionally
segregate the life of the body from the life of the saint.) What is
most striking about this eerie tabernacle, however, is how its very
unorthodoxy renders it spiritually potent: "It was like a short cut to
the dark and magical heart of the faith—to the night when the graves
opened and the dead walked" (154). It is in the nature of short cuts
to offer a quicker arrival at the cost of rougher, more dangerous
traveling, and this accords well with Greene's overall conception
of the mediated and the absolute. Certainly the whisky priest, by
taking his harrowing road to this mysterious temple, has arrived at
a destination that the pious will in fact never reach: "Faith, one was
told, could move mountains, and here was faith—faith in the spittle
that healed the blind man and the voice that raised the dead. The
evening star was out: it hung low down over the edge of the plateau—
it looked as if it was within reach." So convincing is the spiritual
resonance of the place that when the Indian woman's child fails to
return to life, "it [is] as if God had missed an opportunity" (155). The
prayed-for miracle may not be forthcoming, but the novel leaves
little doubt that the priest has finally found a church appropriate to
his singularly absolutistic faith.

   Greene's thematic juxtaposition of the mediated and the absolute
within *The Power and the Glory* would thus appear to paint all vari-
eties of institutionalized religion as fatally inadequate in their self-
proclaimed roles as mediator and conduit between the individual and
God. Granted, this indictment is hurled by omission, but it is quite
audible nonetheless. As in *Brighton Rock,* the existential heights and
depths to be found in the realm of the absolute constitute the one
thing spiritually needful, the sole salvational encounter, and yet as

in the previous novel this necessary experience is available only to the few. Furthermore, the daily workings of the official Church appear to block such access to the absolute rather than promote it. I would agree with S. K. Sharma that "the astonishing thing about [Greene] is that he can talk about doctrinal matters in his novels without being doctrinal. Though he has a latent yearning for the transcendent vision that an authentic religious experience might nourish, he can scarcely disguise his contempt for the moral and theological perversion of institutional religion."[5]

This vision of the Catholic Church's—taken en masse—endemic spiritual inadequacy may never be called up quite so powerfully again in Greene's subsequent novels, but the implications put forward by what many readers consider his masterpiece should at least give pause to those critics who are continually attempting to broaden the definition of Catholic apologist wide enough to cover the man. At a very minimum, *The Power and the Glory* should squarely refute any claim that our author is intent upon demonstrating the enhanced moral capacities—for good and ill—of all Catholics just because they are Catholics. As we have seen, merely belonging to the Church gets you nowhere at all toward either redemptive extreme—spiritual suburbans are spiritual suburbans, whether they drink in Brighton pubs or kneel before Mexican altars. There is in fact a great existential divide that runs through Greene's cast of characters, but it runs parallel to no merely denominational faultline. In fact, given the extent to which the spiritual isolation of the whisky priest is both emphasized and valorized, *The Power and the Glory's* proselytizing cry—appropriately inverse—might be conceived as asserting that there is "no salvation *inside* the Church"—indeed, inside *any* church.

Greene was occasionally fond of subdividing his religious affirmation into two related but distinct parts. As he stated in an interview, "there's a difference between belief and faith. If I don't believe in X or Y, faith intervenes, telling me that I'm wrong not to believe. Faith is above belief. One can say that it's a gift of God, while belief is not. Belief is founded on reason. On the whole I keep my faith while enduring long periods of disbelief." The use of "X" and "Y" in his definition of "belief" suggests something formulaic and enumerated, while "faith" appears more spontaneous and instinctive. As Paul

5. Sharma, *Search for Belief,* 19.

O'Prey glosses this pair of terms, "faith for Greene means an unques-
tioning acceptance of God and a trust in His love and mercy. Belief,
on the other hand, is man's rationalization and institutionalization
of God, through theology and the Church." It would seem that in
The Power and the Glory the distance between these two terms has
increased to a point where, instead of being two modes of a single,
overarching experience, they are two incompatible ways of relating
to God. Faith is religious feeling in its absolutistic—which is to say, its
only acceptable—mode: "Faith, one was told, could move mountains,
and here was faith—faith in the spittle that healed the blind man
and the voice that raised the dead" (155). Belief, on the other hand,
because it entails the workaday rituals and formulas of a religious
establishment, ceases in *The Power and the Glory* to be a supplement
to faith and instead becomes its despised, suburban opposite, reeking
of altar societies and mechanical confession. This intensification of
the faith/belief distinction is important not because it is a master
key to Greene's overall religious vision, but because it is typical of
the way in which ideas raised in his nonfiction become accentuated,
aggravated, and magnified in his novels. When, for instance, our
author asserts to a journalist that he is "inclined to find superstition
or magic more 'rational' than such abstract religious ideas as the Holy
Trinity," and that he "like[s] the so-called 'primitive' manifestations
of the faith,"[6] we are able to see not so much an echo or mere
demonstration of this preference in *The Power and the Glory* as a
vivid and violent intensification of it. This will not be the only time
that a mild assertion of Greene's in one context will be transformed
into a *cri du coeur* in his fictions.

In the previous chapter, we asked why Greene believes it necessary for Pinkie's reaction against bourgeois Brighton to be so extreme
and violent. To a certain extent, the same question directed at the
priest's wanderings from Catholic orthodoxy will meet a similar
answer—that soul-killing habit and routine can infect a confessional
and a vestry as well as a cheap seaside bedroom. But there is another
answer as well, and one that will lead us straight into an exploration
of Greene's conception of the nature of God. As we shall see, the
Lord must be sought out in the high and dangerous places in part

6. Marie-Françoise Allain, ed., *The Other Man: Conversations with Graham
Greene,* 162–63; O'Prey, *Reader's Guide,* 96; Allain, *Other Man,* 146.

because He has *retreated* there—because He is undergoing a process of diminishment and humanization that calls His omnipotence into doubt and seems to presage His ultimate disappearance from the universe altogether. In Greene's world God is not dead—not yet, anyway—but He has shrunk down to a size in which those who see Him face-to-face also find themselves in the troubling position of facing him eye-to-eye.

II

The Power and the Glory is almost universally regarded as Greene's proclamation of Christianity's inevitable triumph over the forces of militant secularism. And surely no one would deny that the novel depicts the priest's supposed "failure" as anything less than the attainment of sainthood (defined, of course, in Greene's own unique terms), or that it represents the lieutenant's "successful" manhunt as anything more than a hollow, Pyrrhic victory. The antagonists' two dreams at book's end bear this out eloquently: in the priest's, the feasting dreamer stands ready to enjoy "the best dish of all," his glass fills with wine, and he is promised hopeful "news" (209–10). As for the lieutenant, "he couldn't remember afterwards anything of his dreams except laughter, laughter all the time, and a long passage in which he could find no door" (207). These portents, combined with the young Luis's change of heart and the arrival of the next, unnamed priest in Tabasco, all point toward a faith that, because it embodies eternal truths about the world that are dismissed by secularist ideologies, will eventually best and outlast all such hankerings after strange gods. And yet, there is a countervailing motif within the novel that suggests that the lieutenant's vision is not altogether mistaken, a motif that insinuates that whatever the durability of the Catholic Church, the Divinity it worships is fast vanishing. I am not talking here about the oft-noted fact that Greene characterizes the lieutenant with a good measure of sympathy, depicting him as a kind of secular priest, sincere in his beliefs, and carrying within himself a genuine if baffled love for the children of his province. It is not the lieutenant's feelings or actions that are at issue in this contrarian theme, but rather his ideas about the structure and destiny of the universe.

What the lieutenant believes about these matters is straightforwardly presented: "It infuriated him to think that there were still people in the state who believed in a loving and merciful God. There are mystics who are said to have experienced God directly. He was a mystic, too, and what he had experienced was vacancy—a complete certainty in the existence of a dying, cooling world, of human beings who had evolved from animals for no purpose at all. He knew" (24–25). A vision of the world's entropic trajectory, similar to that which drove Pinkie to commit acts of cruelty and murder in a more or less reactive fashion, here prompts the lieutenant to pursue a more disciplined program of political terror. Whereas the protagonist of *Brighton Rock* has nothing but contempt for those not among the cognoscenti, the lieutenant wishes to generously spread the word— he too has "news": the children "deserved nothing less than the truth—a vacant universe and a cooling world, the right to be happy in any way they chose" (58). Again, though, our focus is not upon what the lieutenant does as a consequence of his ideas—rather, it is on the novel's evaluation of the truth of those ideas. To investigate the subject further, however, we must first turn to the lieutenant's opponent and the heavenly power he embodies.

The whisky priest is, beyond doubt, a conduit for grace. Many critics have pointed out the ways in which his presence affects those around him for the better, as if a kind of spiritual energy flowed through him, vivifying adjacent souls despite his abject state and lengthy chapter of faults. The priest thus "brings back to . . . secular and desiccated consciousnesses an impression of spiritual greatness and possibility, indirectly moving them, perhaps at an unconscious level, to a greater spiritual moment in themselves."[7] Here, though, it is the other sense of the word *moment* that is crucial, for what seems to have been missed—or at least passed over as too odd and disconcerting—is the tentative, halting, and ultimately attenuated nature of this benign influence. Consider first the case of Mr. Tench. After his chance meeting and interrupted drink with the protagonist, he is strangely motivated to make contact with the wife he has not seen in decades: "an odd impulse had come to him to project this stray letter towards the last address he had. . . . He tried to begin. . . . He started to write" (45–46). As he continues, it is plain that Tench himself does not fully understand what has prompted him to attempt this symbolic escape from his Mexican exile. "It would have been easier if there had been some purpose behind it other than the vague

---

7. Roger C. Poole, "Graham Greene's Indirection," 32–33.

desire to put on record to somebody that he was still alive. . . . How surprised she would be at hearing from him after this long while." Indeed, "Why write at all? He couldn't remember now what had given him the odd idea" (46). The reader guesses, however, and it is not long before Tench's thoughts drift to the true instigator of his new resolution. "A memory stirred. It was as if something alive and in pain moved in the little front room among the rocking-chairs . . . then died, or got away" (47). The soil of Tench's heart may be nearly exhausted, but clearly a seed has been planted—the mere passage through his house of the suffering priest has mysteriously opened a way of escape for the demoralized man, and the character whom we first met seeking out the purely physical balm of his ether cylinder has received an analgesic for the spirit.

In the end, however, this fresh start comes to nothing—moreover, it comes to nothing with a whimper. Towards the end of the novel Tench reappears, having recently received a letter from his wife "out of the blue" (215)—apparently he never completed his note to her. The contents of the wife's missive—she tells him she has joined a religious group and is going to divorce him—leave Tench baffled. Then, watching from his window as he scrapes the Jefe's teeth, he sees the priest taken out and shot. The sight appalls him, and he appears to make another resolution: "currency—he would insist on foreign currency: this time he was going to clear out, clear out for good." Now, however, the memory of his martyred guest imparts no energy whatsoever, and Tench exits the novel on a note of exhaustion and inertia: "an appalling sense of loneliness came over Mr. Tench, doubling him with indigestion. The little fellow had spoken English and knew about his children. He felt deserted" (217). Here, the potential fruits of grace have apparently died on the vine.

Even more suggestive is the case of Coral Fellows, for her encounter with the priest seems to promise much more than Tench's, and yet in an important sense this promise too goes unfulfilled. The prematurely mature girl, after harboring the fugitive priest, discussing religion with him, and receiving the promise of his prayers, seems to be mulling over the faith she abandoned at the age of ten.

> "Mother," the child said, "do you believe there's a God?"
>   The question scared Mrs. Fellows. She rocked furiously up and down and said, "Of course."

"I mean the Virgin Birth—and everything."

"My dear, what a thing to ask. Who have you been talking to?"

"Oh," she said. "I've been thinking, that's all." (52–53)

It is later, however, when she is feeling the onset of her first menstrual pain, that Coral appears to receive a visitation of grace through the agency of the priest, for he has left a hieroglyphic testament behind him. Checking the barn where he spent his frightened night, she makes a discovery.

> The torch lit the back wall: low down near the ground somebody had scrawled in chalk—she came closer: a lot of little crosses leant in the circle of light. He must have lain down among the bananas and tried to relieve his fear by writing something, and this was all he could think of. The child stood in her woman's pain and looked at them: a horrible novelty enclosed her whole morning: it was as if everything were memorable. (54–55).

Coral appears to be at the threshold of some epiphany, some expansion of consciousness and sympathy that seems likely to lead her somewhere important—into closer spiritual sympathy with the priest, perhaps; it is difficult to be more precise.

And yet, what is the issue of all this? Except in the protagonist's final dream, Coral never appears again. We know that she has died, but we are never told how—did Calver shoot her? Did the police? Did she die of a fever? Nor does the later scene involving her parents much clarify her spiritual and emotional growth between the last time we see her alive and the moment of her death: "But the odd thing is—the way she went on afterwards—as if he'd told her things" (214)—this we have already witnessed. Some critics, pointing to her role as cupbearer in the hero's hopeful last dream, assert that we must understand that Coral's "brief contact with the whisky priest . . . has turned her mind back to God in time"—i.e., in time to earn her eternal salvation—for "the 'sesame' to the future, as the priest's dream suggests, has occurred."[8] While I agree that Coral's appearance in the dream reinforces our sympathy with her and gives comfort to those who insist upon speculating about her eternal destination, it

8. Ronald G. Walker, *Infernal Paradise: Mexico and the Modern English Novel,* 215; see also Richard Kelly, *Graham Greene,* 50.

does not much lessen the shock of her otherwise total disappearance from the secular plane of the novel. If *The Power and the Glory* were a postmodern text we might not think her unprepared-for and unexplained erasure so strange, but given the novelistic conventions that Greene normally inhabits, most readers cannot help but find it puzzling. Indeed, the words that accompany Pinkie's exit at the end of his book could almost apply to Coral's in the middle of hers: "it was as if [s]he'd been withdrawn suddenly by a hand out of any existence—past or present, whipped away into zero—nothing" (*BR*, 234). Nothing certainly comes of nothing where Coral's parents are concerned, for the Fellows exit the book in a state of mental paralysis upon which their daughter's all-too-brief acquaintance with grace has left, spiritually speaking, no visible trace: "It was no good. They had both been deserted" (213). Once again, we see a stream rise, only to watch it feebly peter out in the desert.

We can add to this at least one more example of dissipated or feckless grace. The priest makes his most strident and self-conscious effort to carve a toehold for redemption in his daughter, Brigitta. In this case, however, we are informed on several occasions that he is simply too late. When he first recognizes her, it is "as if a grown woman was there before her time, making her plans, aware of far too much. . . . He put out his hand as if he could drag her back by force from—something; but he was powerless" (67). Although she is only a child, "the world [is] in her heart already, like the small spot of decay in a fruit. She [is] without protection—she ha[s] no grace, no charm to plead for her" (81), and the priest despairingly sees her "fixed in her life like a fly in amber" (82). Later, remembering Brigitta during his night in the prison cell, he concludes that "the knowledge of the world lay in her like the dark explicable spot in an X-ray photograph; he longed—with a breathless feeling in the breast—to save her, but he knew the surgeon's decision—the ill was incurable" (127). What is noteworthy here, and what is troubling from an orthodox point of view, is this insistent emphasis on belatedness. Grace *could* have triumphed in Brigitta's soul, it is suggested, had the priest arrived back in the village a month or a week or even a day before he actually did. But, like a benign fluid in the blood that must, by its very chemical structure, dwindle in volume as an invading substance multiplies, it has been slowly, incrementally, and inevitably overwhelmed by a worldly infection. No lighting on the road to Emmaus here—rather, the process of spiritual deterioration seems mechanical, quantifiable, and, most importantly, irreversible.

If, then, God's grace in *The Power and the Glory* resembles nothing so much as a fixed quantity of precious fuel liable to depletion, a finite charge imparted now and again to the soul's battery, as it were, what can we say about God himself? We can say, I believe, that the deity we encounter in this novel lacks omnipotence in one striking regard: He is depicted as being *subject to entropy,* no less so than the universe He presumably created. Divine grace, at the moment of its introduction into Greene's world, takes the shape of a spontaneous and distributive spiritual power to awaken, but from that moment on it begins to behave like more conventional types of energy, rapidly dissipating over time. The priest imparts his gift to those whom he touches, but that gift cannot seem to remain sufficiently concentrated or organized to redeem them, as if it were some fast-decaying isotope, and thus its transformative power seeps away into space. As a result, "the ambiance which permeates *The Power and the Glory* . . . is . . . dominated by the fact of mortality, of loss, of temporal flux tending toward entropy."[9] The Catholic Catechism, of course, makes it clear that grace is a call that the individual must answer if the soul is to be redeemed, and it is understood that many a sinner will not exercise his or her free will in such a way as to adequately respond to the divine invitation. Still, this does nothing to blunt the impact of Greene's repeated depictions of a redemptive vitality insufficient to wrest souls from the entropic malaise that envelops his fictional Tabasco—in a literary text, the instances we actually see are the only ones we may legitimately consider when assessing the author's conception of life. And in Greene's Mexico, spiritual power is radiated away as waste heat more frequently than it is put to productive use. When the mestizo attempts his confession, for instance, the metaphor is strikingly entropic:

> The priest was reminded of an oil-gusher which some prospectors had once stuck near Concepción—it wasn't a good enough field apparently to justify further operations, but there it had stood for forty-eight hours against the sky, a black fountain spouting out of

9. Walker, *Infernal Paradise,* 206; see also John Mills, "The Dog in the Perambulator," 81.

the marshy useless soil and floating away to waste—fifty thousand gallons an hour. It was like the religious sense in man, cracking suddenly upwards, a black pillar of fumes and impurity, running to waste. (96–97)

Likewise, when the Jefe is downing the contraband wine that the priest had hoped to employ during mass, the latter weeps to see "all the hope of the world draining away" (113). And, later, during the protagonist's trek across the mountains, we are told that he and the Indian woman "might have been the only survivors of a world which was dying out" (154). Spillage, seepage, sputtering life—such are the figures that govern the spiritual forces at play in this novel.

Frequently, this waning and wasting of divine energy is defined as abandonment, as if the only decisive act God had lately committed was the purely negative one of turning away, or the entropic one of giving up. We can see this when a stargazing Father José "c[an] not believe that to a watcher there [on another planet] *this* world could shine with such brilliance: it would roll heavily in space under its fog like a burning and abandoned ship" (29). This divine lassitude is mirrored in the somnambulistic attitude of Tabasco's citizens. Mr. Tench, for instance, doesn't really mind not finding his ether cylinder: "It didn't matter so much after all: a little additional pain was hardly noticeable in the huge abandonment" (18). And, in like manner, Luis's father can't work up any anger at his son's scoffing at the pious book, resignedly admitting, "It's not your fault. We have been deserted" (51). It is interesting to note that in *The Lawless Roads* Greene remarked that "one can respect an atheist as one cannot respect a deist" (*LR,* 37), for what seems to be operating through these passages concerning his fictional Mexico is in fact a kind of tough-minded, pessimistic deism. The God of *The Power and the Glory* appears to be a Watchmaker who for some reason has ceased to wind and oil his creation, as if the same entropy that decrees the running down of the mechanism had palsied the hands of the Maker as well.

The Power and the Glory also sees the instigation of a type of scene that appears in all of the subsequent so-called Catholic novels and that goes far toward contributing to this notion of a deity in thrall to the Second Law of Thermodynamics.[10] Desperate at the thought

10. See Roger Sharrock, "Unhappy Families: The Plays of Graham Greene," 81–82.

of his daughter's worldly corruption, the whisky priest addresses a startling petition to his Lord: "He prayed silently, 'Oh God, give me any kind of death—without contrition, in a state of sin—only save this child'" (82). This is a moment that finds an echo eight years later in *The Heart of the Matter,* when Scobie, on the verge of taking communion while in a state of mortal sin, attempts a similar bargain with God: "But with open mouth (the time had come) he made one last attempt at prayer, 'O God, I offer up my damnation to you. Take it. Use it for them,' and was aware of the pale papery taste of an eternal sentence on the tongue" (*HM,* 225). Finally, and perhaps most famously, there is Sarah Miles's reaction to seeing what she believes to be the dead body of her lover Bendrix crushed beneath a door during an air raid:

> I knelt down on the floor: I was mad to do such a thing: I never even had to do it as a child—my parents never believed in prayer, any more than I do. . . . I shut my eyes tight, and I pressed my nails into the palms of my hands until I could feel nothing but the pain, and I said, I will believe. Let him be alive, and I *will* believe. Give him a chance. Let him have his happiness. Do this and I'll believe. But that wasn't enough. It doesn't hurt to believe. So I said, I love him and I'll do anything if you'll make him alive. I said very slowly, I'll give him up for ever, only let him be alive with a chance . . . and then he came in at the door, and he was alive, and I thought now the agony of being without him starts. . . . (*EA,* 95)

Unfortunately, one often encounters an impulse among critics to anxiously trim and flatten even such passages as these until they appear compatible with some conception of Christian orthodoxy. The example below is fairly typical.

> What can be said of the bargaining prayers, the bartering which God seems to accept? . . . Is Greene so badly instructed in the Catholic faith as to suppose that this is sound and acceptable doctrine? . . . It would seem that in this, the farthest extreme of all, he is again saying that nothing can alienate from God those whom he has chosen, that nothing is beyond his mercy. The stark bargain, which the Christian sees as blasphemy and the unbeliever as a proof of the inadequacy of professed faith, even this may become an instrument of grace. You cannot turn away God even by offering

your thirty pieces of silver: he may accept them and save you in spite of yourself."[11]

To my mind, however, these passages bespeak a Greene whose diversions from orthodoxy cannot be so easily papered over. Taken together and considered in light of what has been said of *The Power and the Glory* thus far, such scenes of soul-wagering testify not to a God so merciful that he will accept even the crassest swap of eternal destinies, but to a God who inhabits a zero-sum universe in which any spiritual disbursement from on high must be countered by an equal and opposite payment from the petitioner. It is as if the whole possibility of divine generosity and creativity had somehow lapsed, and that the grace necessary to save even a single soul must now be extracted from that contained within a closed system that is jealously guarded. The cosmos, it appears, is running down, and thus God's inexhaustible love and gratuitous plenitude has been replaced by a scheme of quid pro quo between heaven and earth.

When scrutinized in this manner, *The Power and the Glory,* which has long been considered one of Greene's most strident proclamations of faith and a novel comparatively free of religious doubt—that is to say, one of his most monologic productions—appears in fact to be surprisingly polyphonic. According to Mikhail Bakhtin, in a monologic novel there is only one description of reality that the text depicts as valid, usually that articulated by the protagonist or the narrator. In such a text the author's own ideological positions are the only ones allowed to fully resonate, while opposing perspectives are doled out to obviously secondary characters in such a way that they "no longer [appear] as signifying ideas, but rather as socially typical or individually characteristic manifestations of thought." Labeled as the idiosyncratic products of some special social circumstance, biographical trauma, or psychological lacuna, they become not valid alternatives to the reigning authorial discourse but so many verbal straw men that, by their obvious deficiencies, merely underscore the infallible, unanswerable speech emanating from the novel's ideological center. A polyphonic novel, by contrast, is one in which "a character's word about himself and his world is just as fully weighted as the author's" and in which those figures

---

11. Raymond Chapman, "The Vision of Graham Greene," 92–93.

whose perspectives oppose that of the narrator or protagonist are represented "not only [as] objects of authorial discourse but also [as] subjects of their own directly signifying discourse."[12] This does not mean that an author remains neutral (an impossible undertaking) or fails to sharply differentiate between the ethics of his hero and that of his villain; it means only that he endeavors to present the worldviews of even the chief antagonist as if from the inside, granting that dissenting position its full status as a legitimate competitor with the one he chooses to inhabit.

Now it has long been a critical commonplace that the whisky priest and the lieutenant agree about more things than they realize. It has furthermore been pointed out that some of the latter's accusations against the Church hit home and remain unanswered—that "while bemoaning the Lieutenant's violence, the novel also acknowledges the need for social change and, more readily than *The Lawless Roads,* the excesses of the Church."[13] But what our analysis now points to is something more radical than a claim that the lieutenant is sometimes right about the institution of Catholicism but always wrong about the ultimate nature of the universe. Rather, our conclusion must be that, when looked at wholly and carefully, *The Power and the Glory* also tacitly validates that character's entropic vision of the cosmos, that it exercises a kind of polyphonic fairness vis-à-vis the competing cosmologies of its two main figures. The priest may occasionally best the lieutenant in argument as they ride toward the former's Calvary, but the passages we have discussed above make it clear that as far as the novel as a whole is concerned, the lieutenant's beliefs are not sad delusions, but sadly accurate descriptions of reality. Of course it might be objected at this point that Greene also spares no opportunity to describe the stifling, debilitating heat of Mexico, and thus makes the very notion of entropy seem about as unlikely as the virgin birth. Perhaps, but although "heat stood in [his] room like an enemy" the lieutenant "believed against his senses in the cold empty ether spaces" (25). As the priest would no doubt agree, faith is nothing if not the evidence of things not seen, and it is *The Power and the Glory's* contention that the lieutenant's faith is

---

12. Mikhail Bakhtin, *Problems of Dostoevsky's Poetics,* 82, 7.
13. Judith Adamson, *Graham Greene: The Dangerous Edge: Where Art and Politics Meet,* 62.

justified—that his version of final things is just as truthful as that of the priest.

This is *not* to imply that the novel represents the whisky priest as mistaken in *his* belief. To be precise, we should claim that when the lieutenant affirms that the children "deserv[e] nothing less than the truth—a vacant universe and a cooling world" (58)—he is half right. The universe is *not* vacant, for the merciful God of the whisky priest exists; but the world *is* cooling, and so is the God who created it. Needless to say, the logical contradiction of a deity susceptible to heat-death is in no way detrimental to Greene's novelistic achievement. On the contrary, it is the source of that overriding atmosphere of attenuated hope and tattered sanctity, that sense of a benign yet evanescent and crepuscular providence that renders *The Power and the Glory* so hauntingly powerful. Indeed, the contradiction is precisely what allows the novel to testify without preaching, to allow the sacred and the secular to speak with equal validity. If Greene must be seen as a twentieth-century heir to those Victorians—diagnosed in J. Hillis Miller's *The Disappearance of God*—who frantically attempted to describe the lineaments of a Creator increasingly difficult to locate and fathom, it is fitting that he was able to so seamlessly overlay his own time's prevailing scientific eschatology upon that of Christianity's, and to produce thereby a novel whose theology is not so much agnostic as ambivalent—a novel that, to employ the terminology of Greene's least-favorite Victorian, voices the Everlasting Yea and the Everlasting Nay in the selfsame breath.

In Greene's subsequent fictions, his God continues to diminish in stature and power without, however, relinquishing the ability to motivate human action and transform human hearts—if only by the poignant spectacle of His shattered greatness. And, as we shall see, our author is not averse to reimagining the Christian God as a participant in another of the twentieth-century's scientific master narratives, if such a risky strategy holds any hope of preventing his disappearance altogether.

III

I wish to consider *The Heart of the Matter* and *The End of the Affair* within the frame of Greene's overall conception of a diminished and humanized God. These are the two books of his canon that have historically touched off the most vexed and polarizing critical debates, and with good reason. The volatile ambiguity surrounding Scobie's eternal fate in the first book, and (for some critics) the even more flammable lack of ambiguity concerning God's intrusion into the second, make them natural attractors of heated opinions. While I lay no claim to a cooler head than anyone else, I will attempt to see both texts as part of a continuum, and thereby, at least in this chapter, skirt some partisan battles in the name of keeping an eye on a bigger picture. The two books are very different from each other—indeed, I think that in some ways *The End of the Affair* is Greene's least typical major novel—but they do both put forward a vision of the Deity that can be seen as a continuation of that which we have already discerned in *The Power and the Glory.*

The Heart of the Matter is, to a large extent, a book about be-ing vulnerable, and Greene's conception of a diminished God who approaches closer and closer to the status of the merely human makes for two interrelated kinds of vulnerability. (Christianity, of course, has at its center the drama of God making Himself vulnerable through the earthly ministry of Christ, but when Greene imagines divine weakness, it is not Calvary he has in mind, and no citation of Trinitarian dogma will square the author's views with orthodoxy. As Erdinast-Vulcan remarks, Greene "dispense[s] with the traditional Catholic distinction between the Father and the Son as separate attributes of divinity, and turn[s] the Christian archetype of the self-sacrifice of the Son into an archetype of the self-sacrifice of the Father."[14] Indeed, little has been said about how infrequently Greene's Catholics actually think of Christ, who appears only to wander at the margins of their various religious struggles.) The first, and perhaps the less shocking variety of vulnerability, is that of human beings exposed to unjustified and irremediable suffering in consequence of a God who can no longer adequately shelter His creations. Here, Divinity does nothing in the face of human tragedy except stand by and observe, either because of some lack of needful potency or, it is sometimes hinted, because of some inexplicable moral failing. The second vulnerability is, because it is almost unique to Greene, much more intriguing. According to this notion, God himself is helpless before the woundings inflicted upon Him by sinning human beings, injuries that are represented not as pinpricks

14. Erdinast-Vulcan, *Childless Fathers,* 2.

but as debilitating body blows, insults to the supposedly Immortal of a nearly mortal consequence. Human beings, especially Catholics who boast a tactile relationship with the body of Christ through the taking of the sacraments, have God, so to speak, in the palms of their hands.

Of course any discussion of *The Heart of the Matter*'s presentation of the Deity must first deal with the objection that Scobie's views on the nature of God and the duties of a Catholic are presented by the text as being fundamentally mistaken—and that it is the hero's doctrinal "errors" that cause his tragic downfall. I would counter such an objection in several ways. First of all, Scobie's conception of how to square a world of terrible suffering with a supposedly benign Creator is the only such conception put forward by the text in any detail. I am simply not convinced by the all-too-common critical assumption that Scobie is being roundly criticized by Greene because he has misunderstood or ignored Catholic teachings on various subjects, for it represents an attempt to regulate our response to the hero by means of what Bakhtin would call (derisively) an "authoritative" discourse that a) lies almost wholly outside the text (or the canon, for that matter) we are considering and that b) fails to command Greene's belief in many of its particulars. Scobie is indeed reminded from time to time—or reminds himself—of the official Catholic dogma on this or that issue, but such dogmas are nearly always quickly dismissed as inadequate in the face of his own immediate and visceral experience of human pain. Greene himself likewise disposed of many official Catholic positions that did not square with his own perceptions of reality, as a myriad of his interviews and nonfiction pieces attest. Frankly, I cannot imagine a more uninteresting comment about Scobie than that his doctrine is unsound according to the doctors of the Church. The second reason often heard for discounting Scobie's cosmology is more psychological than religious—here, he stands accused of harboring excessive pity, an emotion that Greene takes special pains to blacken in both *The Ministry of Fear* and *The Heart of the Matter.* A full explanation of why Scobie's pity should do him no harm in our eyes—why it in fact does him no real harm in Greene's—must await the next chapter wherein the distinctions our author rhetorically erects between "love" and "pity" will be, I hope, thoroughly deconstructed. Suffice it to say now, that when Greene's thought is eventually observed in widest perspective, pity will appear as an indispensable component of the moral person, for it will be seen as inseparable from love in those characters who perceive the world wholly and clearly.

It should be apparent from the above that I understand Scobie to be the center of sympathy in his novel in a less hedging and qualified way than many critics would be comfortable with. Does this mean then that I take Scobie as a straightforward spokesman for Greene? Well, never straightforward (so few things are in Greene), and only to this extent: *The Heart of the Matter* is, like *The Power and the Glory* before it, in part a philosophical assay, an attempt to solve — or at least to plumb — the age-old problem of evil. In this novel, it seems to me, Greene is attempting, tentatively and speculatively, to reconcile the belief in a beneficent Creator with a world of endemic physical and emotional agony. This concern apparently leads his aesthetic imagination to augment the vision of a diminished God we encountered in his Mexican novel. I have no wish to finalize Scobie's thoughts and feelings into some codex of Greenean dogma, but his reactions to the harrowing paradoxes of life stand unrefuted elsewhere in his own novel, or indeed in his author's fiction as a whole, and thus they should, in Bakhtin's words, be allowed to fully "sound," to take their place as at least a provisional part of the author's "directly signifying discourse."

Scobie is a policeman, and so it shouldn't surprise us that he is a man in search of an explanation — a man who gets impatient when the facts of a case refuse to add up. The case — or, rather, the crime — in question involves the shipwrecked survivors who are ferried over in extremis from French territory. Among them is a young girl who has lost both her parents in the sinking, spent forty days in an open boat, and is now certain to die. What lays siege to Scobie's orthodox notion of a God who is both omnipotent and all-merciful is made explicit: "it would take all Father Brûle's ingenuity to explain that. Not that the child would die — that needed no explanation. Even the pagans realized that the love of God might mean an early death, though the reason they ascribed was different; but that the child should have been allowed to survive the forty days and nights in the open boat — that was the mystery, to reconcile that with the love of God" (120–21). In the subsequent weeks, the child's horrifically extended suffering weighs on his mind, thoughts of her agony breaking through to the surface at odd moments: "Scobie went down to the jetty and watched the sailing boats move down towards the sea. Once he found himself saying aloud as though to a man at his elbow, 'Why didn't you let her drown?' A court messenger looked at him askance and he moved on" (126). This case is obviously not closed; the perpetrator is still at large.

It is at this point that a kind of temptation is thrown in Scobie's path, and one that has nothing directly to do with Helen Rolt. There are rumors of an attack from French territory, which Scobie considers unlikely, "and yet of course one remembered the Heights of Abraham. . . . A single feat of daring can alter the whole conception of what is possible" (134). Just what kind of daring act he himself might accomplish comes into focus some time later as he performs his penance in church, "a formula" and a "hocus pocus" he considers a troublingly easy route to God's attention: "He went out of the box and knelt down again, and this too was part of a routine. It seemed to him for a moment that God was too accessible. There was no difficulty in approaching Him. Like a popular demagogue he was open to the least of His followers at any hour. Looking up at the cross he thought, He even suffers in public" (154). The likening of God to a demagogue hints at some moral taint in the Deity, and the comments about His vulnerability implicitly liken Scobie to a man plotting an assassination. What I am getting at is this: that the protagonist's subsequent visions of a God so weak as to be open to cruel injuries at the hands of human beings are overdetermined in a psychologically convincing way. Such a debilitated God, on the one hand, could not be held responsible for gratuitous human suffering; on the other hand, such a God could be punished for causing it. God could thus be exonerated of the crime and sentenced for committing it simultaneously. Both these outcomes must have a strong appeal to a born policeman like Scobie.

This desire to both absolve and injure divinity can be seen to operate in a pair of scenes that occur two pages apart on consecutive days. The fantasy of doing violence first drifts into Scobie's mind when he is attempting to explain Catholic doctrine to Helen, and in so doing paints his own behavior as verging on the satanic. "Now I'm just putting our love above—well, my safety. But the other [taking communion without benefit of confession]—the other's really evil. It's like the Black Mass, the man who steals the sacrament to desecrate it. It's striking God when he's down—in my power" (211).

Hard upon this comes the other side the coin, a God whose weakness is an excuse rather than an incitement to violence. "It seemed to him for a moment cruelly unfair of God to have exposed himself in this way, a man, a wafer of bread, first in the Palestinian villages and now here in the hot port, there, everywhere, allowing man to have his will of Him. . . . to put Himself at the mercy of men who hardly knew the meaning of the word. How desperately God must love, he thought with shame" (213). Notice here how eliding the Deity's omnipotence saves His benevolence—the extreme masochism of the figure Scobie imagines is both a tacit protest of divine innocence and an act of divine atonement for human suffering.

As the book nears its climax, Scobie's visions of himself as the batterer of a helpless God intensify. He is now to his own mind a *worse* offender than "those ruined priests who presided at a Black Mass" and who at least insult the Creator "from a hatred of God" (223) that he—quite significantly, as we shall see—says he lacks. "I am the cross" (225), he thinks as he takes his unshriven communion, and the thought of further such occasions calls up "a sudden picture . . . of a bleeding face, of eyes closed by the continuous shower of blows: the punch-drunk head of God reeling sideways" (237). One would think that no image could more vividly conflate the longed-for retribution and the exculpating weakness better than this one, but in a sense Scobie takes things one step further, imagining the final act of aggression and the final proof of mortal frailty when he conflates the person of God with that of his servant Ali, at whose murder he has passively connived. "Oh God, he thought, I've killed you: you've served me all these years and I've killed you at the end of them. God lay there under the petrol drums" (247). In *The Heart of the Matter* it is very much as if the Christian story were all about the Incarnation, leaving the Resurrection as only a vague and fading hope and thus emphasizing the God who suffers over the God who triumphs. As Frank Kermode has pointed out, it is one of the paradoxes of Greene's theology that if God is "strong, [He has] somehow convinced us that he is [also] easily hurt."[15]

---

15. Frank Kermode, "Mr. Greene's Eggs and Crosses," 133. See David H. Helsa, "Theological Ambiguity in the 'Catholic Novels,'" 109; Eagleton, "Reluctant Heroes," 114; and Nadya Aisenberg, *A Common Spring: Crime Novel and Classic*, 170.

In Scobie's final dialogue with what might be the voice of God, the interlocutor who speaks from the "cave of his body" claims to be as "humble as any other beggar" and asks the crucial question: "Can't you trust me as you'd trust a faithful dog?" (258–59). The issue is whether God can be counted upon not to visit Helen and Louise with unbearable suffering if Scobie eschews suicide and remains alive to choose between them. Scobie's reply is forthright: "No. I don't trust you. I've never trusted you" (259). It is significant that the heart of the matter is one of trust, for while one can mistrust someone who is morally deficient in some way, one can also feel a lack of trust in well-meaning souls who simply aren't strong enough to get the job done. But does the fact that Scobie holds the latter attitude render him too fatally confused about theological matters to garner our sympathy? Judith Adamson thinks not: "there may be a monstrous pride here as Greene suggests, but there is also an admirable independence from a God who stands by as man suffers." I would agree, as long as it is understood that Greene's God stands by not from indifference, but from an inability to assist. This, I think, is the bargain that the novel has made—to "solve" the problem of evil by choosing to imagine God as less than omnipotent rather than less than all-loving and all-merciful. And thus Scobie's insistence on suicide even though he believes it will damn him is simply another way of proving that God can plead exculpatory weakness, for "thinking of what he had done and was going to do, he thought, even God is a failure" (254). Furthermore, Scobie asserts, as do several other of Greene's protagonists, that "he love[s] failure: [he] can't love success" (253). Indeed, according to Joseph Kurismmootil, Scobie reads "failure . . . as the final meaning of Jesus' death. Despair was the reason for Calvary, not sacrifice; and this being so there is hardly anything further to hope for: not victory, nor regeneration."[16] In cosmological terms, though, this pessimism is paradoxically consoling: given the state of the world as *The Heart of the Matter* depicts it, conceiving of God as a success would also mean branding him a callous tyrant with a standard of morality below that of his suffering creatures— the option, for instance, that Bryon chose to pursue in *Cain*. Instead, Scobie and Greene determine to preserve that part of the Deity that

16. Adamson, *Dangerous Edge,* 83; K. C. Joseph Kurismmootil, S.J., *Heaven and Hell on Earth: An Appreciation of Five Novels of Graham Greene,* 126.

is most important to them—the fellow sufferer whose all-too-human weakness they can pity and love.

There remains one final thing to be said about this theme in *The Heart of the Matter.* As his fatal overdose takes effect, Scobie is granted a final visitation from his diminished God:

> It seemed to him as though someone outside the room were seeking him, calling him, and he made a last effort to indicate that he was here. He got to his feet and heard the hammer of his heart beating out a reply. He had a message to convey, but the darkness and the storm drove it back within the case of his breast, and all the time outside the house, outside the world that drummed like hammer blows within his ear, someone wandered, seeking to get in, someone appealing for help, someone in need of him. (265)

This passage appears as a kind of bridge linking Greene's first masterpiece, *Brighton Rock,* with perhaps his last, *The Honorary Consul.* The urgency of the warning call is reminiscent of that "something trying to get in; the pressure of gigantic wings" that Pinkie feels accosting him as he drives out of Brighton on his final errand. At the same time the note of divine neediness, the plea not for a worshiper so much as a companion in travail, looks forward to Father Rivas's speculations about a God who "one day with our help . . . will be able to tear His evil mask off forever" (*HC,* 227). However, *The Honorary Consul*'s hopeful gospel of a deity who shall overcome still lies decades in the future, and hard upon *The Heart of the Matter* comes another major novel in which the diminishment of God continues apace.

At first glance, *The End of the Affair* might appear to be an unlikely text to cite as part of a discussion concerning the humanization or disappearance of the Deity. After all, it is a novel in which, on the face of things, God "wins"—wresting belief in Himself out of a pair of committed sensualists who have good reasons to continue, as Thackeray put it, "living without God in the world." However, the very fact that we can speak so securely of Divinity as acting within the borders of a novel is itself the best evidence of how far He has been shrunk down in order to fit inside such an unaccustomed abode. And let us be clear on a crucial point: the conflict that drives *The End of the Affair*—that between God and Bendrix for the attentions of Sarah—is crucially dependent upon the Deity being imagined,

referred to, and grappled with as a human adversary. This is a novel
fueled almost exclusively by the frisson of blasphemy—by Bendrix's
continued insistence that God is nothing more than his sexual rival.
As one critic puts it, "this God is truly a jealous God, in the terms of
human eroticism rather than Mosaic law."[17] Without this conception,
there could be no tension, no suspense, no narrative momentum of
any kind, and when Bendrix at last concedes that it is a fiction, the
novel has no choice but to end then and there. Before he eventually
concedes defeat, however, Bendrix appears to wrestle with a randy
angel who might just lose: "I was cold and wet and very happy. I
could even look with charity towards the altar and the figure dangling
there. She loves us both, I thought, but if there is to be a conflict
between an image and a man, I know who will win. I could put my
hand on her thigh or my mouth on her breast: he was imprisoned
behind the altar and couldn't move to plead his cause" (*EA*, 128).
Bendrix makes much of this supposed corporeal advantage, lording
it over his spectral adversary: "She shut her eyes again, and looking
up at the altar I thought with triumph, almost as though he was a
living rival, You see—these are the arguments that win, and gently
moved my fingers across her breast" (130). Even after Sarah has died
and become immune to the allure of his caresses, Bendrix's rhetoric
still places her in the embrace of a distinctly mortal interloper. When
discussing her funeral arrangements, for instance, Bendrix confesses
that his "jealousy had not finished, like Henry's, with her death. It
was as if she were alive still, in the company of a lover she had
preferred to me. How I wished I could send Parkis after her to
interrupt their eternity" (137). He refuses to view her body, not
wishing to see her in death "any more than [he] would have wished
to see her in another man's arms" (141).

Moreover, when the protagonist turns his eyes directly upon his
opponent, he sees a kind of intrusive Lothario, "a strange relation
returned from the Antipodes" (137) who is "as underhand as a lover,
taking advantage of a passing mood, like a hero seducing us with his
improbabilities and his legends" (173), and who needs reminding
that he is a newcomer on the scene: "You didn't own her all those
years: I owned her. You won in the end, You don't need to remind
me of that, but she wasn't deceiving me with You when she lay here

17. Chapman, "Vision," 87.

with me, on this bed, with this pillow under her back. When she slept, I was with her, not You. It was I who penetrated her, not You" (165). Bendrix's manner of cutting God down to size may be different than Scobie's and spring from different emotions, but the enterprise is just as earnestly pursued.

The End of the Affair also shares *The Heart of the Matter*'s notion that God is only lovable when imagined as less than omnipotent. Bendrix is at his least venomous toward his heavenly competitor when he believes himself victorious over him: "Perhaps the publisher half hoped that my cynical treatment of [General] Gordon's Christianity would cause a *succès de scandale*. I had no intention of pleasing him: this God was also Sarah's God, and I was going to throw no stones at any phantom she believed she loved. I hadn't during that period any hatred of her God, for hadn't I in the end proved stronger?" (132). As the Deity waxes mightier in Bendrix's conception, however, He becomes proportionally the object of anger. "I thought of the stranger I had paid Parkis to track down: the stranger had certainly won in the end. No, I thought, I don't hate Henry. I hate You if you exist" (136). Indeed, of all God's attributes, it is His power that our narrator finds most detestable: "there still remains jealousy of my rival—a melodramatic word painfully inadequate to express the unbearable complacency, confidence and success he always enjoys" (54). Just as Scobie's suicide was a way both of harming God and of proving a lack of omnipotence that alone could render Him sympathetic, Bendrix too plans to use his own soul as a kind of weapon of last resort: "He robbed me and like that king you wrote about I'll rob Him of what he wants in me" (191). However, where Scobie wished to rescue God from his (Scobie's) own polluting companionship (the very claim denies God's omnipotence), Bendrix plans to withhold his love in an act of Byronic revolt—he will refuse to love Big Brother just in order to prove that the dictator's totalitarian regime is not quite total. Thus the novel's ending is precariously balanced at a point of unstable equilibrium. Bendrix exits the book with a prayer—"O God, You've done enough, You've robbed me of enough, I'm too tired and old to learn to love, leave me alone for ever" (192)—which hints that he may soon come to love God (simply because it *is* a prayer) while underscoring the refusal of that love in the present moment. Were God so completely successful as to win Bendrix's love within the novel, Green's paradoxical conception would paint such an all-triumphing deity as unlovable in the selfsame moment.

The suspicion that God might in fact be omnipotent is here always accompanied by dread, because in *The End of the Affair* it is always depicted as incompatible with free will. The book begins, in fact, with Bendrix questioning who is actually writing the narrative we are reading:

> A story has no beginning or end: arbitrarily one chooses that moment of experience from which to look back or from which to look ahead. I say "one chooses" with the inaccurate pride of a professional writer who—when he has been seriously noted at all—has been praised for his technical ability, but do I in fact of my own will *choose* that black wet January night on the Common, in 1946, the sight of Henry Miles slanting across the wide river of rain, or did these images choose me? It is convenient, it is correct according to the rules of my craft to begin just there, but if I had believed then in a God, I could also have believed in a hand, plucking at my elbow, a suggestion, "Speak to him: he hasn't seen you yet." (7)

This "agonized suspicion" of the narrator's "that some other and Omniscient Author is arranging the scenes, imposing a plot on his own life"[18] persists and deepens throughout the text. At one point, for instance, the protagonist likens people such as himself and God's saints to flat and round characters, respectively: "The saints, one would suppose, in a sense create themselves. They come alive. They are capable of the surprising act or word. They stand outside the plot, unconditioned by it. But we have to be pushed around. We have the obstinacy of non-existence. We are inextricably bound to the plot, and wearily God forces us, here and there, according to his intention, characters without poetry, without free will" (185–86). Moreover, the emerging coincidences of the plot—the fact that Sarah began loving God the night that Bendrix ran into Henry again, or that it was Bendrix himself who inadvertently hastened Sarah's death, or that Sarah was baptized a Catholic without knowing it—all contribute to an atmosphere of determinism that is almost suffocating. Indeed,

18. Herbert R. Haber, "The End of the Catholic Cycle: The Writer versus the Saint," 129–30.

whenever God escapes his role as a quasi-mortal lover, he instantly becomes a monstrous pedagogue intent upon proving to Bendrix that "the novel is written through [Bendrix] but not by him."[19] In a text whose narrator is a novelist, this insistence of God's that there are no genuine narratives beyond those He has always already written results in a frightening atmosphere of predestined captivity.

What is curious about this dread is that it is never dispersed or alleviated, even at the book's finale. Bendrix fears many of the consequences and implications of believing in God, and one could say that Sarah's diary is included in part to demonstrate (to the reader if not to Bendrix) that most of those fears are unfounded. In this particular, however, her words provide the opposite of comfort:

> . . . it seemed such a silly thing to write a letter to You who know everything before it comes into my mind. Did I ever love Maurice as much before I loved You? Or was it really You I loved all the time? Did I touch You when I touched him? Could I have touched You if I hadn't touched him first, touched him as I never touched Henry, anybody? And he loved me and touched me as he never did any other woman. But was it me he loved, or You? For he hated in me the things You hate. He was on Your side all the time without knowing it. You willed our separation, but he willed it too. He worked for it with his anger and his jealousy, and he worked for it with his love. (123)

In this regard Bendrix's last words are again important, for his request that God "leave [him] alone for ever" can be read as a terrified plea for the preservation of some last, small arena in which his free will can operate, a vestige that God's very existence promises—under the terms of this novel—to obliterate. There is, of course, a "problem of free will" just as there is a "problem of evil," and perhaps Bendrix's rhetorical deflations of God into the shape of a human lover are designed for the same purpose as Scobie's visions of a fragile God— to ward off a chronically unsettling result of affirming the Deity's omnipotence. Greene has been accused of Jansenism, but in *The End of the Affair* predestination is depicted as a terrifying possibility, and with the concept of an all-powerful God once again conjuring

19. Ronald G. Walker, "World without End: An Approach to Narrative Structure in Greene's *The End of the Affair*," 237.

up a nightmarish vision of life, we can see that Bendrix's discourse is not only appealing because it is titillatingly blasphemous, but also because it keeps at bay a specter raised by the book's own intrinsic theistic conceptions.

Almost everyone who writes about *The End of the Affair* must, it seems, take note of the "miracles" that occur in its closing pages. Most critical discussion has turned upon two questions. First of all, do those events simply demand to be read as genuine divine interventions (through the conduit of a sanctified Sarah) or can a secularly disposed reader opt to dismiss them as coincidences? And secondly, did Greene overstep the structural limitations of the genre when he chose to depict such (possibly) supernatural events within a realistic novel? Now one might suppose that any argument like mine, which asserts that the God of Greene's fiction is a quasi-mortal figure, would have to take a clear stand on the first question, and that a predictable one. However, I think it is only really necessary to turn the second question on its head. Rather than observing how the framework of a novel must stretch and tear to accommodate miracles, I would instead point out the extent to which miracles must be reduced from their traditional dimensions if they are to fit inside so cramped and secular a container as a realistic novel of recognizably Greenean design. Of what, after all, do the miracles consist? Sarah's mother appears at her daughter's funeral and interrupts a seduction; a little boy's stomach aches go away after dreaming of Sarah; a man's birthmark, which Sarah once kissed, suddenly fades. Readers of both the Bible and certain tabloid weeklies might be disappointed at the tasteful modesty of these wonders, as if God were as jealous of the novel's traditional decorums as Greene's much-admired Henry James. Consider in this regard a fairly typical attempt to seize the middle ground on the question of the occurrences' supernatural origin: "A careful reading would reveal that Greene's own attitude to miracles and their place in fiction is ambivalent. He has maintained such a delicate balance between the natural and the supernatural that the reader is kept guessing whether to treat the spectacular events like the healing of Parkis's boy as miracles or coincidences."[20] The very fact that one can reasonably speak of the miracles in this vein obviates any necessity on my part to brand them as mere

20. Sharma, *Search for Belief,* 127.

coincidences, for a God who intervenes so unobtrusively in human affairs seems a God whose power has been somehow attenuated, whose grace is manifested only within the constrictions of entropic decline.

This is only confirmed by the fact that Greene, in *The Power and the Glory,* lays a mine beneath those who attempt to explain away miracles—a mine that significantly fails to go off when brought into proximity with *The End of the Affair.* Here the whisky priest is arguing with the determinedly secular lieutenant:

> "Oh, it's funny, isn't it? It isn't a case of miracles not happening—it's just a case of people calling them something else. Can't you see the doctors round the dead man? He isn't breathing any more, his pulse has stopped, his heart's not beating: he's dead. Then somebody gives him back his life, and they all—what's the expression?—reserve their opinion. They won't say it's a miracle, because that's a word they don't like. Then it happens again and again perhaps—because God's about on earth—and they say: these aren't miracles, it is simply that we have enlarged our conception of what life is. Now we know you can be alive without pulse, breath, heart-beats. And they invent a new word to describe that state of life, and they say science has disproved a miracle." He giggled again. "You can't get around them." (*PG,* 201)

This passage seems almost tailor-made to discomfort those readers who wish to see only coincidences at the end of Greene's later novel, and yet the events there attributable to divine intervention seem of so unprepossessing and genuinely "natural" a character as to exist below the threshold needed to bring the whisky priest's warning into relevance. The word "miracle" derives from the Latin *mirari,* to wonder at, but the happenings in *The End of the Affair* seem capable of arousing only curiosity or annoyance or a quiet satisfaction, depending on the reader's proclivities. They are, if one may hazard an oxymoron, the most mediated of miracles.

IV

For a long time after *The End of the Affair,* speculations within Greene's fictions about the nature of God either disappear or become much more conventional. Most of his protagonists of the fifties and sixties are agnostics, unbelievers, or lapsed communicants, and their comments about the divine, when they emerge at all, carry with them the coolness of philosophical or sociological observations. Here, for instance, is Folwer in *The Quiet American:* "Wouldn't we all do better not trying to understand, accepting the fact that no human being will ever understand another, not a wife a husband, a lover a mistress, nor a parent a child? Perhaps that's why men have invented God—a being capable of understanding. Perhaps if I wanted to be understood or to understand, I would bamboozle myself into belief, but I am a reporter; God exists only for leader-writers" (*QA,* 60). And as with Fowler, so with Querry and his droll allegory of the King and the Jeweler, and Brown with his seemingly airy comment about an "authoritative practical joker" (*TC,* 32) on high who shapes our humiliating ends. But then, without warning, in half a dozen luminous pages of *The Honorary Consul,* it all suddenly resurfaces—the problem of evil, the God with blood on His hands, the Deity with an all-too-human face. But it is as if the submerged obsessions of the forties had undergone some chemical change deep underground, emerging in a newly arranged pattern and with a different coloring altogether. It is as if an answer—of sorts—has been devised to the pressing questions of that earlier decade.

As death, in the form of the Argentine paratroopers, closes in on the hut occupied by *The Honorary Consul's* rebel band, the conversation of Dr. Plarr and his childhood friend, the revolutionary priest León Rivas, turns to final things. It begins, one could say, at the same place that the whisky priest's argument with the lieutenant begins, or that of Scobie's with himself—that is, with the conundrum of evil:

> "I thought the Church teaches that he's love?"
> "Was it love which sent six million Jews to the gas ovens? You are a doctor, you must often have seen intolerable pain—a child dying of meningitis. Is that love? It was not love which cut off Aquino's fingers. The police stations where such things happen . . . He created them."
> "I have never heard a priest blame God for things like that before."
> "I don't blame him. I pity Him." . . . (*HC,* 219)

Pity, that word which will loom so large when we turn to consider Greene's conception of love in the following chapter, here alerts us that we are on moral terrain similar to that explored in *The Heart of the Matter.* Scobie also posits a fallen God whom he can pity, I have suggested, because the only alternative—given a world that he would describe in much the same terms Rivas employs—is hatred of an omnipotent one, and the intervening years of twentieth-century history have only, it appears, exacerbated the dilemma.

To pity God is also, inevitably, to humanize Him, and this we have seen Scobie do as well—but here there is also an important difference between *The Heart of the Matter* and *The Honorary Consul.* Whereas Scobie's conception of a pitied God extended only so far as visions of divine helplessness before the injuries done Him by mortally sinning men, León's admission of pity includes within itself empathy for another, more active human frailty that God possesses—the necessity for struggle with oneself: "He made us in His image—and so our evil is His evil too. How could I love God if He were not like me? Divided like me. Tempted like me" (*HC,* 225). Ironically, though, it is upon this wider justification for pitying the Creator, and upon this larger conception of His human tribulations, that Rivas posits a diminished God who may one day actually *triumph* over the entropy that, in previous novels, seemed to be slowly overwhelming Him.

> The God I believe in must be responsible for all the evil as well as for all the saints. He has to be a God made in our image with a night-side as well as a day-side. When you speak of the horror, Eduardo, you are speaking to the night-side of God. I believe the time will come when the night-side will wither away, like your communist state, Aquino, and we shall see only the simple daylight of the good God. You believe in evolution, Eduardo, even though sometimes whole generations of men slip backwards to the beasts. It is a long struggle and a long suffering, evolution, and I believe God is suffering the same evolution that we are, but perhaps with more pain. (226)[21]

While the idea that evolution is the universe's dialogic answer to entropy may not pass muster with the letter of modern biology

21. The second typescript of *The Honorary Consul* contains the following passage, spoken by Rivas: "But I can see no other way to explain the goodness and love of God, in the life we lead here in the world he made—the massacres and the tortures and the cruel power of wealth—and all the Marxist bureaucrats too, Aquino, who kill the spirit with their little rules" (2d TS, 270, Letters and Papers of Graham Greene, Harry Ransom Research Center, University of Texas at Austin).

and physics, it is easy to see the attractiveness to Greene of appro-
priating a twentieth-century scientific master-narrative to alleviate
(not solve) his theological impasse. It is difficult for most people to
completely divorce the idea of evolution from that of progress—to
segregate the production of increasingly better adapted forms from
some notion of amelioration—and even if science decrees that for
its own purposes they must be kept separate, the aesthetic realm
has more flexible rules of intellectual and moral fraternization. At
any rate, what is important for our purposes is that Rivas's recasting
of God's frailties opens a path for a human response that is more
constructive than that imagined in *The Heart of the Matter.* Scobie, as
he sees it, can do no more than remove the cause of unhappiness—
Louise and Helen's human unhappiness by killing himself, God's
divine unhappiness by the eternal exile from Him that is damnation.
León, however, sees the aid that earth can lend to heaven in much
more expansive terms. Here, God's triumph over his own dark places
will come only "with our help. Because the evolution of God depends
on our evolution. Every evil act of ours strengthens His night-side,
and every good one helps his day-side. We belong to him and He
belongs to us" (226). The future will see its share of atrocities, asserts
Rivas, "but one day with our help He will be able to tear His evil mask
off forever" because "God is joined to us in a sort of blood transfusion.
His good blood is in our veins, and our tainted blood runs through
His" (227). While this is a consanguinity that may paint God as no
less diminished than he appeared to be in the novels of the forties, it
is also a blood tie that radically enhances man's role in an enterprise
that is both secular and millennial—the literal building of a new
heaven and a new earth within historical time, and within a true
and equal partnership with God. In his last moments, Scobie felt the
presence of "someone appealing for help, someone in need of him"
(*HM,* 265), but in Rivas's formulation this divine deficiency is seen to
transcend the aid that any one soul's triumph over sin can possibly
render, and thus it calls for a response that is as much collective and
political as it is private and spiritual.

    But what guarantee can León provide that God will win the battle
over Himself, that the "day-side" will eventually swallow the "night-
side"? Even Dr. Plarr is "not so sure of evolution . . . not since we
managed to produce Hitler and Stalin in one generation" (226). What
is interesting about Rivas's reply is the way it distributes agency

equally between, on the one hand, the willed creation traditionally associated with God, and, on the other, the random mutations proper to blind evolutionary forces. "'But I believe in Christ,' Father Rivas said, 'I believe in the Cross and the Redemption. The Redemption of God as well as of man. I believe that the day-side of God, in one moment of happy creation, produces perfect goodness, as a man might paint one perfect picture. God's good intention for once was completely fulfilled so that the night-side can never win more than a little victory here and there'" (226). Was Christ the product of divine will or blind luck?—seemingly both. Like the rest of León's testament, a religious and secular explanation seem to interpenetrate each another, but then what could be more appropriate than to hear such an amalgam from a priest who has taken up a gun in the name of revolution? And in his divided loyalties and his attempt to meld them, Rivas resembles no one so much as Greene himself, who struggled throughout his career to imagine a politics that would combine compatible strains of Catholicism and Marxism, and to reimagine a religion that might better incorporate a twentieth-century understanding of our condition. That Rivas's idiosyncratic theology is no farther from Greene's own (shifting) beliefs than was Scobie's is made clear by an interview we have quoted from before: "One thing I feel sure, if there is such a thing as life after death it won't be a static state. I think it will be a state of movement and activity. I can't believe in an ultimate happiness which doesn't include a form of development. . . . A kind of evolution. Evolution of the spirit. And an eternity of evolution."[22] As with the absolutistic life, so with the life of the Absolute—ceaseless movement is its and His hallmark, even if—indeed because—it implies a destination not yet attained.

From his earliest days of writing, Greene was always drawn to the idea of a weak or even mortal deity. In pieces of juvenilia such as "The Trial of Pan," for instance, we find a doddering and vengeful God bested by the centaur and his music, while the "Improbable Tale of the Archbishop of Canterbridge" depicts Him dying from gunshot wounds in a bathtub. These fledgling stories suggest that the diminished God we have traced here might be, at base, a figure conceived in anger. But however palpable in the mature fictions is the current of animus directed at the Creator of a world of endemic

22. Cassis, *Man of Paradox,* 252.

pain and suffering, there are other motives in play. First of all, it must be admitted that Greene's fallible and vanishing Deity is simply and straightforwardly one that fits the prevailing spiritual atmosphere of the twentieth-century West. If J. Hillis Miller could claim that in much of Victorian literature God had already "become a *Deus absconditus,* hidden somewhere behind the silence of infinite spaces," how much greater the distance and louder the silence must be for novelists of the century now passing. Greene's furtive and enfeebled Deity is, then, first and foremost a device of realism, in that such a figure is the linchpin of the author's evocation of prevailing cultural assumptions. Thus when one commentator says in reference to *The Heart of the Matter* that "here indeed is the world of [Cardinal] Newman's description, a world without a God, a world from whose terrain the Creator has long since withdrawn and which is now denied both His power and His energizing presence," we can see Greene as another, later link in the chain of modern English novelists and poets testifying to the gradual disappearance of God. When this critic further asserts that our author's Deity "is seen in the far distant horizons, like the faint streak of light that reminds one of stars that once were," and that "the light that shines on Scobie's world is inert," he is doing no more than affirming that Greene is a reflector as well as an interpreter of his age. One may rightly call all this "a strange and startling cosmography,"[23] but as a depiction of our modern subjective reality, it is quite familiar, and surprising only in the way it so accurately articulates our unspoken habits of mind.

But there is more yet, for it is clear that Greene hobbles his God in order to keep him about, that he wounds Him in order to save Him. Discussing the theological speculations with which he would soon be seeding *The Honorary Consul,* he lets slip a motive every bit as important as hatred and a devotion to realism: "Talking as a Catholic, I would argue that Christ was a kind of overpowering expression of the day side—which was a guarantee that the day side could never be swamped. If God is torn as we are between the dark and the bright—and therefore suffers a certain division and

---

23. Miller, *Disappearance of God,* 6; Kurismmootil, *Heaven and Hell,* 125; on Greene's early fiction, see Richard Kelly, *Graham Greene: A Study of the Short Fiction,* 10–13.

anguish as we do—it makes Him a more sympathetic figure."[24] Greene apparently felt that, given the unrelenting horrors of the twentieth century, only a suffering and fallible God—a God fighting alongside us in the trenches—could possibly overcome our skepticism, perhaps retain our allegiance, or ever hope to inspire our love. On the final page of *A Burnt-Out Case*—that "attempt to give dramatic expression to various types of belief, half-belief, and non-belief" (*BC,* 5)—the acute difficulty of theism amidst this century's carnage is succinctly evoked:

> "Your god must feel a bit disappointed," Doctor Colin said, "when he looks at this world of his."
> "When you were a boy they can't have taught you theology very well. God cannot feel disappointment or pain."
> "Perhaps that's why I don't care to believe in him." (199)

Greene's solution of a diminished, half-human God may be heresy, and thus to some eyes a cure as bad as the malady, but if so we must admit that it is unmistakably the heresy of a novelist, of a person who knows what characteristics will arouse or dampen an audience's sympathy for his story's protagonist. Greene seems to have learned what must also have occurred to Milton during the writing of *Paradise Lost*—that there is little in the way of gripping narrative to be garnered from the unfallen and even less of attractive characterization to be discovered in the infallible. And since our author wrote during a century in which "thrillers are like life" and "the world has been remade by William Le Queux" (*MF,* 65), he understood that no Narrator who proclaimed Himself to be wholly above struggle, anguish, and defeat could long hold our interest.

24. Cassis, *Man of Paradox,* 215–16.

3 Love, Pity, Charity

Passions at the Heart of the Matter

I

The fact that Greene's God is fallible, conflicted, struggling, and less than all-powerful has implications for his vision of the course of human love. What, for instance, does it mean to love in a world so imperfectly and precariously governed from on high? To what extent is eros a palliative against the entropic declinations of life? What is the relationship between eros, caritas, and agape? And finally, who are the proper objects of our love, and what form should that love ideally take? These are the questions this chapter will attempt to answer. And whereas up until now it has been occasionally useful to read Greene against the grain of the critical consensus concerning him, here it will be necessary to read our author somewhat against the grain of his own rhetoric, at least for a while.

In *The Ministry of Fear* and *The Heart of the Matter* Greene makes a concerted effort to articulate what love is *not*—to preserve it from contamination by other emotions that he believes are too frequently and harmfully confused with it. It will be my argument that this project fails even within the two novels in which he most vigorously mounts it, and that the remainder of his canon shows both his acknowledgment of this failure and his determination to find something redemptive about a decidedly unpristine love that must admit its own infection by, and compromises with, the burdensome moral ambiguities of our inevitably social lives. This disagreement with himself, however, in no way implies that there is something deficient or fatally incoherent about Greene's vision of love: it is moving and convincing throughout, and only the more poignant for the contradictions that sometimes beset it.

Throughout *The Ministry of Fear* there are two mortal dangers abroad in the land: one is National Socialism, the other is pity. Indeed, the latter sometimes makes Hitler's British fifth column look almost benign by comparison. Arthur Rowe, we come to learn, has committed a mercy killing, proffering his terminally ill wife a poisoned cup rather than allowing her to painfully crawl towards death. Rowe has been let off lightly by the state, but when he recalls his own motives for committing the act he ponders whether it was at bottom himself he really pitied, whether he did it more to save his own eyes the sight of his wife's pain than to end her agony. At any rate, in his present way of thinking about pity that emotion appears inseparable from a kind of violence, and he imagines his wife helplessly "watching from day to day his pity grow to the monstrous proportions necessary to action" (*MF,* 57). In a dream, a childish version of himself kills an injured rat with a cricket bat due to "the horrible and horrifying emotion of pity" (66), and while we are told that his youth afforded him literary outlets for this dangerous proclivity, in adulthood "he could no longer direct his sense of pity towards the fictitious sufferings of little Nell—it roamed around and saw too many objects—too many rats that needed to be killed. And he was one of them" (87–88). Indeed, even the war machine that rages in the skies and streets of a bombed out London finds pity an indispensable weapon: "It wasn't only evil men who did these things. Courage smashes a cathedral, endurance lets a city starve, pity kills . . . we are trapped and betrayed by our virtues" (74, Greene's ellipses). Pity, it seems, is every individual's personal fifth column, beguiling us with false benignity into the hands of our own worst instincts.

What is most dangerous about pity, however, is its corrosive effect upon its emotional cousin, love. Pity shadows love like an evil doppelgänger, invisibly insinuating itself where love should reign in the same manner that counterfeit money drives out genuine coin. As Rowe wishes he could have warned the jury who so lightly judged him, "don't pity me. Pity is cruel. Pity destroys. Love isn't safe when pity's prowling round" (218). Soon after, reviewing his attachments to both his wife and Anna Hilfe, Rowe's thoughts swing "to and fro between two people he loved and pitied. It seemed to him that he had destroyed both of them" (219). Thus Greene's conception of the relationship between the two emotions is a striking one, for love and pity appear to exist as synonyms and antonyms simultaneously. Pity must, on the one hand, display lineaments very similar to love's in order to so easily muscle in on the niche love carves in the heart, but it must be love's stark antithesis as well, since its tendency is to destroy rather than shelter the loved (now the pitied) object. As

W. H. Auden proclaimed under the direct influence of *The Ministry of Fear,* "behind pity for another lies self-pity, and behind self-pity lies cruelty."[1]

While we can certainly understand how the extremity of Rowe's experience leads *him* to demonize pity in such categorical terms, what is surprising is to hear another character in the book mimicking this sentiment. Prentice, the counterintelligence man who adopts Rowe into his hunt for the fifth column, reacts strongly when the latter displays a reluctant admiration for a Nazi spy who coolly killed himself rather than be captured: "Mr. Prentice burst suddenly out as they drove up through the Park in the thin windy rain. 'Pity is a terrible thing. People talk about the passion of love. Pity is the worst passion of all: we don't outlive it like sex.' . . . Mr. Prentice looked at him oddly, with curiosity. 'You don't feel it, do you? Adolescents don't feel pity. It's a mature passion' " (172). It is in passages like these, however, that one begins to sense a slippage, a creeping ambivalence, in Greene's denigration of the emotion in question. The fact that "we don't outlive it like sex" could be taken as praise for its durability in comparison to romantic love, but more importantly, the idea that adolescents cannot feel pity calls into serious doubt its supposed causal relationship to cruelty. Recall that in *Brighton Rock,* "the word murder conveyed no more to [Pinkie] than the world 'box,' 'collar,' 'giraffe,' " precisely because the Boy's "imagination hadn't awoken. That was his strength. He couldn't see through other people's eyes, or feel with their nerves" (*BR,* 45). Furthermore, it is not always the case even in *The Ministry of Fear* that the object of pity is coextensive with the victim of the supposedly concomitant cruelty. When Rowe discovers the body of his fellow patient Stone, for instance, he feels "the awful stirring of pity that told him something had got to be done, that you couldn't let things stay as they were, with the innocent struggling in fear for breath and dying pointlessly. He said slowly, 'I'd like . . . how I'd like . . .' and felt cruelty waking beside pity, its old and tried companion" (180). Rowe's determination to right a wrong is hardly contemptible, whatever its genesis. Is this, then, a chain of cause and effect that civilization can readily do without? In war-torn London it is an open question as to whether a town without pity would stand closer to or farther away from any imagined New Jerusalem.

1. W. H. Auden, "The Heresy of Our Time," 94.

This contentious motif continues in Greene's next novel, *The Heart of the Matter,* where the author makes it clear that the premier cause of Scobie's tragic end is his immense capacity to pity his fellow human beings. At times, pity appears in much the same dark guise it assumed in *The Ministry of Fear*—that of a malign interloper in what should be the exclusive territory of love. When, for example, Scobie detects the sad effects of age in his wife Louise, "these were the times of ugliness when he loved her, when pity and responsibility reached the intensity of a passion" (*HM,* 22). Indeed, at certain moments of introspection, Scobie can be as hard on the emotion as Rowe or Prentice: "Do I, in my heart of hearts, love either of them, or is it only that this automatic pity goes out to any human need—and makes it worse?" (206). A number of critics, taking the hint from Greene's previous novel, have here too claimed to find something more or less malign hiding behind the mask of pity, usually pride. Thus, says R. W. B. Lewis, "Scobie's flaw is an excess of the quality Greene calls pity—an inability to watch disappointment or suffering in others—with this portion perhaps of pride (in Greene's view), that he feels it peculiarly incumbent upon himself to relieve the pain." If Lewis's diction betrays reservations about Greene's view, Francis Kunkel is more enthusiastic: "Pity is the ethic of those who try to substitute themselves for God. Only in the person of Scobie does Greene endeavor to delineate pity in a character committed to a higher moral order. But the deeds that pity inspires in Scobie are ultimately attempts 'to dispense with God, to wrestle with God,' so that the shadow of the lieutenant lies over them." Even those who invert this view and discover "inhuman humility" beneath the whited sepulchre of Scobie's emotion agree with the larger and prior assertions that pity is at best a front for something shadier and that pity and love should be located at opposite extremes of the moral spectrum. Occasionally one finds an admission that "the paradox of pity . . . is that it is a vice born out of love,"[2] but more often than not, Greene's rhetoric (with a boost from Auden's) carries the day: love and pity resemble each other only as do a set of geographical antipodes.

What I would like to suggest is that all the frequent and fervid denigrations of pity that *The Ministry of Fear* and *The Heart of the*

2. R. W. B. Lewis, "The 'Trilogy,'" 71; Francis L. Kunkel, *The Labyrinthine Ways of Graham Greene,* 104; Sharma, *Search for Belief,* 104; O'Prey, *Reader's Guide,* 50.

Matter perform in defense of "genuine" love can usefully be seen as a binary opposition ripe for deconstruction, an analysis that will reveal them as inextricably implicated in each other. As in most such cases, the cracks in the supposedly tidy dyadic hierarchy can be approached through an ambiguity or contradiction in the very language that attempts so hard to construct that hierarchy. Take, for instance, the following passage from *The Heart of the Matter,* which on one level might appear as just another passing swipe at the text's psychological scapegoat:

> He had no sense of responsibility towards the beautiful and the graceful and the intelligent. They could find their own way. It was the face for which nobody would go out of his way, the face that would never catch the covert look, the face which would soon be used to rebuffs and indifference that demanded his allegiance. The word "pity" is used as loosely as the word "love": the terrible promiscuous passion which so few experience. (159)

It is the final sentence that seems to slip free from the dichotomy Greene intends to nail down. First of all, to which term does its final phrase refer? "Terrible promiscuous passion" leads our eye toward pity, but if so few experience it, then whence the touted danger? Perhaps, as the syntax seems to imply, it refers to love, but to listen to the two novels' pronouncements so far, one would think "real" love was the chaste rarity, with pity being the flimsy knockoff peddled on every corner that so often ruins lives. Secondly, the final phrase is internally contradictory, since one would expect a "promiscuous" passion to be shared by many, not by the few, which further clouds the issue of the phrase's grammatical antecedent. In sum, a piece of language that purports to separate emotional wheat from chaff winds up bundling everything back up into the kernel where differentiation becomes impossible. Love and pity are here inextricable, even identical. This passage has vexed others as well—Gerald Levin, for instance, complains of "the indeterminate conception of pity and love" and concludes that "we cannot be certain . . . that pity and love do not intersect at such moments of 'promiscuous passion' as Scobie lives."[3] I would agree and further submit that this instance of the

---

3. Gerald Levin, "The Rhetoric of Greene's *The Heart of the Matter,*" 18.

text's subversion of its own rhetoric is merely synoptic of what goes on throughout *The Heart of the Matter.*

One sign of this self-subversion is that love and pity are paired as often as they are relegated asunder, as if Greene forgot his artificial distinction when his attention was elsewhere. During one of his fantasies of perfect peace, for instance, Scobie imagines a great good place devoid of human entanglements where he can drift "in darkness, alone, with the rain falling, without love or pity" (135). Later, Scobie and Helen, who thought their ages and circumstances would keep them safe from falling in love, find they have been beguiled by "the camouflage of an enemy who works in terms of friendship, trust and pity" (160). And once their affair is well begun, Scobie imagines how absurd it would sound within the confessional to abstractly label Helen "the woman," their meetings "the occasion," and "that moment of peace and darkness and tenderness and pity 'adultery'" (219). Of course it will be objected that it is Scobie who is thus yoking love and pity together, and that Greene no more means to endorse his protagonist's anatomy of love than he does his peculiar theology. The answer to this objection as it applies to religion has been set out in the previous chapter, and many of the same arguments operate here as well.[4] But perhaps the most persuasive reason for likening Scobie's views about these matters to the author's is that *The Heart of the Matter* itself makes a case for the consubstantial nature of love and pity that is both consistent with the odd quality of difference-in-sameness that we have already discerned emanating from the pair of emotions, and that squares with Greene's treatment of love in his later novels. As we shall see, this necessary intermingling of love and pity is connected with Greene's conception of a diminished God and the entropic world He fecklessly administers. Another way of putting this would be to say that the orphaned and dying girl who so strongly rouses Scobie's pity is not a special case in Greeneland, but rather a representative figure for all of us, a fact that Richard Hoggart recognizes when he says that it is not just Scobie but Greene who can "never still the promptings of pity. It is surely this which causes him, whenever his characters are particularly reduced, to slip into the imagery of lost children."[5]

4. Kurismmootil, *Heaven and Hell,* 122.
5. Richard Hoggart, "The Force of Caricature," 82.

When one gets to the heart of the matter, it is not Major Scobie, but Graham Greene who cannot parse pity from love.

To put *The Heart of the Matter*'s counterargument succinctly, pity is love after love's age of innocence has been brought to a close by disappointment, after its naive energy has bled away into the surrounding vacuum left in the wake of God's abandonment of the world. Even Scobie apparently enjoyed a season of belief in the persistence and transformative potential of love, until experience belied such romantic optimism: "When he was young, he had thought love had something to do with understanding, but with age he knew that no human being understood another. Love was the wish to understand, and presently with constant failure the wish died, and love died too perhaps or changed into this painful affection, loyalty, pity . . ." (253). What Greene seems to be doing here is attempting to edit a familiar piece of popular wisdom—in this case, the melancholy but reliable prediction that within monogamy romantic love must always metamorphose into less exciting but perhaps more durable emotions—such as respect and rational affection. (At times, Greene simply blasts such cultural clichés to smithereens: for instance, the notion that "You can't love someone else unless you first love yourself," which can't possibly survive a reading of *The Power and the Glory*.) Why our author insists that "pity" more accurately describes love in its mature and disillusioned phase than "rational affection" or other more conventional labels goes back to the absolutism delineated in the first chapter. Rational affection, esteem, respect—all the things that Edgar Linton claims he feels for Catherine in *Wuthering Heights*—are bourgeois desiderata, promising as they do a life of ordered and essentially plotless equilibrium. But it is an article of faith with Greene that whatever his middle-aged protagonists feel toward their lovers—and it is definitely not "young love" or romantic infatuation—it yet retains the power to move them to desperate and terrible acts: to betrayal, blasphemy, and murder; to heroism, obsession, and suicide. Given the violence of the outcomes attributable to love's living corpse, it must rightly be labeled "pity"— no milder, middle-class euphemism will do it justice. Just as Pinkie's hate can, in Greene's view, exist in close moral proximity to Rose's love because both are felt with absolutistic intensity, so can pity, because of its ability to motivate dire acts, be a falling off from love that nevertheless inhabits love's precincts of extremity.

A second reason for love and pity's conjunction has directly to do with Greene's cosmology. Scobie's youthful belief that "love had something to do with understanding" and his mature admission that "no human being underst[ands] another" is similar to Fowler's speculations in *The Quiet American* about why people believe in a deity: "no human being will ever understand another, not a wife a husband, a lover a mistress, nor a parent a child[.] Perhaps that's why men have invented God—a being capable of understanding. Perhaps if I wanted to be understood or to understand I would bamboozle myself into belief" (*QA*, 60). The Deity is largely absent in Fowler's novel, and as we have already seen, He is removed and weakened in Scobie's. And, just as the impossibility of perfect understanding is apparently associated in Greene's mind with a *deus absconditus,* so too apparently is the inextricability of pity from the vitals of love. This is suggested when Scobie makes the mistake of saying "Poor you" to Helen, who, being young and inexperienced, believes pity and love to be two very different things:

> She said furiously, "I don't want your pity." But it was not a question of whether she wanted it—she had it. Pity smouldered like decay at his heart. He would never rid himself of it. He knew from experience how passion died away and how love went, but pity always stayed. Nothing ever diminished pity. The conditions of life nurtured it. (178)

Just what these "conditions" are, we have seen in the previous chapter—the intolerable suffering of the innocent, a God too weak to protect His creations, a cooling world of pervasive decline, a Hardyesque landscape of endemic frustration. In Greeneland "to act is to initiate a train of consequences which will cause and increase suffering, both for oneself and for others. History is a process of the more or less rapid elimination of the possibilities for realizing whatever good its inhabitants long for; and this is only the more exasperating, since their longing is passionate to the point of being compulsive."[6] Given this state of affairs, love must incorporate pity within itself as a matter of course—it is the only moral response. A love without pity is only imaginable in such a world within the

6. Helsa, "Theological Ambiguity," 102.

hearts of sadists, imbeciles, naïfs, or the willfully blind. Indeed, if one keeps "the conditions of life" in Greeneland firmly before one's eyes, the fact that pity is almost always described negatively—as "painful" or "smolder[ing] like decay"—won't distract one into thinking that Greene is painting it as some sort of avoidable psychological malady, like alcoholism or mental exhaustion. For if one excludes pity for carrying such baggage, all of what we are anxious to label "love" must go too. As Peter Wolfe reminds us,

> Greene does not argue, like Denis De Rougemont in *Love in the Western World,* that sexual love only reaches intensity outside of marriage and at the risk of death. Yet the pain and danger included in Greene's love ethic makes De Rougemont a helpful analogy. Love cannot grow in rich, healthy soil in Greene; nor does it yield bumper harvests. (Greene's fiction abounds in childless marriages.) When it occurs, it is almost always adulterous, short-lived, and indulged in by sad, lost people.

Thus, it is not quite accurate to say that pity is a darker version or a more painful phase of love, since "the conditions of life" decree that darkness and pain are present in love from its first moments, and that therefore "from any tenderness of love in Greene's novels pity is never entirely dissociated."[7] Once again, difference slides toward identity.

At this point, another objection must be dealt with. In his review of *The Heart of the Matter,* Auden attempts to maintain love's quarantine from pity by making a distinction and annexing to that distinction an inflammatory claim: "To feel compassion for someone is to make oneself their equal; to pity them is to regard oneself as their superior and from that eminence the step to the torture chamber and the corrective labor camp is shorter than one thinks."[8] While Auden's statement about the supposedly genocidal effects of pity may be dismissed as a piece of rather silly hyperbole, his distinction between compassion and pity is not wrong. I have not, however, been merely mistaking the latter for the former term: the protagonists whose love I have claimed to be imbued with pity are indeed "superior"

---

7. Wolfe, *Graham Greene the Entertainer,* 134–35; Sharrock, *Saints,* 54.
8. Auden, "Heresy of Our Time," 94; see also Marc Silverstein, "After the Fall: The World of Graham Greene's Thrillers," 41.

to the objects of their affections in one important sense, though they do not gain this dubious eminence through exaggerated self-regard (quite the contrary!) nor do they occupy it in a spirit of callous disdain for the autonomy of their loved ones. Yes, Scobie, for instance, sees the world—the world as Greene imagines it—more clearly than either Helen, who is simply too young and inexperienced despite her trauma, or Louise, whose conventional Catholicism keeps her from worrying her head overmuch about the agony of innocents. His refusal to shut his policeman's eyes to the bitter facts of existence endows him with a gnostic advantage vis-à-vis those around him that is similar, if less aggressively insisted upon, than that possessed by Pinkie over Brighton's pleasure-seekers. This is not an effect peculiar to Greene, since countless protagonists emerge (almost by defini-tion) as the only figures in their respective novels whose knowledge closely approaches that possessed (or better, expressed) by the text as a whole, even when they are fatally deceived or wrongheaded about some crucial issue. The pity Scobie feels toward Helen is at least in part attributable to the fact that he sees farther ahead into life's minefield than she possibly can: "He was more than thirty years the older; his body in this climate had lost the sense of lust; he watched her with sadness and affection and enormous pity because a time would come when he couldn't show her around in a world where she was at sea. When she turned and the light fell on her face she looked ugly, with the temporary ugliness of a child. The ugliness was like handcuffs on his wrists" (159). Is Scobie, as Auden would have it, a step away from locking her up in the Freetown jail for her own good, thus keeping her safe from the depredations of the drunken Bagster? On the contrary, the passage indicates that it is Scobie who is taken into custody.

Gnostic inequality is a common fact of life in Greene's world, and thus it is pity rather than compassion that must accompany his protagonists' love. This is illustrated nowhere better than at the end of *The Ministry of Fear*, which tries so hard and unsuccessfully to sully pity's name. On the final page, Rowe decides to keep Anna ignorant of the fact that he has regained all his agonizing memories, a decision that "pledges both of them to a lifetime of lies"—she to prevent herself from jogging his recollection of his former life, he to keep her from knowing that such cautions are now superfluous. Anna will become "someone perpetually on guard to shield him" as he will be ever on duty protecting her. The couple thus exits the book "like two explorers who see at last from the summit of the range the enormous dangerous plain. They had to tread carefully for a lifetime, never speak without thinking twice; they must watch each other like enemies because they loved each other so much. They would never know what it was not to be afraid of being found out" (*MF,* 221). Here we have both the lovers believing they possess a gnostic advantage over the other, hence it is pity and not compassion that stops their mouths—the pity that dare not speak its name, if you will. Of course such enforced and watchful silence will exact a terrible price.

> It occurred to him that perhaps after all one could atone even to the dead if one suffered for the living enough.
>   He tried tentatively a phrase, "My dear, my dear, I am so happy," and heard with infinite tenderness her prompt and guarded reply, "I am too." It seemed to him that after all one could exaggerate the value of happiness . . . (221, Greene's ellipses)

The ending is unhappy *because* it is suffused with love, and thus because it is necessarily also haunted by love's sad wraith, pity—a ghost joined to love so ineluctably by "the conditions of life" that all the novel's protesting-too-much to the contrary cannot drive a wedge between them.

The famous last words of Scobie also bear looking into in light of this argument. As the fatal dose of sleeping pills takes effect, he hears

> someone appealing for help, someone in need of him. And automatically at the call of need, at the cry of a victim, Scobie strung himself to act. He dredged his consciousness up from an infinite distance in order to make some reply. He said aloud, "Dear God, I love . . ." but the effort was too great and he did not feel his body when it struck the floor or hear the small tinkle of the medal as it span like a coin under the ice-box—the saint whose name nobody could remember. (*HM,* 265, Greene's ellipses)

Greene's intentionally provocative ellipses have left a lacuna into which many interpreters have rushed. Among the camp of the lenient is Grahame Smith, whose "stress would fall on the nature of a man who dies with the world 'love' on his lips," while at the other end of the spectrum lies Jan Tips Rowe, insisting that "the preferable reading of the line is to read exactly what is there, I love _____, or blank, or nothing."[9] In attempting to fill in the blank, as it were, critics are merely continuing the hermeneutical dialogue begun among Scobie's survivors in the book's final pages, where Father Rank says that "from what [he] saw of [Scobie], . . . he really loved God," and Louise bitterly replies that "He certainly loved no one else" (272). For my part, I too would like to read "exactly what is there," though my definition of "exactly" may not exactly match another's. Scobie's last utterance, I would argue, is best understood not as a sentence fragment, a statement-in-progress broken off by the onset of unconsciousness, which we are then asked to complete ourselves. Rather, it is a finished declarative utterance: "Oh, God, I love . . . ," period. The ellipses, rather than narrowing the direct object down to a nullity, stand as the mark of objects too numerous to be iterated in extremis. Scobie is a man who loves—that is his nature. If, as has been said, *The Heart of the Matter* is the one novel of Greene's whose structure most resembles Aristotelian tragedy,[10] we should remember that it is simply a convention that, at their final moment of life, most heroes of classical tragedy are not deceived about their moral situation. As Greene once replied to an interviewer who asked whether Scobie and Pinkie were redeemed in the end, "Yes, though redemption is not the exact word. We must be careful of our language. They have all understood in the end. This is perhaps the religious sense."[11] We know that Scobie pities, and now we know, despite Louise's once and future doubts, that he loves just as strongly. What I am claiming is that Scobie's final assertion resembles the "promiscuous passion" passage because it is another admission on Greene's part that pity and love are one and the same, though this final admission is more forceful and perhaps more self-conscious than the former.

But let us also not forget that this declaration is addressed to someone in particular, to God in fact, the personage "wander[ing], seeking to get in, . . . appealing for help . . . in need of him" (263).

9. Smith, *Achievement*, 102; Jan Tips Rowe, "The Heart of the Matter: Blasphemy by Allegory," 6.

10. See Sharrock, *Saints*, 139.

11. Martin Shuttleworth and Simon Raven, "The Art of Fiction: Graham Greene," 159.

The fact that this God is, as we have seen in the preceding chapter, a weakened and struggling being, includes Him within the scope of Scobie's pity. And once we admit that the God of *The Heart of the Matter* is a fitting recipient of pity, all the assertions by critics that Greene is painting that emotion as "a sort of egoism," in which "the individual assume[s] responsibility for his fellow man without consulting the referents of religion"[12] are reduced to half-truths at best. Greene may in fact have attempted, as he once claimed, to write a book about "the disastrous effect on human beings of pity as distinct from compassion," and to show that "pity can be the expression of an almost monstrous pride," but the implications of his own conception of God and "the conditions of life" that must necessarily prevail under such a deity defeated him. No wonder, then, that our author found that "the effect on the readers was quite different. To them Scobie was exonerated, Scobie was a 'good man'" (*WE,* 125). Indeed, if we take seriously Greene's cosmology as it is actually represented in the novels—which it has been my endeavor previously to do—then we can formulate a reply to another of this book's most provocatively open questions: "If one knew, he wondered, the facts, would one have to feel pity even for the planets? if one reached what they called the heart of the matter?" (*HM,* 124). The answer—if one is to hearken, as D. H. Lawrence insists we must, to the tale rather than the teller—is Yes, absolutely.

But why then this labored attempt to separate them? Why does Greene expend so much energy to build a wall with his right hand that his left hand is all the while busily demolishing? Several explanations are plausible. One might, for instance, put it down to a struggle with his own assumptions about gender. Greene's protagonists are male and the objects of their affections female. Perhaps his insistence that love can—somewhere—exist unalloyed with pity is an effort to claim that there are circumstances under which men and women can love without the presence of a male gnostic advantage, without the man enjoying a surplus of what Foucault would term power/knowledge. This in effect would represent an attempt by Greene to argue for something within his novels that he apparently had trouble actually representing there. If there is any merit to this notion then as a corollary we must see *The End*

12. A. A. DeVitis, "Religious Aspects in the Novels of Graham Greene," 85.

of the Affair as occupying a special place in Greene's canon, because it is the only major novel in which a woman enjoys a distinct and sustained power/knowledge advantage over a man (though it happens frequently in his comic narratives). There it is Sarah who has access to gnostic enlightenment, and Bendrix—despite all his cynical worldliness—who inhabits the role of the naïf and eventually, perhaps, the neophyte. Certainly we can say with confidence that Bendrix never pities Sarah: when that emotion does emerge, it is directed toward the narrator himself, a fact that infuriates him.

> "She could put blinkers on any man," I said, "even on a priest. She's only deceived you, father, as she deceived her husband and me. She was a consummate liar."
>
> "She never pretended to be what she wasn't."
>
> "I wasn't her only lover—"
>
> "Stop it," Henry said. "You've no right . . ."
>
> "Let him alone," Father Crompton said. "Let the poor man rave."
>
> "Don't give me your professional pity, father. Keep it for your penitents."
>
> "You can't dictate to me whom I'm to pity, Mr. Bendrix." (*EA*, 180)

The gender of pity's recipient is not the only thing that sets this novel apart from *The Heart of the Matter*, for love's alchemy also proceeds on different principles. When Father Crompton claims in regard to Bendrix that he "know[s] when a man's in pain," Bendrix replies: "I'm not in pain, I'm in hate. I hate Sarah because she was a little tart, I hate Henry because she stuck to him, and I hate you and your imaginary God because you took her away from all of us" (181). Bendrix's motivations for hatred are genuine and acute, and thus in light of the fact that he exits the novel loving Sarah, loving Henry, and perhaps even loving God, it seems we must label love a "promiscuous passion" if only because of the number and variety of its consorts. Sarah in her diary also appears to insist that hate is here inhabiting the space occupied by pity in the previous novel, claiming that "Maurice who thinks he hates, . . . loves, loves all the time. Even his enemies" (101). Indeed, to establish the fact of love's close connection with its conventional opposite, no better evidence can be cited than Bendrix's own words: "Hatred seems to operate the same glands as love: it even produces the same actions. If we had not been taught how to interpret the story of the Passion, would we have been able to say from their actions alone whether it was the jealous Judas or the cowardly Peter who loved Christ?" (26). If love is thus so intertwined with hatred, is its interpenetration with pity really so hard to accept? It appears that Greene rarely if ever depicts love as roaming the world unattended by a varied and dubious entourage of emotions.

But are there other, perhaps better, reasons explaining our author's doomed attempt to argue his audience into believing in a pristine love? Given that pity is called up and annexed to love by the spectacle of the lover hopelessly entrapped in the prevailing "conditions of life" that are inimical to happiness, I think we must mainly see Greene's truncated enterprise as an attempt to imagine a realm within the psyche (not the soul) immune from the ravages of entropy, in the widest sense of that term. Recall that in our early discussion of English literary history, one of the definitions of an absolutistic novel was a text in which love is portrayed as a transcendent force beyond the writ of normal social constraints. What we encounter in Greene is that and more—something like an attempt to imagine love as existing beyond the writ of physical and biological constraints as well. Even this is quite within the pale of Greene's intertextual genealogy as it was delineated in the first chapter: as Mr. Lockwood says after becoming acquainted with the Heights's inhabitants, "They do live more in earnest, more in themselves, and less in surface change, and frivolous external things. I could fancy a love for life here almost possible"[13]—and indeed *beyond* life, as the rhetoric surrounding Heathcliff and Catherine so blasphemously implies. Lawrence likewise gropes his way toward a passion that is decidedly carnal and of this world and yet simultaneously transcendent, though whether he ever convincingly embodies it in his novels is open to argument. Does Greene successfully represent this all-sufficient passion, this love that, though born in the loins, is deathless and salvational? I would say no, but I would also claim that his argument in *The Ministry of Fear* and *The Heart of the Matter* for a love unbesmirched by pity is his attempt to prepare the ground for its coming. And if these novels are in fact a kind of prologue, we must again look to *The End of the Affair* as the locus of any supposed fulfillment.

13. Brontë, *Wuthering Heights,* 58.

Grahame Smith finds that *The End of the Affair* "remind[s] one irresistibly of *Wuthering Heights*" in its desire to " 'convey the sense of passion,' " and one knows immediately what he means, for the romantic bond between Sarah and Bendrix is beyond doubt the most intensely rendered and exhaustively detailed in Greene's canon. Before God arrives on the scene, it has the same iconoclastic power as Catherine and Heathcliff's passion, having managed, as one critic puts it, "to discard the soggy notions of romance, pity, morality, and spiritualized psychology. It requires no justification and does not resort to abstraction. It simply is."[14] Certainly the scenes of Bendrix and Sarah's lovemaking glow with the Brontësque beauty of a transgression that continually aspires to transcendence:

> There was never any question in those days of who wanted whom—we were together in desire. Henry had his tray, sitting up against two pillows in his green woolen dressing-gown, and in the room below, on the hardwood floor, with a single cushion for support and the door ajar, we made love. When the moment came, I had to put my hand gently over her mouth to deaden that strange sad angry cry of abandonment, for fear Henry should hear it overhead.
> . . . I crouched on the floor beside her and watched and watched, as though I might never see this again—the brown indeterminate-coloured hair like a pool of liquor on the parquet, the sweat on her forehead, the heavy breathing as though she had run a race and now like a young athlete lay in the exhaustion of victory. (*EA*, 49)

And yet even over this affair the shadow of entropic decline hovers, for Bendrix cannot keep from dwelling on the fact that, one way or another, this too shall pass: "for once we had hours of time ahead of us and so I squandered it all in a quarrel and there was no love to make. . . . I had come into this affair with my eyes open, knowing that one day this must end, and yet, when the sense of insecurity, the logical belief in the hopeless future descended like melancholia, I would badger her and badger her, as though I wanted to bring the future in now at the door, an unwanted and premature guest. My love and fear acted like conscience. If we had believed in sin, our behavior would hardly have differed" (56). As Herbert R. Haber puts it, Bendrix

14. Smith, *Achievement,* 103; John Atkins, "Sex in Greeneland," 52.

suffers from an "inescapable sense of duration" and an Augustinian "recognition . . . of that harrowing . . . transiency of thought, memory, and desire, which keeps man from holding fast to *any* mode of love or truth."[15] One thus understands Bendrix's motivation for intentionally destroying the relationship he cherishes, for if time will kill it eventually, then roughly manhandling the affair towards its end is a way of taking destiny back under one's own control (or of appearing to do so). At least, Bendrix seems to be saying, I shall destroy our love according to my own timetable rather than waiting helplessly for life's tendency toward dissolution to do it by and by.

To digress for a moment, this desire to wrest control of the where and when of human endings from the blind forces of the universe may also go some way toward explaining Greene's lifelong attraction to betrayal as a subject and his striking sympathy for those who betray. He certainly seems, in the following excerpt from an essay on Henry James, to be making a similar connection concerning that author: "We shall never know what it was at the very start of life that so deeply impressed on the young James's mind this sense of treachery; but when we remember how patiently and faithfully throughout his life he drew the portrait of one young woman who died, one wonders whether it was just simply a death that opened his eyes to the inherent disappointment of existence, the betrayal of hope" (*CE,* 60). In the eyes of someone imbued with a sufficiently acute sense of "the inherent disappointment of existence" the betrayer can indeed become a kind of existential hero, for if love affairs, friendships, mentorings—all our bonds, in fact—are doomed to die before our eyes, don't we at least express a modicum of freedom when we murder them ourselves, even if the result too often looks like a kind of suicide? It is a bleakly negative sort of affirmation, to be sure, but in a world as deeply in thrall to entropy as Greene's it may be one of the few that is regularly available.

Be that as it may, this desire to murder love so that it won't just expire in due course is a mind-set we shall see again in Greene's later novels. At present, however, the important question is how *The End of the Affair* attempts to face squarely the inevitable cooling of love— and other quite serious worldly pleasures—without having recourse to tincturing love with pity. The text's solution is to shift the energies

15. Haber, "Catholic Cycle," 139.

the lovers devote to eros upward into agape, a transformation that is painful for both parties, but that Sarah in fact accomplishes before the end of the book, if Bendrix doesn't quite. The former's diary is quite explicit about how complete immersion in carnal love can usher one unexpectedly but irrevocably toward a love of God: "Did I ever love Maurice as much before I loved You? Or was it really You I loved all the time? Did I touch You when I touched him? . . . For he gave me so much love, and I gave him so much love that soon there wasn't anything left, when we'd finished, but You" (123). As H. M. Daleski would have it, "Sarah's readiness to give herself to a lover . . . prefigures her willingness to give herself to God, for her capacity for abandon may be seen as proleptic of that for renunciation. . . . And she comes to apprehend sexual love as virtually an expense of flesh in a conservation of spirit." Once eros has been left behind for agape, Time's wingèd chariot ceases to be the enemy of love, and Bendrix exits the novel with a "bitter conviction that love still holds him and Sarah together," having "come to feel the reality of a term like 'forever.' "[16] And as for pity? Sarah can by definition feel only compassion for God since His agony is seen as a greater version of the Christian's who wanders in the "desert" of renunciation—"I am kissing pain and pain belongs to You as happiness never does" (122). Bendrix, of course, until the novel's finale, feels nothing but hatred for the Deity, and thus the vilified emotion of pity doesn't seriously contaminate this new kind of love. Agape means never having to say you're sorry for anyone, but more importantly, it means never having to look forward—as all those who possess Greene's melancholy gnosis cannot help but do—to the dreadful day when eros must die.

II

That this solution troubled Greene is attested to not so much by his published doubts concerning *The End of the Affair*'s "miraculous" ending—he grumbled about many of his novels after their publication—but by the fact that he never repeated this transubstantiation of eros into agape despite the fact that his subsequent protagonists' complaints about the inevitable end of eros echo Bendrix's

---

16. H. M. Daleski, *The Divided Heroine: A Recurrent Pattern in Six English Novels,* 146; Joseph Hynes, "Two Affairs Revisited," 245.

almost to the letter. Here, for instance, is Fowler from *The Quiet American* explaining why he left a previous lover: "I was terrified of losing her. I thought I saw her changing—I don't know if she really was, but I couldn't bear the uncertainty any longer. I ran towards the finish line just like a coward runs toward the enemy and wins a medal. I wanted to get death over" (*QA*, 103). Interestingly, Fowler speaks elsewhere of romantic love's inevitable heat death in a way that specifically rules out the solution proffered by *The End of the Affair:* "Always I was afraid of losing happiness. This month, next year, Phuong would leave me. If not next year, in three years. Death was the only absolute value in my world. Lose life and one would lose nothing again for ever. I envied those who could believe in a God and I distrusted them. I felt they were keeping their courage up with a fable of the changeless and the permanent. Death was far more certain than God, and with death there would be no longer the daily possibility of love dying" (44). In this novel, clearly, any outpouring of the spirit that can hope adequately to take the place of a too-mortal eros will have to be directed at objects within this world rather than the next.

As with Bendrix and Fowler, so with Mr. Brown in *The Comedians,* for he too would rather get the worst over with quickly than wait in fear for the required end, an end whose approach he perceives in even the best moments he shares with Martha: "This is one of the pains of illicit love: even your mistress's most extreme embrace is a proof the more that love doesn't last" (*TC*, 49). At times Brown's knowledge that his affair with Martha will one day conclude—that they will "grieve and separate and find another" (161)—leads him into a deeper and more general skepticism about the entire category of romantic love and its conventional valorization. As he says to Martha, "I suppose if we were still young we'd think it was life or death for us too. But now—'men have died and worms have eaten them, but not for love'" (239). It is this more thoroughgoing questioning of a central cultural myth that ties Brown to Querry in *A Burnt-Out Case* and Dr. Plarr in *The Honorary Consul.* As for the former, one of Querry's motivations for exiling himself upriver is a self-disgust that springs from a realization that he has covered over his own selfishness by calling it love, or lazily collaborated with his bedmates when they did the same. Thus he addresses in thought a young man whose lover he once stole: "I am sorry. I really believed that I meant you no harm.

I really thought in those days that I acted from love" (*BC*, 118). In expiation, he has taken a sort of monastic vow: "I can promise you, Marie, *toute à toi*, all of you, never again from boredom or vanity to involve another human being in my lack of love. I shall do no more harm" (118). In *The Honorary Consul*, Plarr resembles Querry in that he straightforwardly treats what the world calls "romantic passion" as at best a cosmetic for our instincts or an opiate for ennui. When Charlie Fortnum brings up the subject, for instance, Plarr assumes the voice of a disinterested medical investigator, and follows his Greenean predecessors in drawing attention to the scandal of "eternal" love's actual evanescence.

> "But it was real love, not brothel love I wanted. I don't suppose you can understand that either."
> "I'm not quite sure what the word love means. My mother loves *dulce de leche*. So she tells me."
> "Has no woman ever loved you, Ted?" Fortnum inquired. A kind of paternal anxiety in his voice irritated Doctor Plarr.
> "Two or three have told me so, but they had no difficulty in finding someone else after I said good-bye. Only my mother's love of sweet cakes isn't likely to change. She will love them in sickness and in health till death do them part. Perhaps that's the real true love."
> "You are too young to be a cynic."
> "I'm not a cynic. I'm curious, that's all. I like to know the meaning which people put on the words they use." (*HC*, 71)

Plarr is perfectly willing to diagnose his own emotions as well, but the prognosis is the same: "If for once he had been aware of a sickness he could describe in no other terms, he would have unhesitatingly used the phrase 'I love,' but he had always been able to attribute the emotion he felt to a quite different malady—to loneliness, pride, physical desire, or even a simple sense of curiosity" (139–40). Because of passages like this, some critics have in turn diagnosed Plarr as a physician who needs to heal himself, as a sufferer from "a more serious kind of impotence than Charley Fortnum's. It is a form of spiritual as opposed to physical powerlessness, a petrification of the soul." One understands this reaction, but in the world of Greene's later novels, where in fact physical passion always dies and people do move on and the phrase "I love you" rings increasingly hollow, the only malady Plarr can fairly be accused of harboring is that epidemic among Greene's protagonists, a dangerously acute insight into the uncompromising "conditions of life."[17]

If, however, *The Honorary Consul* contains some of Greene's most explicit and extended critiques of the florid pretensions of eros, it also attests to the possibility of a third form of love—neither eros nor agape—which can channel visceral human passions toward objects wholly of flesh and blood, and objects whose need for our affections, given our state of existential abandonment, will never cool. The following paragraph must be quoted at length, for its unhurried trajectory from a dissatisfaction with the unspoken selfishness inherent in conventional romantic posturing, and toward an attraction for the more rigorous expenditures of self demanded by broader political commitments, recapitulates the signature narrative arc of Greene's "post-Catholic" fictions.

> "Love" was a claim which he wouldn't meet, a responsibility he would refuse to accept, a demand . . . So many times his mother had used the word when he was a child; it was like the threat of an armed robber, "Put up your hands or else . . ." Something was always asked in return: obedience, an apology, a kiss which one had no desire to give. Perhaps he had loved his father all the more because he had never used the word or asked for anything. He could remember only a single kiss on the quay at Asunción and that was the kind of kiss one man can give to another. It was like the formal kiss he had seen French generals give in photographs after they have presented a decoration. It claimed nothing. His father would sometimes pull at his hair or tap him on his cheek. The English phrase "Old fellow" was the nearest which he ever came to an endearment. He remembered his mother, as she wept in the cabin while the ship pulled into the current, telling him, "I have only you to love me now," she had reached at him from her bunk, repeating "Darling, my darling boy," as Margarita had reached at him years later from her bed, before Señor Vallejo had come to take his place, and he remembered how Margarita had called him "the love of my life" as his mother had sometimes called him "my only boy." He felt no belief at all in sexual love, but lying awake in the overcrowded flat in Buenos Aires he had sometimes recalled, as his

---

17. Thomas, *Underground Fate,* 185–86; see Allott and Farris, *Art,* 93.

mother's footsteps creaked towards the privy, the illicit nocturnal sounds which he had heard on the *estancia* in Paraguay—the tiny reverberations of a muffled knock, strange tiptoes on the floor below, whispers from the cellar, a gunshot which rang out an urgent warning from far across the fields—those had been the signals of a genuine tenderness, a compassion deep enough for his father to be prepared to die for it. Was that love? (169–70, Greene's ellipses)

The martial atmosphere surrounding Plarr's remembrances of his father and the looming violence inherent in the elder man's political commitments does not prevent Greene from denominating the motivations for such commitments as a genuine form of love. This idea is forcefully echoed by the nameless priest in *The Comedians* who officiates at the memorial service for the slain Haitian rebels: "though Christ condemned the disciple who struck off the ear of the high priest's servant, our hearts go out in sympathy to all who are moved to violence by the suffering of others. The Church condemns violence, but it condemns indifference more harshly. Violence can be the expression of love, indifference never. One is an imperfection of charity, the other the perfection of egoism" (*TC,* 283). Hatred, according to Greene, is not an emotion to which those who love their neighbors need be a stranger, for hatred toward one thing is often motivated by an equally strong love for another. This imperfect form of love, then, is for Greene an emotion that may redemptively channel the self-expansive impulses that fuel eros without, like agape, leading us out of the suffering world altogether or toward some sort of merely private salvation. Let us, in order to incorporate the widest sweep of its possible meanings, call it caritas—that love whose human objects are broader and whose motives are (perhaps somewhat) purer than those of eros, and that, according to Greene, can harness even our hatred to higher purposes.

If we now cast our eyes back along the line of protagonists whom we have followed hither to Dr. Plarr, we can see several of them grope or merely stumble toward some form of caritas as an alternative to an eros too fatally subject to exhaustion, hypocrisy, and self-delusion. Certainly Brown, for all his talk of noninvolvement and spiritual dryness, finds himself a willing accomplice in the rebel's cause, and for reasons that his intense sexual jealousy of Jones cannot fully explain. Even before he believes that Jones may be enjoying Martha's bed, Brown's affection for his barman Joseph and for all the suffering people of Haiti prompts him to challenge the Tontons Macute in ways too reckless and indignant for us take him at his word when he swears he is permanently uninvolved.

> "I'm acting under orders," he said with a hint of weakness. I could understand why it was these men wore dark glasses—they were human, but they mustn't show fear: it might be the end of terror in others. The Tontons Macoute in the car stared back at me as expressionless as golliwogs.
>
> I said, "In Europe we hanged a lot of men who acted under orders. At Nuremberg." (125)

> "Haiti belongs by right to any Third Force," Captain Concasseur said. "We are the true bastion against the Communists. No Castro can succeed here. We have a loyal peasantry."
>
> "Or a terrified one." (145)

And are we to swallow whole his self-depreciatory assertions that he helps Jones escape from the embassy—a desperate act that nearly gets Brown killed—in order to salvage a love affair that we have already seen he knows to be doomed? Brown is not quite the stranger to political enthusiasm that he pretends to be, as the first page of his narrative indicates. "I can find no reason to mock the modest stone that commemorates Jones on the far side of the international road which he failed to cross in a country far from home. . . . At least he paid for the monument—however unwillingly—with his life. . . . Whenever my rather bizarre business takes me north to Monte Christi and I pass the stone, I feel a certain pride that my action helped to raise it" (9). Brown enjoys his neutralist posing, but he is the son of a woman who fought in the French Resistance, and by the end of the novel there is good reason to conclude that he inherited more from her than the crumbling Hotel Trianon.

Much the same thing can be said about Fowler. It is one of the endearing qualities of Greene's heroes that they are better men than they know themselves to be. Fowler, for instance, thinks of himself as the human embodiment of journalistic neutrality: " 'You can rule me out,' I said. 'I'm not involved. Not involved,' I repeated. It had been an article of my creed. The human condition being what it was, let them fight, let them love, let them murder, I would not be involved. My fellow journalists called themselves correspondents; I preferred the title of reporter. I wrote what I saw. I took no action—even an opinion is a kind of action" (*QA*, 28). And yet throughout the novel Fowler evidences a keen concern for the lives and fates of the Vietnamese people, both en masse and individually, as is evidenced by his words and actions during the nocturnal attack on the watchtower. His behavior there leads Pyle to make a "sentimental assumption" about the older man that Fowler is at pains to correct: "I know myself, and I know the depth of my selfishness. I cannot be at ease (and to be at ease is my chief wish) if someone else is in pain, visibly or audibly or tactually. Sometimes this is mistaken by the innocent for unselfishness, when all I am doing is sacrificing a small good—in this case postponement in attending to my hurt—for the sake of a far greater good, a peace of mind when I need think only of myself" (114). Fowler himself may be taken in by this, but surely we are not meant to be. After all, it is a recognizably British kind of modesty—akin to writing superb novels and then labeling them "entertainments." We have already seen in a previous chapter how Fowler's descriptions of a beautiful and suffering Vietnam are unmistakably imbued with love. When he sees firsthand the dead and broken bodies that are the results of Pyle's political schemes, he is moved to action much more by caritas than by the desire to regain the object of eros with whom Pyle has made off. When Mr. Heng tells him that "sooner or later . . . one has to take sides. If one is to remain human" (174), he is doing no more than appealing to Fowler's sense of charity—a charity that has been watered inevitably, Greene would insist, by hatred (for the United States, for reckless innocence, for war) as well as love. Of course giving rein to caritas does not ensure Fowler's happiness, even though "everything ha[s] gone right with [him] since [Pyle] died" (189). This must necessarily be the case, not only because Fowler's motivations include "lower" elements such as sexual jealousy, but also because caritas, like the other "higher" virtues, "smashes a cathedral, . . . lets a city starve, . . . kills" (*MF*, 74); as the priest in *The Comedians* asserts, the violence that we do to save others is at best "an imperfection of charity"—in truth there doesn't seem to be any other kind. This is perhaps the hardest lesson of *The Quiet American*: that if caritas is in some ways an outlet for our best impulses that is superior to romantic love, it is, no less than romantic love, always already contaminated by the very emotions and consequences from which we yearn to keep it sacrosanct.

What the journey from eros to caritas does indisputably win for Greene's heroes is a chance to participate in a type of love that can survive entropy's depredations. Love dies, lovers die—but victimhood in Greeneland is an ever-renewable resource, for there "anguish is inseparable from the daily experience of human life; like the act of breathing it amounts almost to an involuntary accompaniment to existence."[18] Indeed, the very "conditions of life" that cause Scobie, Bendrix, Fowler, Querry, Brown, and Plarr to so keenly perceive the inevitable end of the affair are the same conditions which ensure that occasions requiring caritas will always be with us, for whereas entropy is romantic love's nemesis, it is the nourisher, the raison d'être, of charity. And though agape is also a route by which our need to love may slip the bonds of mortality, in a world whose God is too weak to be trusted "to see that the suffering isn't too great" (*HM,* 259), charity toward our fellow creatures appears both more urgent and in some ways more justified than a love of the Deity.

As we have already begun to see, this needful caritas often takes the form of a political commitment, and it will be the aim of the next chapter to delineate in detail Greene's vision of just what a personally redemptive commitment and a socially redemptive politics might entail. What I wish to do now, however, is to investigate a different sort of potential escape from a pity-tainted eros, from commitments shadowed by entropy, and indeed from entangling human claims altogether. If Greene's heroes invariably find themselves, to use Charley Fortnum's words, "caught up" by some form of love, "kidnapped . . . by mistake" (*HC,* 265), they also at times yearn desperately to escape from their captor, to flee at whatever cost toward an imagined sanctuary that all of them call by the name of "peace."

III

"Peace," like "love," is a word that can contain a multitude of meanings. When fervently longed for by Greene's heroes, however, "peace" always seems a kind of psychic island paradise called up from the sea in response to a pair of bleak circumstances central to our

18. Smith, *Achievement,* 216.

author's conception of reality. First of all, it is the imagined antidote to an exhaustion or disgust with love's inevitable contamination by other, complicating emotions, chiefly pity and the terrible sense of responsibility for others that pity entails. Second, it embodies a desire to exist outside of the temporal flux whose inevitable trajectory is that of declension and that decrees the death of all human connections. In other words, the hunger for "peace" is motivated by the same circumstances that compel the diversion of psychic energy from eros to caritas, and the goal of this yearning is therefore another potential solution to the problem of love under Greene's God and Greeneland's "conditions of life." As we shall see, though, this supposed remedy is one that, in the novels of the forties, exists for the most part as a fantasy that even the most fervent striving cannot quite make flesh, and that the texts themselves finally reject as overly private and inward looking. In the novels of the fifties, sixties, and beyond, however, Greene attempts to recast his heroes' visions of peace in a more social and outward-looking direction, a move that parallels his increasing emphasis on caritas as the only sufficient mode of love.

In *The Ministry of Fear,* the land of peace is largely equated with the time of childhood. Arthur Rowe enters the neighborhood fete that eventually involves him with the Nazi fifth columnists because it allows him to "ste[p] joyfully back into adolescence, into childhood," a realm evocative of "the sound of brass, the sense of glory, [and] of a future that would be braver than today" (*MF,* 12–13). Indeed, "it all seemed perfect in the late summer Sunday afternoon. 'My peace I give unto you. Not as the world knoweth peace . . .' " (11). This recreated childhood is a world of moral simplicity, where "God is good, the grown-up man or woman knows the answer to every question, there is such a thing as truth, and justice is as measured and faultless as a clock" (89). Furthermore, because visiting it represents a temporal regression, it stands as an oasis outside the winnowing effects of time: "in childhood we live under the brightness of immortality— heaven is as near and actual as the seaside" (88). This is all very Wordsworthian, but Rowe's actual life is lived under the perpetual shadow of Peele Castle, and therefore this dream of peaceful simplicity and stasis is always on the brink of a plunge into the buffeting waters of adult complication. Even in the novel's opening scene, the idyll cannot last, for as soon as Rowe mistakenly wins the cake that unbeknownst to him contains stolen microfilm, the odd "intensity" of the stares he receives alert him that "the experience of childhood renewed had taken a strange turn, away from innocence. There had never been anything quite like this in Cambridgeshire" (18). This is the pattern from now on: Rowe's haven in remembered youth— or, later, in temporary amnesia—is continually broken in upon by an adult present that is permeated with violence, treachery, and emotional ambiguities. Even in sleep, the present erupts to puncture the fantasy, for Rowe's dream in the air-raid shelter of "having tea on the lawn at home behind the red brick wall and his mother . . . lying back in a garden chair eating a cucumber sandwich" (63) is punctuated by his own anxious attempts to get her to understand that he has killed his wife, that the previously discrete simplicities of love and pity have become intertwined to a literally fatal degree. Later in the dream, his Edenic remembrance of first love is also cut short when "without warning the dream twisted towards nightmare" and "a policeman stood at his elbow and said in a woman's voice, 'You had better join our little group,' and urged him remorselessly towards a urinal where a rat bled to death in the slate trough" (67). Sleeping or waking, Rowe may be "filled with horror at the thought of what a child becomes" (65), but the novel insists that even the awakened imagination, like childhood and fetes, is at best only an evanescent and falsely comforting escape from adult realities. It is in fact all very un-Wordsworthian.

The same movement is writ large upon the structure of the novel itself, as the titles of its four books—"The Unhappy Man," "The Happy Man," "Bits and Pieces," and "The Whole Man"—trace a blissful forgetting that cannot be sustained. Amnesia is almost literally a return to childhood (Rowe only remembers his life up till eighteen), but the sanitarium, headed by the fifth columnist Dr. Forester and invaded by newspapers carrying war news, is the vehicle of Rowe's return to his own and his century's dire history. And while "the whole man" at the novel's end is much the same "unhappy man" of its beginning, in the final analysis the novel refuses to straightforwardly mourn the irrevocable loss of Rowe's peaceful cloud of unknowing. Witness, for instance, the following passage describing the moral effects of the protagonist's amnesia (and note as well how pity is once again subtly rehabilitated): "none of the books of adventure one read as a boy had an unhappy ending. And none of them was disturbed by a sense of pity for the beaten side," and so therefore London's bombed-out

> ruins from which [Rowe and Prentice] emerged were only a heroic back-cloth to his personal adventure; they had no more reality than the photographs in a propaganda album: the remains of an iron bedstead on the third floor of a smashed tenement only said, "They shall not pass," not "We shall never sleep in this room, in this home, again." He didn't understand suffering because he had forgotten that he had ever suffered. (176)

There is for Greene a tinge of selfishness about those unaccustomed to adult pain, a hint of solipsism about the childish incapacity to empathize with suffering—to pity the casualties, in short. By the end of the book, though, one might say, again with Wordsworth's aid, that the full return of a deep distress hath humanized Rowe's soul. And what about happiness, that other boon of youth? We have already seen that the novel's last page, where the love of Rowe and Anna is thoroughly "contaminated" by pity, suggests that here too the things of childhood must be put aside for higher, less self-centered commitments: "It occurred to him that perhaps after all one could atone even to the dead if one suffered for the living enough. . . . It seemed to him that after all one could exaggerate the value of happiness" (221). As Richard Kelley insists, "the whole man . . . is the man steeped in suffering, who faces the terror of life with an isolating pity and a wistful longing for lost innocence."[19] But more than this, he faces it as a man who knows that the pity he feels will be his lifelong companion, and that the innocence he mourns is irrevocably lost.

The Ministry of Fear's deployment of a fantasized "peace" as an alluring yet unsustainable refuge from a fully adult cognizance of love's failures and time's triumphs is bound up with politics and history in a way that none of the subsequent novels quite duplicates. Alongside the text's assertions that a hard-eyed look at pity and entropy are a requirement of "the whole man" runs a parallel argument that such tough-mindedness is also the price of living through a century in which war has become the familiar fabric of reality. Rowe can think

---

19. Kelly, *Graham Greene*, 132.

of himself, murderer though he is, as a "good man" in part because "his early childhood had been passed before the first world war, and the impressions of childhood are ineffaceable" (88). Earlier, during his dream, much of his difficulty in convincing his mother that he has killed arises from the fact that "she had died before the first great war, when aeroplanes—strange crates of wood—just staggered across the Channel" (64–65). Thus he tries in vain to assure her that though she "used to laugh at the books Miss Savage read—about spies, and murders, and violence, and wild motor-car chases," that absolutistic fictional world is now "real life: it's what we've all made of the world since you died. I'm your little Arthur who wouldn't hurt a beetle and I'm a murderer too. The world has been remade by William Le Queux" (65). When the dream finally ends, the emphasis is on a waking life that is nightmarish but which has become familiar, mundane, habitual.

> He woke and the sirens were sounding the All Clear. One or two people in the shelter sat up for a moment to listen, and then lay down again. Nobody moved to go home: this was their home now. They were quite accustomed to sleeping underground; it had become as much part of life as the Saturday night film or the Sunday service had ever been. This was the world *they* knew. (68)

War has transformed the absolute into the mediated and made terror a simple produce of the common day. Adulthood may be horrible, but horror is inescapable in part because it is nothing special these days. This conception of the post-1914 world as one of endemic warfare, actual and metaphorical, is one that Greene acquired early—as the title of *It's a Battlefield* indicates—and never really abandoned. As Dr. Hasselbacher in *Our Man in Havana* answers when questioned about why he occasionally still dons his pre–World War I uniform, "Do you ever have a desire, Mr. Wormold, to go back to peace? Oh no, I forgot, you're young, you've never known it. This was the last peace for any of us" (*OM*, 140). There will be more to say in a subsequent chapter on Greene's changing conception of the relationship between the Victorian and the modern eras, but clearly "peace" for him is relegated to the realm of fantasy by history's atrocities as well as by the complexities of the mature and cognizant heart.

Of all Greene's protagonists, none desires peace more fervently than Scobie. "Peace seemed to him the most beautiful word in the language: My peace I give you, my peace I leave with you: O Lamb of God, who takest away the sins of the world, grant us thy peace. In the Mass he pressed his fingers against his eyes to keep the tears of longing in" (*HM,* 60). There are in fact periods of time during his daily routine, such as when he is "crouched under the rusting handcuffs in the locked office, reading the reports from the sub-stations" (60) that he comes close to attaining it; and there occur a few special instances, such as his first return to the home his wife has recently vacated, during which he actually feels its healing presence. But peace in *The Heart of the Matter* is most memorably represented in two of Scobie's dreams, the first of which is recalled during one of his frequent arguments with Louise: "For he dreamed of peace by day and night. Once in sleep it had appeared to him as the great glowing shoulder of the moon heaving across his window like an iceberg, Arctic and destructive in the moment before the world was struck" (60). This image, with its haunting yet disconcerting imagery, seems to cry out for interpretation.[20] To my mind, the passage can be usefully read as Scobie's half-conscious admission of the dubious allurements held out by his imagined paradise. The moon is coolly remote and can well signify Scobie's desire to distance himself from all the human claims we have seen impinging upon him,[21] but its metamorphosis into an iceberg clearly communicates a dire and immanent threat, suggesting that such emotional divestiture is at best a dangerous solution. Furthermore, the vision's setting in the moment preceding catastrophe intimates that even momentary indulgences in reveries of detachment can court disaster in the same way a negligent lookout may endanger a ship. After all, we know how thickly laid with traps for the heedless the protagonist believes his world to be.

Scobie's second vision offers the same mélange of beauty and hazard:

Scobie slept and woke, slept and woke. When he woke he thought of [the suicide] Pemberton and wondered how he would feel if he

20. See A. F. Cassis, "The Dream as Literary Device in Graham Greene's Novels," 102–3.
21. Chase, "Spies," 162.

were his father—that elderly, retired bank manager whose wife had died in giving birth to Pemberton—but when he slept he went smoothly back into a dream of perfect happiness and freedom. He was walking through a wide cool meadow with Ali at his heels: there was nobody else anywhere in his dream, and Ali never spoke. Birds went by far overhead, and once when he sat down the grass was parted by a small green snake which passed on to his hand and up his arm without fear, and before it slid down into the grass again touched his cheek with a cold, friendly, remote tongue. (83)

The scene is clearly Edenic, its almost frozen tableau suggesting an unfallen state in which the passage of time is irrelevant. Scobie's isolation with only his silent and subordinate helpmate Ali also contributes to the Adamic unhurriedness that seems to envelop him. The transit of the snake, however, strikes an ambiguous note, as it must in any scene so clearly evocative of an earthly paradise. On the one hand, the fact that the serpent passes over Scobie "without fear" is reminiscent of the lion lying down with the lamb (though who is which?), and renders the bush a peaceable kingdom in stark contrast to the human community Scobie polices and is policed by, so red in tooth and claw. At the same time, though, the "cold, friendly, remote" contact between Scobie and the snake suggests an unspoken conspiracy with something inhuman and heartless, a fraternization with something akin to evil.

All I really wish to establish is that both visions of peace are ambiguous, that the great good place of Scobie's imagination is shadowed by an inkling that, given the way of the world, such peace is only obtainable at the cost of someone's safety, even if it is not that of the satisfied dreamer himself. Peace is here imagined as a solitary, even a solipsistic pleasure, and thus it shares with agape the fault of threatening to overlook our fellow sufferers in a rush toward a genuine good, of seeking our own well-merited rest and reward at the expense of our most valuable—which in Greene's parlance means our most painful—human ties. It is not merely coincidence, I think, that the plot of *The Heart of the Matter* involves shipwrecks and tales of survival in open boats. What Scobie is being tempted with is, I would argue, the equivalent of making off alone in a dinghy in order not to witness, and thus not to take responsibility for, one's fellow castaways. And it is precisely Scobie's decision not to heed this call of "every man for himself" that damns him according to the Church but redeems him according to the novel. Here is the moment when he chooses to exile himself from God rather than throw either Louise or Helen overboard:

> And myself, he thought, watching the priest pour the wine and water into the chalice, his own damnation being prepared like a meal at the altar, I must come last: I am the Deputy Commissioner of Police: a hundred men serve under me: I am the responsible man. It is my job to look after the others. I am conditioned to serve.
> *Sanctus. Sanctus. Sanctus.* The Canon of the Mass had started: Father Rank's whisper at the altar hurried remorselessly towards the consecration. "To order our days in thy peace . . . that we be preserved from eternal damnation. . . ." *Pax, pacis, pacem:* all the declinations of the word "peace" drummed on his ears through the Mass. He thought: I have left even the hope of peace for ever. I am the responsible man. (224, Greene's ellipses)

Scobie acts in a way that he believes will rob him of tranquillity for all eternity in order to protect those with whom he has become entangled and for whom he has shouldered responsibility; the fact that those he seeks to shelter may be heartier—and harder-hearted— than he understands does little to alter the moral weight of his sacrifice. While some critics may harp on the fact that Greene's hero here violates the Church's instruction that each individual is first and foremost responsible for his or her own salvation, there are other canonical texts one can appeal to on Scobie's behalf. For example, his situation is, structurally speaking, remarkably similar to Adam's in Book 9 of *Paradise Lost,* at the point where Eve has confessed to eating from the Tree and Adam decides to join her in sin rather than leave her to suffer the consequences alone. In Greene's novel, as in Milton's poem, the theologically correct reaction is ethically (not to mention dramatically) impossible, and Scobie's fall is also a fortunate one if we will recognize how far Greene's conception of redemption is from that laid out in the Catholic Catechism. Kai Laitinen appreciates the distance involved when he states that "Scobie breaks the rules of the Church, although he acts in the spirit of Christianity," an opinion Allen Warren Friedman seconds in asserting that "salvation awaits" Greene's protagonists "despite, or even because, they elect damnation."[22] Indeed, one could even say that Scobie is Greene's object lesson about the need for the spirit to trump the letter of the law not only in the reading of Scripture itself but in regard to all the Church's subsequent glosses as well. To return to the subject at hand, however, *The Heart of the Matter* appears to go some way towards confirming what was hinted at in *The Ministry of Fear*—that however beautiful the protagonists' visions of peace, they represent, morally speaking, little better than the negative peace of the grave.

This association of a sufficient peace with something deathly is made more explicit in *The Quiet American,* where, as we have seen, Fowler conceives of death as the only safe refuge from love's exhaustion and the decline of the body.

> I hoped it was an attack—it increased our chances [of being killed].
> "Are you scared, Thomas?"
> "Of course I am. With all my instincts. But with my reason I know it's better to die like this. That's why I came east. Death stays with you." (*QA,* 105)

Closely associated with death in Fowler's mind are his opium— " 'Aren't we all better dead?' the opium reasoned" (18)—and his mistress Phuong, the preparer of his pipes.[23] The Ammonite woman is sexually available to Fowler, but because she also prepares the drug that kills his desire—"when [he] had smoked four pipes [he] would no longer want her" (14)—the act that most graphically underscores their difference in ages is somewhat elided. Moreover, when Fowler is under the influence, the line between the woman and the drug appears to waver: "I thought that if I smelt her skin it would have the faintest fragrance of opium, and her colour was that of the small flame" (14). Sometimes, in fact, Phuong "seem[s] invisible like peace" (45). Finally, because she is childlike and because what she feels for Fowler is not what the Western mind would recognize as "love," their relationship seems to exist outside the writ of physical and emotional decline altogether:

22. Kai Laitinen, "The Heart of the Novel," 179; Alan Warren Friedman, " 'The Dangerous Edge': Beginning with Death," 134; see also Georg M. A. Gaston, *The Pursuit of Salvation: A Critical Guide to the Novels of Graham Greene,* 35–36.
    23. See Thomas, *Underground Fate,* 35.

"But she loves you, doesn't she?"

"Not like that. It isn't in their nature. You'll find that out. It's a cliché to call them children—but there's one thing which is childish. They love you in return for kindness, security, the presents you give them—they hate you for a blow or an injustice. They don't know what it's like—just walking into a room and loving a stranger. For an aging man, Pyle, it's very secure—she won't run away from home so long as the home is happy." (104)

The way in which Fowler, like his predecessors, turns away from his particular version of comforting serenity in order to affirm wider human ties is thick with Greenean irony. Having lost his human embodiment of peace to Pyle, he sets in motion a train of events that will eliminate his rival and bring Phuong back to his bed. By the time he does this, however, his motivation is just the opposite of a desire to retreat into a solipsistic bower. His former "creed"—"the human condition being what it was, let them fight, let them love, let them murder, [he] would not be involved" (28)—has been replaced by a determination to choose sides politically in order to stop the human suffering that Pyle's zealous innocence will continue to cause. Below, what Fowler is "mad" about and what he and Pyle "disagree" over is now a political, not a personal matter.

"Can you have dinner with me, Pyle?"

"I'd love to, Thomas. I'm so glad you aren't mad any longer. I know you disagree with me, but we can disagree, can't we, and be friends?"

"I don't know. I don't think so."

"After all, Phuong was much more important than this."

"Do you really believe that, Pyle?"

"Why, she's the most important thing there is. To me. And to you, Thomas."

"Not to me any longer." (177)

Thus, in a further turn of the ironic screw, Fowler abandons his deathlike vision of peace in order to save lives, though saving those lives demands his collusion in the death of Pyle and results in bringing Phuong back to him. Perhaps this is the real significance of the characters' names: the novel's fowler regains his bird (*Phuong* means "phoenix"), but in accordance with the myth of the phoenix rising from its own ashes, this second capture represents a kind of rebirth for the protagonist, for along the way to it his former commitment to "a profound confusion of erotic and thanatopic impulses"[24] has evolved into a tentative caritas that has begun to make itself felt in the world at large. It is certainly true that even though Fowler exits the novel in possession of Phuong, his solipsistic peace is forever shattered: "Everything had gone right with me since [Pyle] had died, but how I wished there existed someone to whom I could say that I was sorry" (189). For Greene, this is moral progress, for our author seems to have little patience toward those who cry "Peace, peace!" when there is no peace.

One gets a sense that *The Quiet American* represents a turning point in Greene's pursuit of this theme. In the novels of the forties, whatever ambivalences infected the heroes' dreams of solitary calm, the spaces they imagined seemed to have something of the transcendent about them, to be charged with an ethereal glow that promised to lift one altogether out of the here and now, at least for those happy stolen intervals when one could elude one's daily responsibilities. However, having come, in the mid-fifties, to associate such ways of escape with physical death and spiritual solipsism, Greene appears in subsequent novels to attempt a redefinition of peace that purges it of its troublingly solitary character, a process that also entails the shedding of a good deal of the visions' otherworldly transcendence. As the locales in which we may cast off our mental burdens are reimagined as places we can or must share with others, they necessarily become precincts that take on the recognizable lineaments of everyday human habitations. This new conception of peace, like the Greenean caritas that manifests itself as political action, will come to be very much a creature of this world.

We can perceive this new direction in *A Burnt-Out Case,* for on the novel's first page Querry's purely solitary tranquillity is already represented as inadequate: "if no change means peace, this certainly was peace, to be found like a nut at the centre of the hard shell of discomfort" (*BC,* 9). Querry himself, though, does share several important traits with Greene's earlier protagonists, such as a revolted exhaustion at the transitory nature of eros. When, for instance,

---

24. Thomas, *Underground Fate,* 32; on the characters' names, see R. E. Hughes, "*The Quiet American:* The Case Reopened," 42, 48.

Dr. Colin remarks that his nocturnal chase into the jungle after the fleeing Deo Gratias "must have been a long bad night," Querry replies: "One has had worse alone . . . Nights when things end. Those are the interminable nights." His hours with the frightened leper, though, have constituted something altogether different: "In a way you know this seemed a night when things begin" (57). This new commencement springs from Deo Gratias having told Querry during the vigil of his own vision of peace, a place he calls Pendélé: "I am certain he meant a place—somewhere in the forest, near water, where something of great importance to him was happening. . . . He had been taken there once by his mother when he was a child, and he could remember how there had been singing and dancing and games and prayers" (58). For our purposes, the relevant attributes of Pendélé are two. First of all, Greene leaves it ambiguous throughout the novel as to whether it is a real place or merely a product of Deo Gratias's fancy—that is to say, it exists halfway between the purely imaginary Eden of Scobie's reveries and, say, the Caribbean golf club that Jones longs to purchase in *The Comedians*. Second, it is always conceived of as a communal locale. When, for instance, Querry asks Deo Gratias "what happened" there, he replies, *"Nous étions heureux"* (78). In fact, the sharable, social nature of Pendélé is insisted upon in other ways, for not only does Querry eventually take it up as the place—geographical and spiritual—that he is himself attempting to get to (as his frustrated questions to Deo Gratias about it attest), but the novel makes it clear that Querry approaches Pendélé only in proportion to his increasing life of useful service to the leper colony. When he arrives at the hospital, Querry is seeking the peace of utter solitude and is eventually forced to explain to Dr. Colin why he is reluctant to use his architectural skills to help the sick: "Don't talk to me of human beings. Human beings are not my country. . . . I will do anything for you in reason, but don't ask me to revive . . ." To which the doctor replies, "Scruples. . . . Just scruples. . . . Who cares?" This response, dwarfing and shaming a private proclivity by juxtaposing it to an immense communal need, might equally be aimed at Fowler's scruples against political involvement. At any rate, "that question 'Who cares?' [goes] echoing obsessively on in Querry's brain like a line of verse learnt in adolescence" and "bob[s] up again, like a cork attached to some invisible fishing-net below the water" (51–52). The next morning he relents and begins his work, at which point Colin observes, "you have been trying an impossible experiment. A man can't live with nothing but himself" (52). By the novel's end, Querry may or may not have reached his own version of Pendélé, but what is beyond question is that by then the location of Greene's peaceable kingdom has shifted dramatically earthward.

This process only accelerates in *The Comedians,* where Smith, Jones, and Brown's visions of peace are each social, even gregarious. What is more, whether it be at Smith's golf club, Jones's vegetarian center, or Brown's pre-Duvalier hotel, all three men conceive of themselves as the hosts, even as the servers, of others. Here is Brown remembering his season in paradise:

> Few in the good days drank anywhere else but the Trianon, except for those who were booked on round tours and chalked everything up. The Americans always drank dry Martinis. By midnight some of them would be swimming in the pool naked. Once I had looked out of my window at two in the morning. There was a great yellow moon and a girl was making love in the pool. She had her breasts pressed against the side and I couldn't see the man behind her. She didn't notice me watching her; she didn't notice anything. That night I thought before I slept, "I have arrived." (*TC,* 51)

The contrast between Scobie's moonlit scene of arrival and Brown's couldn't be more different, and yet they are continuous in that the mantle of deep serenity pervades both. Nor does the fact that Jones— and perhaps Brown—eventually reach, through political commitment, great good places that outshine their former commercial dreams (a subject for the next chapter) interfere with the progression of our theme. Whether one wants to nominate their initial or their eventual Pendélés as the genuine article, all their peaceful Edens are thickly settled with others.

Finally, in *The Human Factor,* that novel in which so much familiar Greenean material seems to get turned inside out, we meet a character who, to some extent, actually lives within his redemptive vision day after day. Castle in effect is already in possession of his tranquil demesne, though it is perpetually threatened from the outside.

> He poured himself a triple J & B and the murmur of voices upstairs began to give him a temporary sense of peace. A door was closed

softly, footsteps passed along the corridor above; the stairs always creaked on the way down—he thought how to some people this would seem a dull and domestic, even an intolerable routine. To him it represented a security he had been afraid every hour he might lose. He knew exactly what Sarah would say when she came into the sitting room, and he knew what he would answer. Familiarity was a protection against the darkness of King's Road outside and the lighted lamp of the police station at the corner. (*HF*, 189)

Of course it is true that, given this ever-encroaching threat, Castle, no less than Scobie, is forced to visit a landscape of fantasy in his dreams: "He didn't want to sleep until he was sure from her breathing that Sarah was asleep first. Then he allowed himself to strike, like his childhood hero Allan Quartermain, off on that long slow underground stream which bore him on toward the interior of the dark continent where he hoped that he might find a permanent home, in a city where he could be accepted as a citizen, as a citizen without any pledge of faith, not the City of God or Marx, but the city called Peace of Mind" (141). The difference now is that the key to this longed-for citadel will be used to lock a door rather than open it— to barricade the consequences of Castle's secret political allegiances firmly outside its gates. Still, Castle resembles figures like Querry and Brown in that his conception of peace embraces others, though because this is the first of Greene's noncomic novels to valorize the mediated world, the vision of peace is social in the special sense of being domestic. Concerning the trajectory of the theme we have been following, though, *The Human Factor* represents no reversal at all but rather a completion, for here we see the culmination of that process whereby Greene's heroes have increasingly sought, and eventually found, their promised lands of peace closer and closer to home.

What we have witnessed in this chapter are the results of a war between Greene's idealistic Romanticism and his tough-minded realism, between the hopes of his heart and the evidence of his eyes. His failed attempts to argue for a transcendent eros and to imagine a peace separate from the dangerous claims of this world are the gambits of a man who wishes to escape from his own unblinking estimate of the human predicament, and fashion by force of will a hope his reason and experience tell him is illusory. And yet neither of these attempts ends up being merely a narrative of foiled escapism or a retreat into sour disillusionment, for they both conclude with clear-eyed efforts to make the most of what remains, to imagine a high road toward love and peace that never strays outside the confines of the possible or takes detours into the falsely comforting. When the author reluctantly concluded that our need to love and our desire for peace are stifled and thwarted by the attempt to keep them unsullied by contact with our century's violent political realities, he ushered them into Greeneland's noisy and often noisome public square and found there much needful work for them to do. And is it then so certain that this represents something second-best, something merely settled for? After all, in Greene's later novels, love has a way of redeeming not just the lovers, and dreams of peace embrace and sometimes shelter more than the solitary dreamer—perhaps we should talk of fulfillment rather than compromise or consolation. As Greene's Dr. Magiot insists, "if you have abandoned one faith, do not abandon all faith. There is always an alternative to the faith we lose. Or is it the same faith under another mask?" (*TC*, 286).

4 Comedians, Commitment, and *Commedia*

I

This chapter centers around two redemptions, both involving characters named Brown, and both to some extent shadowed by ambiguity. Taken separately, Pinkie's salvational moment is recognizably religious, and underscores how heterodox is Greene's personal recasting of Christianity, while that of *The Comedians'* narrator is mainly political, and allows us to grasp the author's vision of what shape the moral life must assume in a largely secular world. By examining them loosely in tandem, however, I also wish to attempt a description of something rather difficult to articulate: the extent to which, and the manner in which, the presence of God manifests itself in Greene's later fiction. His novels of the fifties and beyond are in an undeniable sense "post-Catholic" and even "post-Christian"—at least when contrasted with those of the forties—and yet at the same time most readers understand that in an important way spiritual energies are still in play . . . somewhere, somehow. Mr. Brown of *The Comedians* is not pursued, as Pinkie may be said to be, by the bloodhounds of heaven, but neither is his status in the eyes of God entirely moot: we feel the shadow of a vague presence; we sense the slow shifting of an obscure providence. At any rate, readers inevitably speak of Brown as either redeemed or lost, saved or cast out, and it will be the business of this chapter to discover just what such words can and cannot mean in Greene's later, more secular fiction.

We may commence by returning to Greene's first "Catholic"—that is, recognizably heretical—novel. Concerning *Brighton Rock,* the big, inevitable, and (for a secularly minded critical establishment) often distinctly uncomfortable question has always been, Is Pinkie, in a conventionally Christian sense, saved or damned?—after his death, is he bound for heaven or hell? While Greene himself angrily asserted that, concerning the eternal destinies of his protagonists, he "was not so stupid as to believe that this could ever be an issue in a novel" (*WE*, 126), in the critical reactions to *Brighton Rock* it has indeed become an

129

issue—often *the* issue—and for three good reasons. First of all, Pinkie, and to a lesser extent Rose, spend a good deal of time discussing what kind of reception they, and the human race in general, may expect after death.

> "But you believe, don't you," Rose implored him, "you think it's true?"
>
> "Of course it's true," the Boy said. "What else could there be?" he went scornfully on. "Why," he said, "it's the only thing that fits. These atheists, they don't know nothing. Of course there's Hell. Flames and damnation," he said with his eyes on the dark shifting water and the lightning and the lamps going out above the black struts of the Palace Pier, "torments."
>
> "And Heaven too," Rose said with anxiety, while the rain fell interminably on.
>
> "Oh, maybe," the Boy said, "maybe." (*BR*, 52)

Second, Pinkie's steps are dogged throughout the book by something that can, without irreparably distorting the general realistic texture of the novel, be called grace or the Holy Spirit or heavenly mercy—though it could as easily be conceived of in secular terms as, say, a repressed psychological yearning to love others and himself and to be loved by the same. This pursuer takes several forms: the band music that "vibrate[s] in [his] heart . . . like . . . other people's experience battering on the brain" (45); the "faintest stirring of sensuality" (138) that Rose inspires in him despite his sexual revulsion; the "enormous emotion . . . like something trying to get in; the pressure of gigantic wings against the glass" (239). All this discourse about heaven's hunt for the fleeing soul leads, of course, to an inevitable curiosity about whether the quarry is or is not bagged at the final moment.

And finally, most importantly, there is the famous final moment itself—or rather its provocative prolongation. The manner of Pinkie's death is significant—as opposed to being merely melodramatic—because of the careful way in which the text has been previously seeded by speculations about the redemption of sinners in extremis.

> "You know what they say—'Between the stirrup and the ground, he something sought and something found.'"
>
> "Mercy."

"That's right: Mercy."

"It would be awful, though," she said slowly, "if they didn't give you time." (91)

Thus Pinkie's final plunge off the (note the name) Peacehaven cliffs ("it was as if he'd been withdrawn suddenly by a hand out of any existence—past or present, whipped away into zero—nothing" [243]) has proved hermeneutically fertile precisely because the "moment" of death is stretched considerably (but indeterminately) beyond that expended between the stirrup and the ground, allowing the scene to provide rich fodder both for those who argue that Pinkie is damned and for those who wish to see him as redeemed. The former explain the extended agony of the Boy's fall as testament that during even so prolonged an exit from this world he can neither seek nor find mercy for his crimes, while the latter affirm that the long drop is there precisely to underscore that even Rose's tormentor may receive divine forgiveness and that, as the priest later says, no one can conceive the "appalling . . . strangeness of the mercy of God" (246) Greene may in fact have known that such matters cannot be decided *within* a novel, but he also must have realized that he was rigging things in a way that guaranteed they would be heatedly discussed afterward.

Few critics have been comfortable consigning Pinkie to flames everlasting, but those who have tend to write him off with a tone of calm assurance. Robert O. Evans, for instance, informs us that salvation "requires a conscious effort of will, and Pinkie finds that in the instant of death there is no time, though for him there has always been plenty of time to make an effort of will directed towards evil." Furthermore, "Greene never allows any real possibility of saving Pinkie. As a moralist he could not do so, and in the end Pinkie gets what he deserves." The bloodhounds of heaven aside, "Pinkie has fled [God] down the nights and days and successfully evades Him."[1]

Much more common are critics who, reading the physical circumstances of Pinkie's end alongside the priestly warnings against damning judgments that close both *Brighton Rock* and *The Heart of the Matter,* find cause for hope. Georg Gaston, for instance, suggests that the Catholic novels "end with the suggestion that grace has been the

1. Evans, "Satanist Fallacy," 161, 162, 167–68.

ultimate means of salvation, not primarily because the characters have been spiritually responsive, but because of the haunting mercy of God," a state of affairs that renders all Greene's fictions of the period "comedies of salvation." Likewise, Paul O'Prey insists that these texts "questio[n] the traditional concept of divine punishment" and that the Church's dogmas about who is fit for damning are "undermined by the overriding and anarchic power of love," a notion seconded by John Spurling, who suggests that in Greeneland "all might be secretly justified when infinite love rather than human reason [is] the judge."[2]

Certainly these more lenient commentators can take heart in Greene's own pronouncements about Pinkie's fate, which became more uncompromising with the passing years. In 1971 Greene states that "only in one book had [he] tried to write about a wholly unpleasant character, and then at the end one put in a doubt whether even he was as theologically damned as he seemed." By the late seventies, Greene has apparently come up with a scholastic argument against the existence of hell that, when applied with an eye towards Pinkie's social deprivation, seems to get the Boy off the hook. According to the Church, damnation is occasioned by mortal sin, but the author finds the whole concept of mortal sin "difficult to accept because it must by definition be committed in defiance of God. I doubt whether a man making love to a woman ever does so with the intention of defying God. . . . I don't think that Pinkie was guilty of mortal sin because his actions were not committed in defiance of God but arose out of the conditions to which he had been born." Finally, by 1980, an interview with Anthony Burgess elicits a blanket pardon for his protagonists:

> Superficial readers say that I'm fascinated by damnation. But nobody in my books is damned—not even Pinkie in *Brighton Rock*. Scobie in *The Heart of the Matter* tries to damn himself, but the possibility of his salvation is left open. The priest's final words are that nobody, not even the Church, knows enough about divine love and judgment to be sure that anyone's in hell.[3]

2. Gaston, *Pursuit,* 17, 48–49; O'Prey, *Reader's Guide,* 82; Spurling, *Graham Greene,* 32.
3. Cassis, *Man of Paradox,* 215; Allain, *Other Man,* 149; Cassis, *Man of Paradox,* 322.

Of course all these pronouncements were made well after the publication of *Brighton Rock,* and are therefore open to the charge of being attempts to amend a relatively orthodox text in light of a later attenuation of faith. Precisely because it has been my intention to read Greene as synchronically as possible in regard to his major themes, I don't wish to gloss over this possibility. What I would say to allay such suspicions, however, is that sufficient evidence exists, both within *Brighton Rock* itself and within the novels that precede and follow it, to allow us to see them as in fact Greene's earliest arguments against the whole notion of theological—that is, posthumous—damnation. To my way of thinking, Greene's fictions are his most important statements about philosophical and intellectual matters, and I would also contend that they are the places where many of his most important ideas first come to light—that they frequently anticipate his later statements in essays and interviews, forming the advance guard of his overall view of life.

Conveniently, this argument against hell within the novels themselves can be looked at under a trio of heads that correspond to the motifs traced in the three preceding chapters. Take, to begin with, the moral superiority that Pinkie's absolutistic career confers upon him vis-à-vis the mediated moral dullards of bourgeois Brighton. When Terry Eagleton considers this superiority and then tries to square it with the Boy's apparent damnation, the result is puzzlement: "Pinkie may be 'evil,' but he is not 'corrupt': his evil is a pure, pristine integrity, a priestly asceticism which refuses the contaminations of ordinary living. . . . Pinkie cannot understand human reality, but the human reality we are shown has nothing substantial about it to be understood." Thus, while Pinkie is

> damned because of his incapacity to surrender himself to life[,] . . . we are nowhere shown that life is particularly worth surrendering to. We condemn his murders, of course, but not from any standpoint of sympathy with his brutal or broken victims. If Ida Arnold and Pinkie's underworld friends are truly representative of the human condition, then it is difficult to avoid feeling that Pinkie is damned by his author for holding a view of life which the novel validates.[4]

4. Eagleton, "Reluctant Heroes," 117, 116.

Of course this contradiction immediately disappears if the salvational suggestions of the Boy's last moments are factored into the equation. Indeed, Pinkie's end is every bit as absolutistic as his life, and thus, in the eyes of the novel, his death is—to use the relevant theological phrase—a good death.

The fact that the Deity who presides over Greeneland is a diminished and struggling figure also makes it difficult for our author to construct even the most tenuous or implicit hell of the conventional variety anywhere in his imagined universe. Paradoxically, though, this is so only because God, however much He falls short of omnipotence, is never imagined as anything less than omniscient. Thus O'Prey is moved to declare that "Greene's God, as we meet him in the novels, is not God enough to damn anyone anyway," though in the next breath he declares that this "God is omniscient" and quotes the following passage from an interview with Greene: "God's justice derives from total knowledge. This is the reason why I don't believe in hell: If God exists—I'm not convinced He does—He is omniscient; if He is omniscient, I can't bring myself to imagine that a creature conceived by Him can be so evil as to merit eternal punishment. His grace must intervene at some point."[5] Just *why* Greene should be willing to credit God with omniscience when he will not allow Him to be omnipotent is difficult to answer, except perhaps by admitting that to our earthbound imaginations omniscience cannot help but appear (however illogically) as a more passive attribute than omnipotence, and thus somehow more within the probable capacities of a less-than-perfect deity. But this much *is* clear: nowhere in the novels is this God of Greene's—this God who is subject to entropy, who is unable to protect the innocent from terrible suffering, who is not above being dragged into a lovers' triangle—nowhere is He imagined as being ignorant of so much as a single sparrow's fall. Indeed, the whole notion of a deity who merits our pity rather than our hatred rests on the assumption that He intimately knows and feels our pain without being able to relieve it. As León Rivas says, "the God I believe in suffers as we suffer while He struggles against Himself—against his evil side," for "God is suffering the same evolution as we are, but perhaps with more pain" (*HC*, 226). Thus even those critics who (wrongly, I believe) see Greene's diminished God as evidence that

5. O'Prey, *Reader's Guide*, 72; see Allain, *Other Man*, 152.

the author is a Gnostic in the classical sense of that term grapple with the notion of a deity who, even in the midst of his weakness, knows all and thus forgives all:

> If [man] is what he is because he was made that way by an evil creator-god, by "beings that by nature are no gods," there can be no justifiable limit to the mercy of the Redeemer-God. Hence one does not often come across in the novels any notion of God's justice, for if mercy is to be limited, its limitations will be determined by justice. But since the Redeemer's mercy must be infinite, it cannot be limited, and justice cannot be one of the attributes of the Deity; and the definition of God which seems to emerge from the novels is, "God is suffering love"; or—if mercy and love are identical, as they seem to be—"God is suffering mercy."[6]

This brings us to the brief against hell that springs from Greene's ideas about love, human and divine. If, as we have seen, the entropic fate of the universe demands that pity is wedded to love at the very marrow, and that "if one reached what they called the heart of the matter" one would "have to feel pity even for the planets" (*HM,* 124), and by implication even for the Deity who made them—then it seems evident that God's pity for his suffering creations would be most unlikely to flag. This world is, by Greene's lights, so filled-to-brimful with suffering that it becomes a kind of hell and purgatory combined, obviating the need for any posthumous punishment for even the most grievous of sins. The point is illustrated by Greene's fascination with an anecdote concerning the two heroes of his youthful reading, Stevenson and Haggard, an anecdote he returned to several times in his essays:

> Fishing together for trout at Bateman's, these two elderly men . . . suddenly let out the secret. "I happened to remark," Haggard wrote, "that I thought this world was one of the hells. He replied he did not think—he was certain of it. He went on to show that it had every attribute of hell; doubt, fear, pain, struggle, bereavement, almost irresistible temptations springing from the nature with which we are clothed, physical and mental suffering, etc., ending in the worst fate man can devise for man, Execution!" (*CE,* 212)

6. Helsa, "Theological Ambiguity," 107.

That Greene was given to repeating this conversation is an indication of how closely it resembles his own view of human existence. Even in the last years of his life, the brookside exchange can be heard echoing in his own statements: "I don't believe in [a posthumous] hell. I never have believed in hell. I think it's contradictory. I think there may be *nullity,* and for others something that is conscious. But I don't believe in hell and I feel that purgatory may happen in *this* life, not in a future life." Certainly some critics have discovered such a cosmology implicit in the pages of his fiction. Alan Warren Friedman, for instance, believes that Greene's "eschatological obsession presents earthly reality retrospectively, as limbo or purgatory, where we are constrained to wander in search of an ending—or, rather, a better beginning." And Kurismmootil deftly sums up this structure of feeling by asserting that "Greene would seem to consider suffering the true baptism."[7] The notion that this world is so awful that it might be the only hell that human beings need anticipate, the only purgatory they need endure, is one that also affirms God's unfaltering pity for the human condition—a statement that will seem odd only if we forget God's inability to prevent human suffering in the first place. If Greene alters the position of Dante's hell by insisting that we already inhabit it during our lives, he also alters the *Commedia*'s overall vision by insisting that, thanks to a God who can pity where He cannot presently help, *all* journeys through the hell of this world will resemble Dante's own in its promise of eventual passage beyond to better things.

Allied to this notion that our ordinary lives are a kind of purgatorial ordeal is Greene's focus on Pinkie's environment as an extenuating factor in his life of crime. It is, after all, poverty that forces the Boy to witness his parents' Saturday-night copulations and thus that perverts his sexual energies into sadistic channels. In other ways as well, Greene makes it clear that Pinkie has been fashioned by social deprivation:

"Where's home?"
"Nelson Place. Do you know it?"
"Oh, I've passed through," he said airily, but he could have drawn its plan as accurately as a surveyor on the turf: the barred and

---

7. Cassis, *Man of Paradox,* 461; Friedman, " 'Dangerous Edge,' " 131; Kurismmootil, *Heaven and Hell,* 87.

battlemented Salvation Army gaff at the corner: his own home beyond in Paradise Piece: the houses which looked as if they had passed through an intensive bombardment, flapping gutters and glassless windows, an iron bedstead rusting in a front garden, the smashed and wasted ground in front where houses had been pulled down for model flats which had never gone up. (*BR,* 90)

As Neil Nahring admirably puts it, "the weight of secular indignation in *Brighton Rock* makes it more a political novel than an exercise in Jansenism. . . . Depravity does indeed originate at birth, as a Jansenist would have it, but as a result of birth into the bottom of the pernicious English social structure"[8] If this world is indeed "one of the hells," then Greene's Brighton, with its pervasive kitsch and intermittent "carving," is surely one of the lower circles. After such knowledge, what condemnation?

But if all are saved, what becomes of the notion of sin? Does God's inability or indisposition to damn His creatures mean that moral issues, on the theological level, are simply moot? What acts are pleasing in the sight of God?—what counts as an abomination?—and does it make any real difference if we commit one as opposed to the other? I have previously argued that Pinkie's absolutistic career is redemptive where a life of bourgeois piety and liberal tolerance is not, and that within the absolutistic sphere intense love and intense hate, ecstasy and agony, are all near allied, while a great gulf is fixed between these admirably violent emotions and the bridled, cautious feelings of a mediated, law-abiding citizenry. Under such a regime, sin becomes in effect both its own painful punishment and ecstatic reward combined, as it is in that important precursor of *Brighton Rock, Wuthering Heights*.

> The most paradoxical consequence of Emily Brontë's view of the human condition is her belief that the suffering sin brings will be sufficient expiation for that sin. Each person is fated to commit a certain number of sins and to suffer a certain amount of pain before he can escape to heaven. The passive, obedient people, the Edgar Lintons of this world, do not really act within the law. They eke out over a longer period the necessary allotment of sin. . . . A certain number of sins are necessary to complete the great work of the

8. Nehring, "Revolt," 229.

exhaustion of evil which will make possible resurrection into the
new life.

. . . Between this life and the world to come there is no likeness,
even though this life with all its horror and discord is a necessary
prelude to the harmony of heaven.[9]

Once we realize how impossible an orthodox hell is in Greene's
view, the similarities between the Brontëan vision and that of
Brighton Rock become striking. Sin retains a place in the individual's
spiritual drama, but becomes a kind of virtue in disguise, expiation-
ally scourging the sinner in the very moment it is committed. After
all, given Pinkie's embittering loneliness, his chronic and enervating
anxiety, the slashing he receives on the racecourse, and his final
agony with vitriol, it is quite easy to imagine the Boy, along with
Heathcliff, as a figure who has already done his time in hell. Thus, to
quote Marlowe's Mephistopheles, though—or rather because—"this
is hell nor are we out of it," it is also true, in Faustus's words, that
"hell's a fable"; and likewise, though damnation is not a genuine
possibility for Greene's protagonists after death, "salvation awaits
them despite, or even because, they elect damnation."[10]

This conception of an afterlife without hell and a road toward
it through holy sinfulness is broadly useful in sorting out the final
status of Greene's protagonists in the "Catholic" novels: once we fully
understand Greene's heretical brand of Catholicism, we can argue
with some confidence that Scobie is saved because of the sheer enor-
mity of his love (or, if one insists, his pride), just as Pinkie and Bendrix
are presumably saved by the violence of their hatred. They all lead
exemplary lives because they live absolutely; God loves extremists,
and pities the agony that is extremity's reward. However, in Greene's
fictions of the fifties, sixties, and seventies, the signs of election are
harder to discern, for the actions and emotions of the later heroes
are simply not as steeped in absolutistic grandeur as those of their
predecessors: what do Fowler, Querry, or Brown feel or perform that
equals the chronic Gethsemanes of Pinkie, Scobie, or the whisky
priest? Just as importantly, in these later fictions God seems to have
retreated, surviving now only as a hovering possibility rather than a

9. Miller, *Disappearance of God,* 200–201.
10. Friedman, "'Dangerous Edge,'" 134.

hectoring presence. Meanwhile, the protagonists have almost ceased to ponder—or even to recognize—the question of whether they are redeemed or damned in a conventional sense. And yet—and here is the crux—it is also undeniable that at one level of implication within these later texts, the issue of what constitutes "salvation" in some sense *beyond the secular and political* remains acutely central. The question, "Is he, in the end, redeemed; is he among the chosen or the lost?" arises with as great an urgency in the cases of Fowler, Querry, Brown, and Plarr as it does in those of the Catholic heroes, only now the question is double voiced, reverberating in both a political key and in one that is still religious, but religious in an attenuated rather than a vigorously heretical mode. Here, to choose one example from among many, is the climactic scene of *The Honorary Consul:*

> The voice said a word which sounded like "Father." Nothing in their situation seemed to make any sense whatever.
> "Lie still," Doctor Plarr said. "If they see either of us move they may shoot again. Don't even speak."
> "I'm sorry . . . I beg pardon . . ."
> *"Ego te absolvo,"* Doctor Plarr whispered in a flash of memory. He intended to laugh, to show León he was only joking—they had often joked when they were boys at the unmeaning formulas the priests taught them to use—but he was too tired and the laugh shriveled in his throat. (*HC,* 251)

It has long been a critical commonplace that secular redemption in the later Greene is largely a matter of undertaking a dangerous political commitment—though attainments such as self-knowledge and an ability to love are also involved. But this is not the whole story, a fact also recognized by critics, even if the specifics of Greene's mature religious vision are left largely unmapped. Witness, for instance, Georg Gaston's eloquent yet representative observation that "in Greene's later eschatologies there is sufficient reason to be gay because the resurrection of the heart is an endless possibility if one is willing to take the risk of human involvement."[11] The risk Gaston speaks of here is that mentioned above—the risk of political engagement, the risk of love and trust. But what if it were possible to examine Greene's concept of political redemption while keeping

11. Gaston, *Pursuit,* 71.

another question in mind: what exactly *are* the author's "later eschatologies" in a specifically religious sense?—and how exactly do
they intertwine with his secular, political concerns? The remainder
of this chapter will attempt to infuse some new life into familiar
material by answering these questions. As *The Comedians'* Dr. Magiot says of Communism, "there is a *mystique* as well as a *politique*"
(*TC*, 286)—and what I intend to do is to trace both simultaneously.
In what follows we shall discover that the mystery that shadows
political struggle in Greene's novels of the fifties and beyond has
much to do with his previously established ideas concerning the
absolutistic life, the impossibility of hell, a diminished God, and the
ineluctable nature of love and pity. The final result, I hope, will be
the illumination of as yet unobserved strands of thought that link
the "Catholic" Greene of the thirties and forties to the "political"
author of subsequent decades, and a demonstration of how the ideas
that fueled an earlier religious heresy also undergird a later political
theosophy.

II

Let us begin what will soon become a stereoscopic discussion by
first covering one eye and asking whether *The Comedians'* Mr. Brown
is, in a purely secular and political way of speaking, redeemed? On
this issue, opinions markedly differ. On the one hand, we are told
that he exemplifies "the death of the heart," and that his "failure in
the novel can be seen as an inability to accept the reality of love, let
alone die for it; it is perhaps best explained in existential terms as
a failure of engagement." Furthermore, his becoming an undertaker
at novel's end renders him "a comic Baron Samedi" who "belongs
to the world of the dead and not to that of the living," for his mode
of employment "recalls Christ's judgment: 'Let the dead bury their
dead.'"[12] Commentators of a different humor, however, are equally
convinced that because "writing can be a form of action," Brown "not
only establishes a permanent monument to Jones but also discovers
the identity and commitment that he has always lacked." To their
way of thinking, Brown as undertaker is "a man who has risen from
the world of the dead in order to honor the dead" and "redeem death

12. A. A. DeVitis, "The Later Greene," 65; DeVitis, "Religious Aspects," 96;
Kelly, *Graham Greene*, 83.

from nothingness" and to perform "penance for past insincerities by mourning the victims of life."[13] Thus, those who disparage his new job simply fail to see its political import in the Haitian context: "If Papa Doc can be seen as a vampire or as a roaring lion seeking whom he may devour, then resistance to him becomes the essentially symbolic gesture of protecting the graves of those who are buried from his renewed depredations."[14] It would seem that the question of Brown's status as he is summoned by Mr. Fernandez "to [his] first assignment" (*TC*, 287)—the question of whether he is one of the secular saints of political commitment or has damned himself through indifference— is as fraught with controversy as Pinkie's last fall toward either fire or divine forgiveness.

Alas, the best road toward a resolution of this critical dispute leads immediately into another one, this time concerning the likely meaning or meanings of the novel's title. Here, there seem as many interpretations as interpreters. The words refer, we are informed, to "survivors . . . who understand that in order to get on in the world . . . one must learn to shift into various roles and to mask feelings"; or, to "those, like Brown and Jones, who pretend or act and who thus avoid not only their true selves, but any involvement or commitment"; or yet still, to those "playing parts forced on them by circumstance."[15] If one is a comedian, then "one is uncommitted," though "Brown is partially absolved from belonging to this category through his knowledge that he does belong to it," and yet "what Brown fails to understand is that when one accepts [one's] part in the comedy with a total commitment, the word 'comédian' becomes a title of honour."[16] Comedians "play a part . . . neither good enough nor grand enough for tragedy," or better yet they "simply *play* various roles" while "the non-comedians . . . are actually *committed* to their roles." Finally, the term "can refer either to author or actor, enabl[ing] Greene implicitly to question conventional distinctions between the world and the

13. Randall Craig, "Good Places and Promised Lands in *The Comedians*," 324; Thomas, *Underground Fate*, 157; Erdinast-Vulcan, *Childless Fathers*, 84; Gaston, *Pursuit* 100.

14. Thomas, *Underground Fate*, 143.

15. Miller, *Understanding*, 120; O'Prey, *Reader's Guide*, 117; Kelly, *Graham Greene*, 81.

16. Pendleton, *Conradian Masterplot*, 129–30; Erdinast-Vulcan, *Childless Fathers*, 76.

stage."[17] It is not my purpose to ridicule these interpretations—so rudely plucked from their proper contexts—most of which are to some extent enlightening. Rather, their sheer number and variety should serve to indicate that there is wide agreement on at least one important prior question—that the title of this novel is centrally significant to its content in a way that even the many other suggestive and resonant titles in Greene's canon cannot approach. The phrase *the comedians* is a synoptic statement of extreme compactness, and most critics feel obliged to try their hand at cracking it open and teasing out the much longer sentence they suspect dwells within it. I shall myself follow suit, for I believe that a proper understanding of what Greene means by "comedy" is a key to what might be called his political eschatology.

In our culture, comedy exists as one member of a binary opposition that also includes tragedy. And, while it would be interesting to speculate, as Umberto Eco does in *The Name of the Rose,* how the history of the West might have differed had Aristotle pronounced the former to be a genre of equal stature with the latter, the fact remains that for a number of cultural and historical reasons the two inhabit a hierarchy that valorizes tragedy at the expense of comedy. There is then, inevitably, something second best about naming an action a comedy or a person a comedian, if only because the unspoken dominant counterparts—tragedy and tragedian (or tragic hero)—are always summoned to attention at the selfsame moment. This much is tacitly admitted at the reception held by Ambassador Pineda during which young Philipot ridicules his youthful literary pretensions by saying, "Wasn't I a comedian with my verses smelling of *Les Fleurs du Mal,* published on handmade paper at my own expense?"—an utterance that prompts the following apology for the comedian's perpetual second-class status from the ambassador: "We mustn't complain too much of being comedians—it's an honourable profession. If only we could be good ones the world might gain at least a sense of style. We have failed—that's all. We are bad comedians, we aren't bad men" (133, 134).

What it might mean to be a tragedian in the world of this novel is immediately suggested by Martha: "I'm no comedian. . . . You talk so

---

17. A. A. DeVitis, "Greene's *The Comedians:* Hollower Men," 130; Michael Larson, "Laughing till the Tears Come: Greene's Failed Comedian," 184; Craig, "Good Places," 316.

much. Such rubbish. My child vomited just now. You can smell it still on my hands. He was crying with pain. You talk about acting parts. I'm not acting any part. I do something. I fetch a basin. I fetch aspirin. I wipe his mouth. I take him into my bed" (134). The simple, domestic nature of Martha's actions should not distract us from the clue that is here being planted: she is, it appears, no comedian because she takes action to alleviate the pain of another. Young Philipot also seems to believe that the way to shed his comic mantle is to "do something" for the suffering, for he muses that "the same money [he expended on his poetic career] would have bought [him] a Bren perhaps" (133). His thoughts are turned to violence, but recall the priest's sermon for the dead guerrillas in which it is asserted that violence can be "an imperfection of charity" while "indifference" will always remain "the perfection of egoism" (283). This then is the text's first, though not its final, definition of the "comedian"—a person who has yet to shoulder any dangerous responsibility for those who suffer, who refuses to commit to what the priest terms a "political solution" against oppression and who instead remains safe with "the cold and the craven" (283).

To become a tragedian in *The Comedians* means to risk death through commitment to a cause, to encounter mortal dangers by heeding the incautious promptings of caritas. Comedy, of course, ends safely in marriage and a dance rather than with an expiatory or sacrificial death, and this in part explains why it is said to lack the seriousness and gravitas of tragedy. As if to underscore this distinction, a recurring motif in the novel locates a genuine and suffi-cient dignity almost exclusively among the dead. Brown and Martha's affair, for instance, is declared to be comic when juxtaposed to the deceased: "the corpse in the pool seemed to turn our preoccupations into comedy. The corpse of Doctor Philipot belonged to a more tragic theme; we were only a sub-plot affording a little light relief" (57). Later, the couple attempts to make love "in a shallow declivity under the palms like bodies in a common grave," causing Brown to recall his mother's lover "Marcel hanging from the chandelier" and to bitterly remark that "neither of us would ever die for love. We would grieve and separate and find another. We belonged to the world of comedy and not of tragedy" (161). Marcel, Brown eventually concludes, was "no *comédian* after all," for "death is a proof of sincerity" (253). Nor is even the experienced playactor Jones immune from feelings of this kind, for he understands that death renders even the pitifully comic Mr. Baxter "sort of respectable, doesn't it?" (211). Later, his own end approaching, Jones declares that "Death's a bloody serious affair. A man doesn't feel quite worthy of it. Like a decoration" (263). And before the novel ends, we are told that both Jones himself and Dr. Magiot have joined the "dignified and disciplined ranks" of the dead, who "rebuk[e] our levity" (285).

Two of the dead who reappear again and again are Martha's father and Brown's mother. Though the former was a Nazi and the latter fought against Nazism in the French Resistance, there is throughout the novel a quiet suggestion that, on one level, they share something important. When, for instance, Martha complains of her own and Brown's status as mere spectators toward Haiti's struggle with barbarity—"Yes. That's all it means to us. We aren't concerned"—the conversation eventually turns to their parents' more active involvement in political causes:

> "Haven't the French a word for going into the street?"
>   "My mother must have gone into the streets I suppose, unless it was her lover who gave her the Resistance medal."
>   "My father went into the streets too in 1930, but he became a war-criminal. Action is dangerous, isn't it?"
>   "Yes, we've learnt from their example." (189)

The example of Martha's father might in fact easily stand as a cautionary exception to Greene's general promotion of commitment, as an admission that not all political engagements are redemptive. It *might,* that is, were it not for an unsettling mistake that Brown makes in reference to him, and for an accompanying undercurrent of envy and ambivalence that becomes audible from time to time. When the Ambassador first tells Brown about Martha's father, our protagonist's thoughts range widely:

> Haiti was not an exception in a sane world: it was a small slice of everyday taken at random. Baron Samedi walked in all our graveyards. I remembered the hanged man in the Tarot pack. It must feel a little odd, I thought, to have a son called Angel whose grandfather had been hanged, and then I wondered how I might feel . . . We were never very careful about taking precautions, it

could easily happen that my child . . . A grandchild too of a Tarot card. (130, Greene's ellipses)

In later scenes, Brown again invokes the image from the Tarot pack of the Hanged Man, noting that Angel does not have "the blue Saxon eyes of the hanged men" (136), and wondering, in a bitter mood, why he should "trust a German, the child of a hanged man?" (245). What is disturbing about this is that Brown is mistaken about the Hanged Man and his function in Tarot fortune-telling. As Greene certainly knew, the Hanged Man is suspended not by his neck but by his leg, and more importantly, there is nothing sinister or derogatory about the card's meaning within the Tarot's divinatory patterns—indeed, his still and inverted form is a symbol of peace of mind and serenity of soul. Furthermore, there are other subtle suggestions in the book that political commitment is in some sense an *absolute* good, regardless of the cause being served. Notice, for instance, the ambivalence toward the executed father in the following conversation between Brown and Martha, and how Christianity, Nazism, and Communism seem almost as interchangeable as the names Brown, Smith, and Jones:

She said, "I envy you and Luis. You believe in something. You have explanations."

"Have I? Do you think I still believe?"

She said, "My father believed too." (It was the first time she had ever mentioned him to me.)

"In what?" I asked.

"In the God of the Reformation," she said. "He was a Lutheran. A pious Lutheran."

"He was lucky to believe in anything."

"And people in Germany too cut their throats to escape his justice."

"Yes. The situation isn't abnormal. It belongs to human life. Cruelty's like a searchlight. It sweeps from one spot to another. We only escape it for a time. We are trying to hide now under the palm trees."

"Instead of doing anything?"

"Instead of doing anything."

She said, "I almost prefer my father."

"No."

"You know about him?"

"Your husband told me."
"At least he wasn't a diplomat."
"Or a hotel-keeper who depends on the tourist trade?"
"There's nothing wrong with that."
"A capitalist waiting for the dollars to return."
"You speak like a Communist."
"Sometimes I wish I were." (162–63)

This brings us back to the last letter from Dr. Magiot, whose eloquent but unsettlingly broad endorsement of political commitment was discussed in the first chapter: "Catholics and Communists have committed great crimes, but at least they have not stood aside, like an established society, and been indifferent. I would rather have blood on my hands than water like Pilate" (286). Just what is our author trying to suggest by putting these words in the mouth of so noble and attractive a character, and by the hints and insinuations noted above? Is he really saying that all political causes are equal, and that there is no real difference between joining the Resistance and joining the Nazi party, so long as one puts one's whole heart into it? I don't think Greene intends us to suspend our political judgments or to cease discriminating between the Ho Chi Mins and Papa Docs of the world. I do, however, believe that he is putting forward a provocative thesis: that there is something salvational (we are still for now speaking in a purely secular vein) that accrues to the engaged individuals themselves from *any and all* dangerous political commitments, even if their particular cause promotes evil. This is certainly an implication one could draw from Dr. Magiot's earlier discussion with Brown concerning his mother, where the circumstances, practicalities, and outcomes of political engagements seem to pale beside the spiritual benefits of submersing oneself in them completely.

"If your mother had lived to see these days she would not have been so indifferent; she might well be up in the mountains now."
"Uselessly?"
"Oh yes, uselessly, of course."
"With her lover?"
"He certainly would never have let her go alone." . . .
"What do you want out of life, Brown? I know how your mother would have answered."

"How?"

"She would have laughed at me for not knowing the answer. Fun. But 'fun' for her included almost everything. Even death." (234)

Taken together, the passages here discussed do seem to suggest that even though "action is dangerous" and the politically committed life can potentially turn one into a war-criminal, those who put themselves at risk can be sure of some sort of spiritual recompense—perhaps defined in psychological terms as a life of heightened vividness and intensity. If, however, our author's idea strikes us as potentially scandalous in its apparent lack of discrimination between fascists and freedom fighters, this is in itself a strong hint that the economy of rewards Greene envisions in some way transcends even the most self-evident human judgments and enters the jurisdiction of a higher court. There do occur moments in the later novels where the implied fruits of the spirit accruing to the committed individual approach that frontier where the psychological turns imperceptibly into the religious, where an invigorated mind (or soul) appears to owe its robustness to something very like divine grace. Certainly Dr. Magiot himself blends matters political and religious at the very moment that he seems to equate several disparate wavelengths of the political spectrum: "if you have abandoned one faith, do not abandon all faith. There is always an alternative to the faith we lose. Or is it the same faith under another mask?" (286). Could it be that all the politically committed live a life whose very precariousness is somehow pleasing in the sight of God?

There is no way to inch closer to what I am going to propose, so let us review some facts, make a leap, and see if the evidence bears out the claim. If we are at all convinced that God's presence is obscurely felt in Greene's later novels, and if we then recall the absolutional quality of Pinkie's absolutistic existence in *Brighton Rock,* and *The Power and the Glory*'s argument that God forgives large and violent sins more readily than small and workaday ones, and the unlikelihood of Greene's God damning the creatures he cannot aid—what emerges is a moral order in which those who abandon the banal comedy of noncommitment and become politically engaged tragedians also become participants in a higher comedy of redemption. We can rightly call this third genre of life a *Commedia* in the Dantean sense, for it requires of us that, by becoming politically engaged, we cease to shield ourselves from the hellish and purgatorial menaces of this world in order to eventually inhabit the paradisical state—in *both* a secular and religious sense—vouchsafed to all who choose the committed life.

To flesh out this political eschatology we must inquire as to precisely what, in Greene's later novels, is pleasing in the eyes of God. Again, while this is a question we are not compelled to ask of the "post-Catholic" fictions, I believe it is one that can be asked if we so choose. The answer—if our proposed *Commedia* of commitment really reflects Greene's vision—is not radically different from that hinted at in *Brighton Rock:* people discovering the courage to act on their convictions to the uttermost, *whatever those convictions may be,* and, as a corollary, human lives possessed of a shape large and compelling enough to approach the condition of narrative art. This last claim may seem a bit dilettantish in a religious context, but consider in this regard the prediction out of *Old Moore's Almanac* that the *Medea*'s purser looks up in connection with Jones—a character who unmistakably finds his "great good place" of political engagement and martyrdom: "an artistic temperament. Ambitious. Successful in literary enterprises" (203). And successful in a literary mode he certainly is, not because of his lies about his past, but because he exits the book having found, according to Brown's dream, his proper role in that higher, sadder comedy that springs from our tragic commitments, at which "everyone laughs till the tears come" (287). God, it seems, likes a good thriller, and He wants our mortal spans to resemble one, in part because the times demand it: these days, after all, "the thrillers are like life" (*MF,* 65)—unless, that is, we have closed our eyes and hearts to the horrors of our century and those who suffer from them, making of ourselves comedians in the inferior sense. Granted, we may still leave God out of it altogether and assert that this *Paradisio* of the committed is simply a matter of having found a life of sufficient meaning and moment, for that it certainly is: as Mr. Heng says to Fowler, "Sooner or later . . . one has to take sides. If one is to remain human" (*QA,* 174). But Greene has always been a master at suggesting a spiritual realm enveloping even the most realistically rendered of locales, and thus it seems a pity to strip his novels of this final level of implication, especially since the unobtrusive God we are allowing in can do no more than watch—and perhaps laugh until He cries.

It should be emphasized here that even if one chooses to read *The Comedians* in a manner that posits its characters' drama as being religious as well as political, one will find no indication that anything resembling a conventional heavenly reward awaits anyone after their calvary. The only postmortem recompense held out to the committed is—perhaps—the knowledge of having somehow pleased Greene's weakened and suffering God, and thus the reward is purely symbolic, or, if you will, literary. Some critics maintain that genuine tragedy is impossible in Greene's world because Christian salvation is available to all, while "tragedy in its real sense can exist only in a world stripped of the Christian amenities, one in which heaven, paradise, and salvation are pleasant but meaningless terms. . . . Give men even the limited 'escape' that Greene permits his characters, and they forsake their tragic roles."[18] While this is yet another unfortunate attempt to corral Greene into an orthodox pen that simply won't hold him, it does offer a phrase we can bend into a more accurately explanatory shape. What is implicit in Greene's later novels is precisely—if paradoxically—a Christianity stripped of its amenities. In this theology the emphasis falls heavily on the Incarnation at the expense of the Resurrection, and furthermore, the Incarnation and subsequent Crucifixion exist not as a promise of anything, but rather as an example of how to live a fully human—which is to say a committed and thus tragic and thus ultimately comic—life. One undertakes the *Imitatio Christi* not because it is the high-road to eternal felicity, but for the same reasons one dedicates oneself to a hopeless political cause: to affirm solidarity with our fellow Sufferer, to alleviate if even for a moment His terrible pain. There are no beatific smiles among the "dignified and disciplined ranks" of the dead.

And what then of Brown himself? Are we to understand that he too finds a goodly part to perform in the arduous *Commedia* of commitment, or is he one of those forever consigned by his supposed "lack of sufficient zest" (*TC,* 279) to the *Inferno*'s vestibule, where the lukewarm forever shuffle back and forth without purpose? Taking up his case in detail will, I believe, clearly show how the secular and religious strands of Greene's political eschatology continually interweave themselves. Thus in what follows, the *mystique* and *politique* of his progress toward salvation will be given equal weight.

18. Karl, "Demonical Heroes," 56–57.

To determine whether Brown finally belongs among the sheep or the goats, we should look first of all at his reasons for returning to Haiti, for what prompts him appears to be a longing for a life in closer proximity to the realm of the absolutes. When Jones queries him aboard ship as to why he is going back, "conditions being what they are," he answers: "I found I missed the place. . . . Security can get on the nerves just as much as danger" (41). What enchants him about the island is reminiscent of Fowler's loving catalog of a war-torn Vietnam, which, recall, included "the gunfire traveling like a clock-hand around the horizon" (*QA*, 68). Thus Brown says he feels "a greater tie here, in the shabby land of terror, chosen for [him] by chance" (*TC*, 223), than in any of the other locales in his peripatetic life. Brown, for all his talk of his own "timidity" (279), puts himself conspicuously in harm's way, both by returning to Haiti in the first place, and then, as previously discussed, by bearding the Tontons Macoute with a seemingly reckless disregard for his own safety.[19] Just as it was impossible to take Fowler at his word concerning his purported selfishness, so too does it seem we must assess Brown's self-proclaimed cowardice with a good deal of suspicion.

Brown's attraction for danger is, in Greenean terms, auspicious, and appears to endow him with a seedy version of the Romance-hero's mantle,[20] though he might equally be seen as a sinner under the special protection of divine grace, for as the novel opens our protagonist is accompanied by various signs and omens that presage a pilgrimage to Beulah that will be successfully completed, a temptation in the wilderness that will be finally overcome. First of all, the ship that carries Brown and the other comedians back to Haiti is named the *Medea*, after that figure whose aid allowed the ocean-borne quester Jason to capture the coveted Golden Fleece. Secondly, there is the mysterious demeanor of his fellow passenger and future employer, Mr. Fernandez, whose disconcerting responses paint him as an oracular figure: "he kept very much to himself, and at table he answered politely and ambiguously in monosyllables," replying only "Yes" when Brown inquires about a port of call and "No" when asked how he finds the weather. Furthermore, in an observation whose

19. See C. S. Ferns, " 'Brown is Not Greene': Narrative Role in *The Comedians*," 64.

20. See Thomas, *Underground Fate,* 132–36.

diction foreshadows our narrator's later meditation on the dignified dead, Brown tells us that Fernandez "never himself asked a question and his discretion seemed to rebuke our own idle curiosity" (14, 15). Strangest of all, of course, is his unexplained fit of crying, during which he sits "straight upright in his chair" and "we[eps] with great dignity" (38). As Jones remarks, "it was as though he saw things. In the future" (40). And Brown is also willing to view him as prophetic, for "there was plenty for all of us to weep for where we were going" (38). But there is one odd encounter that occurs between Brown and Fernandez alone, and that seems to promise something other—or more—than tears:

> Again I drowsed and found myself alone in a blacked-out room and someone touched me with a cold hand. I woke and it was Mr. Fernandez who had, I suppose, been surprised by the steep roll of the boat and had steadied himself against me. I had the impression of a shower of gold dropping from a black sky as his spectacles caught the fitful sun. "Yes," he said, "yes," smiling an apology as he lurched upon his way. (18)

We need not deny that Mr. Fernandez has deathly associations to see this as a kind of benediction, for can't it be said that part of what Brown learns from events is that "the awareness of one's mortality . . . lends significance to life?"[21] The idea that one must lose one's life (literally or figuratively) in order to gain it is, apparently, never far from Greene's mind.

A final omen of the opening section is the name of Brown's own half-serious method of divining the future—propitious indeed in connection with our proposed *Commedia*—the *Sortes Virgilianae.* When he attempts this rite with Jones's trashy paperback, which bears the politically animating title of *No Time Like the Present,* the word revealed to him is "Trust?" (24). Perhaps this is the password that will eventually release him from the infernal regions of the uncommitted.

We also find that our narrator's earlier career has not been devoid of favorable signs and auguries. Brown, for his part, asserts several times that he left all faith—not just the religious variety—behind

---

21. Erdinast-Vulcan, *Childless Fathers,* 84.

him when as a teenager he escaped from his Catholic school run by the Fathers of the Visitation: "somewhere years ago I had forgotten how to be involved in anything. Somehow somewhere I had lost completely the capacity to be concerned" (182). When Martha points out that Dr. Magiot is a Communist, for instance, Brown replies, "I suppose so. I envy him. He's lucky to believe. I left all such absolutes behind me in the chapel of the Visitation. Do you know that they once even thought that I had a vocation?" (225). Of course we get the full story of his romantic departure from the school—how he bluffed his way into the Casino wearing makeup from his role as Father Lawrence and how he wound up that same evening losing his virginity to an older woman. The irony of this "breakout" (60), as he calls it, revolves around the oft-repeated name of his schoolmasters' order (mentioned over a half-dozen times in the course of the novel), for the moment of his liberation is accompanied by, well—a Visitation. And whereas Pinkie only feels "the pressure of gigantic wings against the glass" (*BR*, 239), this divine messenger gains entrance at the crucial moment:

> An odd thing happened as we lay on the bed. She was finding me shy, frightened, difficult. Her fingers had no success, even her lips had failed their office, when into the room suddenly from the port below the hill, flew a seagull. For a moment the room seemed spanned by the length of the white wings. She gave an exclamation of dismay and retreated: it was she who was scared now. I put out a hand to reassure her. The bird came to rest on a chest below a gold-framed looking-glass and stood there regarding us on its long stilt-like legs. It seemed as completely at home in the room as a cat and at any moment I expected it to begin to clean its plumage. My new friend trembled a little with her fear, and suddenly I found myself as firm as a man and I took her with such ease and confidence it was as though we had been lovers for a long time. Neither of us during those minutes saw the seagull go, although I shall always think that I felt the current of its wings on my back as the bird sailed out again towards the port and bay. (62)

The sexual context of this occurrence need not prevent us from seeing it as concerned with matters religious, for the conjunction is common enough in Greene. But what exactly is the significance and resonance of so startling a set-piece for the rest of Brown's

career? I think we must take it as the visible, prophetic sign of
what becomes clear only incrementally as the novel unfolds—that
Brown underestimates himself in declaring that he has long since
lost interest in "all such absolutes" and "forgotten how to be involved
in anything." That this sign takes the form of a lowly seagull rather
than the more traditional and ethereal dove is simply an indication
that the salvation it promises is at least halfway a thing of this
world. Brown's "vocation"—not for the priesthood, but for paying
due acknowledgment to the _"lacrimae rerum"_ (31) and for genuine
commitment to a political struggle that might ameliorate it—may
have been lost sight of during his rootless life, but it is rediscovered
as the narrative progresses. Brown, of course, talks frequently about
his unfitness for the _Commedia:_ "When [he] was a boy the fathers of
the Visitation had told [him] that one test of belief was this: that
a man was ready to die for it," and that while "once [he] might
have taken a different direction," it is "too late now" (286–87). But
of course Brown does in fact risk his life, though he would have us
believe he does it out of sexual jealousy rather than his love for the
mangled Joseph, for suffering Haiti, for the "tarts" as against the
"toffs" generally. ("Perhaps he [Jones] thought that my allegiance
in the last event would not necessarily be to the toffs" [26].) When
Brown puts himself at mortal risk in smuggling Jones to the rebels, it
is at the promptings of that "never quiet conscience which had been
injected into [him] without [his] consent, when [he] was too young to
know, by the fathers of the Visitation" (270). Caritas, we discover, is
no spent force within the protagonist, for even as he pushes aside the
beggars who are mobbing Mr. Smith, he feels "revolted by [him]self,
as though [he] were rejecting misery. The thought even [comes] to
[him], What would the fathers of the Visitation say[?]" (156). As with
Fowler and Querry, he is, "in the last event," a better man than he
knows and does not turn his back on the miserable of the earth.

Before leaving the subject of portents, we must touch on Brown's
dreams. As it happens, both express fear—but a fear of apathy and
sterile quietism, not a fear of involvement. In the first, the protagonist walks by the side of a moonlit lake while dressed as an altar boy,
all the while feeling

> the magnetism of the still quiet water, so that every step I took
> was nearer to the verge, until the uppers of my black boots were

submerged. Then a wind blew and the surge rose over the lake like a small tidal wave, but instead of coming towards me, it went in the opposite direction, raising the water in a long retreat, so that I found I walked on dry pebbles and that the lake existed only as a gleam on the far horizon of the desert of small stones, which wounded me through a hole in my boots. (74)

What is striking about this vision is that even though it seems to take a turn away from the expected nightmare—the waters desert rather than engulf the dreamer—it turns into a kind of nightmare nevertheless. This contrariness, it seems to me, is all of a piece with Greene's overall paradox of commitment: the still waters of peace are to be found through immersing oneself in danger, while the safety of the shore is the abode of a desiccating spiritual dryness. Here, the dreaming Brown gets his feet wet, so to speak, but then sees the opportunity for a sufficient baptism in peril retreat out of reach. A similar sense of exclusion from something needful arises in the second dream:

I fell asleep and dreamed I was a boy kneeling at the communion-rail in the college chapel in Monte Carlo. The priest came down the row and placed in each mouth a bourbon biscuit, but when he came to me he passed me by. The communicants on either side came and went away, but I knelt obstinately on. Again the priest distributed the biscuits and left me out. I stood up then and walked sullenly away down the aisle which had become an immense aviary where parrots stood in ranks chained to their crosses. (207)

I would agree with Brian Thomas's opinion that in this dream Brown's "cherished anonymity is now transformed into a sort of dreadful invisibility."[22] In terms of the *Commedia,* the fact that God desires from each of us a lived narrative of absolutistic intensity means that the price of noncommitment is to cease to count in the eyes of the Lord, to be etched out from the Book of Life—to be passed by at holy communion. Our protagonist thus here encounters his fear of excommunicating himself through caution and detachment. That he retreats from the altar rail toward an aviary of parrots is also significant, for the birds can be seen as so many comedians

22. Thomas, *Underground Fate,* 154.

of the baser variety, mouthing rote humorous lines over and over again. Parrots, of course, live longer lives than human beings, and perhaps this is a further comment on—given Greene's overall view of existence—the dubious reward of continually playing things safe.

Brown has a third vision at the novel's end that some have taken as an admission that he has failed the great test and consigned himself to the *Inferno*'s anodyne anteroom: "I had felt myself not merely incapable of love—many are incapable of that, but even of guilt. There were no heights and no abysses in my world—I saw myself on a great plain, walking and walking on the interminable flats" (286). This, however, is a waking vision, and thus it is less candid than the dreams that state their case uncensored by Brown's self-depreciating modesty. How much authority can we confer upon this confession of a supposed inability to feel guilt when it is so obviously motivated by, and redolent of, the guilt of being a survivor? The truth is that Brown's life is flat only in comparison with those who have actually died in the cause, and thus whose tragic fall and subsequent rise through the Dantean strata have been that much the greater. Here again, wisdom resides in trusting the tale above the teller.

Perhaps the place where Brown comes closest to admitting that he might be a genuine member of the *Commedia*'s cast is on the novel's first page, in a passage whose location perhaps accounts for the number of critics who seem to have forgotten about it. There he "can find no reason to mock the modest stone that commemorates Jones on the far side of the international road which he failed to cross in a country far from home. . . . *Exegi monumentum.* Whenever [his] rather bizarre business takes [him] north to Monte Christi and [he] pass[es] the stone, [he] feel[s] a certain pride that [his] action helped to raise it" (9). The Latin tag is significant, for, as with other evidence that Brown is at heart one of the engaged, it has remained with him from the schooling he claims to have disowned: "I find it strange to think now of my Latin verses and compositions—all that knowledge has vanished as completely as my father. Only one line has obstinately stuck in my head—a memory of the old dreams and ambitions: '*Exegi monumentum aere perennius . . .*'" (59, Greene's ellipses). The passage in question is from Horace:

> I have achieved a monument more lasting than bronze, and loftier than the pyramids of kings, which neither gnawing rain nor

blustering wind may destroy, nor innumerable series of years, nor the passage of ages. I shall not wholly die . . . [23]

At the time that Brown recalls this line, he is conceiving of his monument as "the most popular tourist hotel in the Caribbean" (60), and in fact it looks for a while as if he has there achieved his great good place: "Once I had looked out of my window at two in the morning. There was a great yellow moon and a girl was making love in the pool. She had her breasts pressed against the side and I couldn't see the man behind her. She didn't notice me watching her; she didn't notice anything. That night I thought before I slept, 'I have arrived'" (51). Alas, there is a crack in this monument, as Brian Thomas again explains:

> The sexualized tourist paradise presided over by the spirit of a spellbinding woman with an inexhaustible hunger for love symbolizes the "making" of Brown's fortune in the very precise sense that it represents the realization of an endless erotic dream. The figure of arrival is consummation; Brown has again glimpsed a promised land.
>
> The fact remains, however, that he takes possession of this great good place as a kind of outsider or voyeur. [24]

I think it is therefore no coincidence that in the following paragraph Brown describes his annoyance at discovering that his "small brass paper-weight shaped like a coffin, marked with the letters R.I.P." (51) is missing. It turns up, of course, in the pocket of Doctor Philipot, who has chosen to commit suicide in the very pool that once enclosed Brown's erotic epiphany, an act that begins the protagonist's inevitable progress toward involvement and risk in the rebel cause. The paperweight is thus another paradoxical symbol—Brown cannot "rest in peace" among the recreations of the Trianon, for true peace comes only through a more intimate involvement with that more "serious" and "respectable" phenomenon, death. By the time of his final dream, where he is vouchsafed a vision of Jones and his "good place" for a soldier's death, Brown has exchanged his outsider status for that of insider, his voyeurism for participation. His trajectory,

23. Horace *Odes* 3.30.
24. Thomas, *Underground Fate,* 139–40.

then, is from *hotelier* to undertaker, from one who temporarily houses the frivolous living to one who permanently shelters the "dignified and disciplined ranks" of the dead. Given the chronic horrors of Papa Doc's "nightmare republic," this is progress.

Thus *The Comedians'* uncanny power, like that of *A Burnt-Out Case* and *The Honorary Consul,* springs from Greene's ability to tell the same story on two levels simultaneously while yet avoiding the mechanical creakiness of allegory or fable. The figure of Brown, motivated by the most earthy of sexual and political passions, and yet shadowed at every step by a fitful providence, implies a God who is something more than a spectator, something less than a playwright, a deity who watches the stage of this world with an intensely interested, sympathetic, and painful eye, but whose only succor—aside from an occasional omen or dream—arrives in the form of satisfying applause at the performance's end. Indeed Brown seems to understand that, despite the obscurity suggested by his name, he is a man caught in some manner of spotlight, and has even formed an opinion concerning the dramatic taste of his invisible audience:

> Surely there must be a power which always arranges things to happen in the most humiliating circumstances. When I was a boy I had faith in the Christian God. Life under his shadow was a very serious affair; I saw Him incarnated in every tragedy. He belonged to the *lacrimae rerum* like a gigantic figure looming through a Scottish mist. Now that I approached the end of life it was only my sense of humor that enabled me sometimes to believe in Him. Life was a comedy, not the tragedy for which I had been prepared, and it seemed to me that we were all, on this boat with a Greek name (why should a Dutch line name its boats in Greek?), driven by an authoritative practical joker towards the extreme point of comedy. (31–32)

Just as he is only half right about himself, so he is only half right here. Life *is* a comedy—though not the degraded kind he imagines—and it can be so precisely because it is, more often than he guesses, just the kind of tragedy for which he has been prepared. Another way of putting it might be to say that whereas Brown believes himself to be a character in a light "entertainment," Greene's achievement lies in convincing us that he—and we—are all the while writing ourselves into tragicomic novels.

III

On the subject of the literary qualities we have discerned in Greene's eschatology, several critics have argued that the "monument" Brown rears can also refer to the story he narrates, to the novel he writes for us. Randall Craig, for one, is convinced that this memorial is also redemptive, that "the text itself becomes [Brown's] great, good place."[25] Perhaps—though while one can certainly agree that Brown's narrative is not the solipsistic and "dark Brown" (230) tale of Martha's accusation, one can yet hold that the text is rather more cautious about the question of whether, and to what extent, writing by itself can count as an act of sufficient engagement. This matter appears to get its airing in Brown's most extended meditation on commitment, a passage notable because in it the protagonist seems to both claim and disclaim the burden that has become his novel's touchstone:

> The rootless have experienced, like all the others, the temptations of sharing the security of a religious creed or a political faith, and for some reason we have turned the temptation down. We are the faithless; we admire the dedicated, the Doctor Magiots and the Mr. Smiths for their courage and their integrity, for their fidelity to a cause, but through timidity, or through lack of sufficient zest, we find ourselves the only ones truly committed—committed to the whole world of evil and of good, to the wise and to the foolish, to the indifferent and to the mistaken. We have chosen nothing except to go on living, "rolled round on Earth's diurnal course, With rocks and stones and trees." (279)

While this can be read as yet another example of Brown's modest self-depreciation, the notion of being committed to "the whole world of evil and of good, to the wise and the foolish, to the indifferent and the mistaken" makes one suspect that Greene here is also mulling over his own situation as a writer whose subject is all of life—and as a writer who champions the committed life, but who always lives to write another day. Can such an author participate in the *Commedia,*

---

25. Craig, "Good Places," 324; see also Thomas, *Underground Fate,* 158–59.

or is he the sacrificial man whose "damnation" is necessary in order to save others—a figure familiar in the pages of his own books? Perhaps "timidity" and "lack of zest" are the inevitable price to be paid for the objectivity necessary for aesthetic achievement. Though at the same time there seems to be something grand about committing to the whole world of evil and of good—it doesn't sound at all the equivalent of being insufficiently committed to anything, even if that is a plausible interpretation of the phrase. Or is Greene here using "committed" in its other, incarceratorial, sense, punning thus in order to claim that the unsought gift of literary genius sentences one almost against one's will to neutrality, irony, and cool ecumenical sympathy?

Craig, playing devil's advocate to his own argument, observes that by concluding the passage with a quotation from the end of one of Wordsworth's "Lucy" poems, Greene may be implying that Brown's uncommitted life (if that's what it is) is a kind of survival but also a kind of death, since such is the ambiguous state in which the lines leave the woman of whom the poet sings. I wonder, though, whether the quotation might more fruitfully be taken as a tentatively hopeful comment on the office of the artist? Doesn't Wordsworth bestow a shape and a meaning upon the heretofore "unknown" life and death he so briefly narrates,[26] building a monument to a once obscure existence that has, so far at least, outlived bronze? If God in fact desires that our lives approach the condition of art, but is at the same time too weakened and constrained to effectively shape our ends according to His frustrated intentions, perhaps the sympathetic author who declaims His *Commedia* may be credited with practicing, at the very least, "an imperfection of charity" sufficient to number him among the cadre of those who have committed their lives to a cause. After all, who could profit from the example of life's obscure or seedy saints such as Smith or Jones without the efforts of their "committed" hagiographer?

IV

Just as Greene's view of the relationship between love and pity changes over the years, so too does his notion of the connection

26. Craig, "Good Places," 319; William Wordsworth, "A Slumber Did My Spirit Seal," ll. 7–8.

between innocence and political action. And just as he singled out and (unsuccessfully) attempted to discredit pity in *The Ministry of Fear* and *The Heart of the Matter,* so in *The Quiet American* does he set his sights on innocence, only to reassess his criticism in *The Comedians.* To some extent, his shifting attitude toward the naïfs who stumble through his novels can be seen as a marker of his increasing insistence on the centrality of political commitment to the adequately moral life.

In *The Quiet American* it is, of course, the title character who embodies the mortal (and moral) dangers of innocence, and Fowler's attack upon him—and it—is as strident as it is relentless. Convinced from his college reading that he knows what is best for the Vietnamese people—no matter how many of them have to die in order to prove it—Pyle is "too innocent to live," with "no more of a notion than any of you [Americans] what the whole affair's about" (*QA,* 31–32). The only adequate solution to his violent meddling is in turn a violent one, for "you can't blame the innocent, they are always guiltless. All you can do is control them or eliminate them. Innocence is a kind of insanity" (163). And while Pyle may be the immediate flesh-and-blood focus of Fowler's fear and anger, the state of mind itself is represented as a danger no matter in whom it lodges: "Innocence always calls mutely for protection when we would be so much wiser to guard ourselves against it: innocence is like a dumb leper who has lost his bell, wandering the world, meaning no harm" (37). It can even affect whole nations as well as individuals, as is evidenced by the United States, a country of moral if not physical "virgins" (102) who "might understand a little more about human beings" if they "sometimes . . . had a few bad motives" (133). Given the maddeningly cocksure portrait of Pyle and his countrymen that emerges during the course of the novel, and the tenor of Greene's anti-American statements elsewhere at this period, it is not oversimplifying to assume that Fowler is speaking for the author of the mid-fifties on this issue.

As compared with the sometimes oblique and slippery assault on pity, there is nothing very complicated about the gist of Greene's critique of innocence. It holds up to distrust any "initiatives supported [only] by theoretical premises," and ridicules any "belief [that] ideals hav[e] a reality quite apart from the facts of experience." Also, the text's assessment of the dangers of innocence are straightforwardly practical—innocent people who get notions in their heads and a fire in their bellies cause more human damage than do more worldly enthusiasts—though that last phrase, in the world of *The Quiet American,* is in fact an oxymoron. Indeed, this polarization between the innocently active and the knowledgeably indolent results in an ambivalence about political commitment that Terry Eagleton, ever sensitive to such things, articulates: "Fowler's action [becoming engaged by facilitating the assassination of Pyle] substantiates a humanity which is, in the last analysis, more worthy than Pyle's fanaticism, and at the same time, through Fowler's guilt at having killed a kind and honourable man, serves to ratify the wisdom of his previous detachment. Both involvement and detachment are therefore criticized."[27] This is supported by Fowler's own ambivalent last words, affirming that while "everything ha[s] gone right with [him] since [Pyle] ha[s] died," he nevertheless "wishe[s] there existed someone to whom [he] could say that [he] was sorry" (189). Still, the scale does not rest at dead center, for there is a surprising moment in the midst of Fowler's world-weary superiority when he momentarily revalues naïveté in a way that looks forward to that term's more favorable reception in *The Comedians:* "All the time that his innocence had angered me, some judge within myself had summed up in his favour, had compared his idealism, his half-baked ideas founded on the works of York Harding, with my cynicism. Oh, I was right about the facts, but wasn't he right too to be young and mistaken, and wasn't he perhaps a better man for a girl to spend her life with?" (156).

In *The Comedians,* such a judgment in favor of the ingenuous over the jaded occurs early, in one of Brown's first encounters with a character who has kept his innocence remarkably inviolate despite his advanced age:

> "Vegetarianism isn't only a question of diet, Mr. Brown. It touches life at many points. If we really eliminated acidity from the human body we would eliminate passion."
> "Then the world would stop."
> He reproved me gently, "I didn't say love," and I felt a curious sense of shame. Cynicism is cheap—you can buy it at any Monoprix store—it's built into all poor-quality goods. (*TC,* 21)

27. Sharrock, *Saints,* 209, 154; Eagleton, "Reluctant Heroes," 112–13.

Brown would like to attribute narrow and intolerant ideas to both the Smiths, feeling that such must be the natural concomitants of single-mindedly pursuing a cause as high-minded and impractical as theirs. By this time, however, Mrs. Smith has saved Brown from death at the hands of Captain Concasseur by the sheer force of her moral presence, and he begins to see their innocence as more a benign than a sinister weapon on the battlefield of existence: "I had assumed them to be puritan because they were vegetarian. Yet it was not the passion of love which was caused by acidity, and they were both enemies of hate" (189–90). Furthermore, as Sharrock points out, while Pyle's innocence consists of "a sublime inability to learn," the Smiths are amenable to the lessons of experience.[28]

> "I'm sorry about the [vegetarian] centre. But, you know, Mr. Smith, it would never have done."
> "I realize that now. Perhaps we seem rather comic figures to you, Mr. Brown."
> "Not comic," I said with sincerity, "heroic." (192)

This exchange is perhaps the clearest indication of Greene's change of heart. And it is not only a matter of the innocent becoming merely less pernicious in his eyes, for in *The Comedians* it is they and not the worldly who are fittingly costumed to take up roles in the *Commedia* of commitment. In fact, the Smiths emerge as paragons of a sort, embodying several Greenean desiderata rarely if ever found outside the bounds of wishful thinking elsewhere in his canon: that is, a political engagement whose motives and likely effects are pristinely benign; an eros directed toward each other that is seamlessly connected to a caritas directed at a suffering world; and a profound peace that has nothing to do with unburdening themselves of responsibility for others. "In the school chapel at Monte Carlo we prayed every Sunday, *'Dona nobis pacem,'* but I doubt whether that prayer was answered for many in the life that followed. Mr. Smith had no need to pray for peace. He had been born with peace in his heart instead of the splinter of ice" (246). Brown is not being quite accurate here in regards to himself, for his splinter of ice is no inherited trait, but rather another label for that worldly experience

28. Sharrock, *Saints,* 230–31.

that warns that "action is dangerous." What keeps Brown from being merely the victim of his education in disenchantment is something he shares with the Smiths—an ability to learn uncomfortable lessons. Witness Brown's tone of painful revelation as he reluctantly drags himself toward a reevaluation of the virtues of innocence and, simultaneously, the necessity for action. When Martha, for instance, says his enervating, "dark Brown" cynicism moves her to pity him as she pities her father, he lies in bed "a long while and wonder[s] what [he] could possibly have in common with a war criminal responsible for so many unidentified deaths" (230). Likewise, when Jones remarks that he (Jones) and Smith have "a bit in common" and are "horses out of the same stable," Brown at first "listen[s] with astonishment. What could a saint possibly have in common with a rogue? Jones gently closed the cocktail-case, and then, taking a cloth from the table, he began to stroke the leather, as tenderly as Mrs. Smith had smoothed her husband's hair, and [he] thought: innocence perhaps" (105). Later, on the road to the rebels, Brown thinks that "perhaps [Jones] really was as innocent as Mr. Smith, and that was the reason they had liked each other" (260).

It is all to the point that the specific form that Jones's innocence takes is that of an unarticulated longing for an absolutistic life, a secret yearning for commitment. As he and Brown approach the graveyard meeting with Philipot and his guerrillas, Jones's excitement at the prospect of his previous fabrications becoming flesh is palpable.

> "Shall we make your rendezvous on time?" Jones asked.
> "I doubt it. You may have to keep under cover till tomorrow night. I brought you some sandwiches in case."
> He chuckled. "It's the life," he said. "I've often dreamt of something like this."
> "I thought it was the life you'd always led."
> He fell silent again as though aware of an indiscretion. (257)

During the subsequent night amid the tombs, Jones confesses to all his previous lies about his career, explaining that despite the mediated reality of his life the spirit was always willing: " 'I only wanted my chance,' he added, and I wondered whether perhaps in all his devious life he had been engaged on a secret and hopeless love-affair with virtue, watching virtue from a distance, hoping to be noticed, perhaps, like a child doing wrong in order to attract the attention of virtue" (267). Such a buried desire for absolutistic engagement is, as we have seen, evident in Brown's own otherwise inexplicable courting of hurt and hazard, and thus he comes to see himself and Jones as comrades of a sort. "It was like meeting an unknown brother—Jones and Brown, the names were almost interchangeable, and so was our status. . . . [W]e had swum from very far apart to come together in a cemetery in Haiti. 'I like you, Jones.' I said" (266). And thus at the novel's end it is in truth "only natural that [Brown] should dream of Jones" and his "comic line" by which he evaluates the site of his death in battle: "This is a good place" (287). It is natural because they have both discovered a hidden fund of innocence within themselves, the innocence that is willing to undertake dangerous action in behalf of a cause, despite all the well-founded cautions of worldly experience.

There is also another sense in which the protagonists of Greene's later fictions are innocent, in that figures like Querry, Brown, and Plarr do not seem to understand where their resources of courage and commitment come from. Querry, for instance, keeps defining his condition negatively, as an absence, and thus determines "never again from boredom or vanity to involve another human being in [his] lack of love" (*BC*, 118). This leads him to misidentify his motivation for following Deo Gratias into the bush, seeing it as an interest of the head rather than the heart: "His own presence here was hardly more explicable than that of Deo Gratias" and "now that he cared for nothing, perhaps he was being driven by a vestige of intellectual curiosity. . . . He had lived with inertia so long that he examined his 'interest' with clinical detachment" (55–56). Querry simply fails to recognize that what he truly desires is not a safely loveless and stationary existence, but a life of love and service in a mode and scale radically different from those that have heretofore made him into an empty public institution. Rycker and Parkinson may be utterly mistaken as to what he is about, and burden him with imaginary virtues, but Querry himself does not understand Querry, and unfairly strips himself of credit for the genuine measure of empathy and charity that still fitfully operate beneath the hard shell of his self-loathing.

Brown's delusion about his own motives involves his reiterated claims that he is an incorrigibly rootless man and that he has not freely chosen to come to Haiti. Significantly placed after one of his loving descriptions of the country's beauty, he asks, "Why was I here? I was here because of a picture-postcard from my mother which could easily have gone astray—no odds at any casino could have been higher than that." And yet even here he is led to admit more than he realizes: "There are those who belong to a province, a county, a village, but I could feel no link at all with the hundred or so square kilometers around the gardens and boulevards of Monte Carlo, a city of transients. I felt a greater tie here, in the shabby land of terror, chosen for me by chance." And thus when he goes on to declare that "transience [is his] pigmentation" and that his "roots would never go deep enough anywhere to make [him] a home or make [him] secure with love" (223), we hear a man who fails to understand the depth of his own attachments. A similar self-deception occurs after Brown witnesses the voodoo ceremony: "I should never have gone to this funeral, I should never have come to this country, I was a stranger. My mother had taken a black lover, she had been involved, but somewhere years ago I had forgotten how to be involved in anything. Somehow somewhere I had lost completely the capacity to be concerned. Once I looked out and thought I saw Philipot beckoning to me through the rain. It was an illusion" (182). But is it? In the end Brown answers Philipot's beckoning call to engagement, telling himself all the while that he is doing it merely to remove a sexual rival. If Brown is in fact a stranger, it is not to the Haiti he loves but to the better angels of his own nature, whom he refuses to properly acknowledge.

This motif also wends its way through *The Honorary Consul,* where Dr. Plarr is unaware of the extent of his love for the father he barely knew and of his admiration for the political cause for which the elder man died. "Not one of [Plarr's] friends in the capital or his coffee-house acquaintances came near to understanding his motive" for moving to the city across the river from Paraguay, in part because the doctor cannot articulate them even to himself. He "c[an] not measure himself exactly how much he had been influenced to return to the small river port by the sense that here he would be living near the border of the country where he had been born and where his father was buried," though he feels "sometimes like a watchman waiting for a signal" (*HC,* 12). As to why he agrees to help León Rivas and his revolutionary bumblers with a plan that involves so much personal risk, we are airily and unconvincingly informed that "it was that very sense of [their] amateurism which had persuaded him to become involved" (27). And even as death closes in, Plarr is still unaware of his deepest motivations, telling himself that if "afterwards people . . . say he ha[s] followed in his father's steps," then "they would be wrong" (209). The doctor, a man of science, is rightly skeptical of invoking the word "love" to explain our basically selfish behavior, and to his credit he does not exempt himself from this doubting scrutiny: "We all of us seem to live with dead fathers, don't we? Fortnum hated his. I think I may have loved mine. Perhaps. How can I possibly tell? That word love has such a slick sound. We take credit for loving as though we had passed an examination with more than the average marks" (215). But Plarr, like Brown before him, simply—and, from a reader's perspective, attractively—underestimates the extent to which caritas compels him toward sacrifice: "What effect did it have on a child to have a cold fish for a father? It might have been better if they could have exchanged fathers. A cold fish would have been his own proper parentage rather than a father who had cared enough to die. He would have liked the little bastard to believe in something, but he was not the kind of father who could transmit belief in a god or a cause" (210). In the end, of course, Plarr does care enough to die, and he, no less than Brown, earns the blessing of a politically committed parent—"you really are a son of mine" (*TC,* 72).

It may be useful to consider this theme in connection with various claims that the generic flavor of Greene's novels changes over the course of time—from tragedy in the thirties and forties to either romance or tragicomedy in the fifties, sixties, and beyond. Certainly what Greene appears to be doing in creating protagonists who are unaware of their own capacity for love, engagement, and sacrifice is endowing them with something that might be considered the generic opposite of a tragic flaw—a "comic virtue," if you will, with "virtue" being understood as a singular noun. Just as hidden from consciousness as the supposed tragic flaw, the comic virtue is responsible for unforeseen salvation as surely as the flaw brings about unlooked-for ruin. And while there is something mechanical and oversimple about baldly opposing, say, *The Heart of the Matter* and *The Comedians* in this way—(aren't Scobie's "tragic flaws," in the end, exactly what redeem him in the eyes of Greene's God?)—it is true that the author's later heroes, as Charley Fortnum puts it, "get caught up by love" (*HC*, 260), "get kidnapped . . . by mistake" (265), and wind up hostage to an insistent charity they did not know they harbored within themselves. That this is, in the end, always a fortunate abduction, is perhaps the most urgent and hopeful pronouncement of Greene's "post-Catholic" fictions.

To view Greene's changing assessment of innocence in light of his larger *Commedia* of commitment is to see how close beneath the surface of his political preoccupations runs a diffuse but nutritive current of religious implication. After all, one could paraphrase much of the above discussion of innocence by saying that to enter the heavenly kingdom of the genuinely engaged, his protagonists must become again as little children. Of course in the seedy environs of Greeneland, experience comes early and hard, and a certain jaded exhaustion with the futility of human aspirations seems to be a prerequisite for Greene's later heroes. What this means, then, is that when such characters opt at last to act and commit themselves to causes that only the innocent believe can succeed, they are to a certain extent playing a part, adopting a role, becoming a comedian. If we consider Oedipus as our culture's quintessential tragic figure in his movement from vigorous innocence to terrible and immobilizing knowledge, then the essentially comic nature of what Greene is about stands out in contrast. Thus it is intriguing in this regard to recall how Fowler, that scourge of all things innocent, attempts to pass the time on the night he knowingly sends Pyle to his death:

> I . . . went into the cinema next door—Errol Flynn, or it may have been Tyrone Power (I don't know how to distinguish them in tights), swung on ropes and leapt from balconies and rode bareback into technicolor dawns. He rescued a girl and killed his enemy and led a charmed life. It was what they call a film for boys, but the sight of Oedipus emerging with his bleeding eyeballs from the palace at Thebes would surely give a better training for life today. No life is charmed. (*QA*, 181–82)

What the later novels actually strive to assert, though, is that even lives lived in the full knowledge of bleeding Oedipus can in fact be charmed, that some of the innocent energies and heroic aspirations of the author's boyhood reading can indeed be recaptured, if only

we will let down our guard of sad experience long enough to perceive the outlines of a comedy, secular and divine, which subsumes
and transfigures the endemic tragedies of our necessary political
entanglements. If, to conflate a pair of Yeats's poems,[29] we will only
"resig[n our] part / In the casual comedy" of non-engagement, in
which only "polite meaningless words" are spoken and "motley is
worn," we may be able, if the risk we undertake is sufficient, to
achieve that broader comic vantage point occupied by those who
look down "on all the tragic scene," and yet whose "glittering eyes . . .
are gay." As Mr. Jones understatedly attests from his own equally
high and rocky prospect, it is "a good place." By ascending to such
difficult elevations, suggests Greene, we may finally comprehend
the revised and completed scripts of lives redeemed from frightened
indifference, and witness "gaiety transfiguring all that dread."

---

29. William Butler Yeats, "Easter 1916," ll. 36–37, 6, 14; "Lapis Lazuli," ll. 52–
56, 17.

5 The Honorary Marxist

Political Philosophy in Greene's Novels

I

Graham Greene's own practical politics are not difficult to describe. He referred to himself as a "social democrat," and, as Brian Diemert has recently put it, he hoped to one day see established "a kind of ideal socialism able to guard and preserve the rights and dignity of the individual."[1] Greene's "final" position on political matters is therefore not nearly as provocative or visionary or idiosyncratic as his theology, or his view of the human passions, or his attitudes toward security and risk. What is of interest, however, is the path by which he arrived at this position. I am not speaking here about some linear development over the decades, or any gradual migration from one point on the political spectrum to another. Rather, I am referring to an ongoing but far from programmatic testing and contesting within his novels of the three systems of thought that contribute to his mature political philosophy: Christianity, liberalism, and Marxism. Throughout his canon, these three worldviews are put into dialogue—sometimes into shouting matches—with one another, and the real interest of Greene's political thought lies in the unexpected parallels, dichotomies, and cross-fertilizations that emerge as a result of this conversation.

Certainly Greene himself bridled at any suggestion that he ever actively propagandized for his own personal political beliefs in the pages of his fiction: "I don't as a rule write to defend an idea. I'm content to tell a story and to create characters. In an article one can try to express a direct point of view but not in a book. I don't want to use literature for political ends, nor for religious ends. Even if my novels happen incidentally to be political books, they're no more written to provoke changes than my so-called 'Catholic' novels are written to convert anyone."[2] Though it has been the practice

---

1. Cassis, *Man of Paradox,* 453; Diemert, *Thrillers,* 49.
2. Allain, *Other Man,* 78.

of this study to listen with a believing ear to the tale rather than the teller, this demurral rings true: Greene, like the vast majority of novelists, is better at making us aware of injustices than at devising specific programs to eradicate them, and thus much of his own social-democratic outlook must be inferred from his disparaging depictions of the often quite different political assumptions and enthusiasms of his characters. But to repeat, it is not really his own social-democratic outlook that is here the object of our attention, but rather his ongoing critiques of the twentieth century's reigning ideologies and the way they shape—and frequently misshape—our daily lives.

Many attempts to articulate Greene's political ideas have taken it as a given that one of his lifelong (if intermittent and uncompleted) endeavors is to imagine some sort of workable synthesis of Catholicism and Marxism. Since these are two philosophies that, in his public statements, his journalism, and his fiction writing, have in general received his continuing sympathy, the assumption is understandable. There are, however, problems with attempting to tease out even the sketch of a Catholic-Marxist concordat from Greene's novels, not the least of which involves the fact that Greene's form of Christianity, at least as it is articulated within those novels, is very much his own construction. Take, for instance, the belief in an apocalypse or a millennium or an endtime beyond history— however one wants to phrase it. Most forms of Christianity (including Catholicism) possess such a belief, and so does Marxism, and in both belief systems it is envisioned as an epoch (if such a temporal term can properly be employed in this context) in which humanity will be finally perfected, though of course in two utterly different ways. Christians, like Marxists, are expected to look forward to such an epoch with joy and longing, but as it happens Greene views both these supposed utopias with something verging on horror. This is perhaps best exemplified by a nightmare that Monsignor Quixote suffers one evening in the course of his extended and peripatetic debate with Sancho, "the Mayor," over the relative virtues of Communism and Catholicism:

> He had dreamt that Christ had been saved from the Cross by the legion of angels to which on an earlier occasion the Devil had told Him that He could appeal. So there was no final agony, no heavy stone which had to be rolled away, no discovery of an

empty tomb. Father Quixote stood there watching on Golgotha as Christ stepped down from the Cross triumphant and acclaimed. The Roman soldiers, even the Centurion, knelt in His honor, and the people of Jerusalem poured up the hill to worship Him. The disciples clustered happily around. His mother smiled through her tears of joy. There was no ambiguity, no room for doubt and no room for faith at all. The whole world knew with certainty that Christ was the Son of God.

It was only a dream, of course it was only a dream, but nonetheless Father Quixote had felt on waking the chill of despair felt by a man who realizes suddenly that he has taken up a profession which is of use to no one, who must continue to live in a kind of Saharan desert without doubt or faith, where everyone is certain that the same belief is true. He had found himself whispering, "God save me from such a belief." Then he heard the Mayor turn restlessly on the bed beside him, and he added without thought, "Save him too from belief," and only then he fell asleep again. (*MQ,* 69–70)

While the dream itself makes no reference to the Second Coming or any postmillennial state, we can easily infer from it what Greene's objection is to both Christianity and Marxism's official eschatologies, for both systems insist upon their own versions of a coming time "without doubt or faith." Such an epoch would also be—necessarily, crucially—one without *narrative,* and this, as we have seen in the previous chapter, flies in the face of Greene's own peculiar theological vision of a God desperately in need of satisfying human stories. Consider, in this regard, just how very fortunate our author believes the Fortunate Fall to have been, for is it not Greeneland's very seediness that demonstrates the infinite pity of a baffled deity (because He must reach so far down in extending His failing grace) and generates the narratives of extremity that alone save us from banality (since men must clutch so desperately at the dangling tatters of His redemption)? As the whisky priest would have it, even Christ's earthly sojourn is only made narratively significant by our pervasive imperfectability: "it was for this world that Christ had died; the more evil you saw and heard about you, the greater glory lay around the death. It was too easy to die for what was good or beautiful, for home or children or a civilization—it needed a God to die for the half-hearted and the corrupt" (*PG,* 97). When the saint is redeemed, there is no story; when the brutalized and brutal murderer *may* be redeemed, there is a gripping story. Thus since both Christianity and Marxism envision themselves as eventually ushering in a state of human plotlessness, a place where narrative will wither as a result of the absence of conflict and obstacle, the writer of thrillers violently rejects their eschatological presumptions. "I don't believe in perfectibility *any* way, on *either* [the Christian or Marxist] side. We can improve conditions, but I don't think we can expect a perfect world."[3]

It may be objected that such scruples are both highly abstract and highly hypothetical, but surely any political program to be derived from a synthesis of Marxism and Christianity would involve devising practical ways of preparing humankind for *some* sort of plotless millennium, since such an endtime is a feature common to both. In truth, though, I cite Monsignor Quixote's nightmare not because it represents the most important of Greene's quarrels with either the Church of Rome or dialectical materialism, but because it illuminates how unproductive it is to conceive of Greene's attempts to meld the teachings of Marx and Christ as some sort of straightforward "take-the-best-from-both" affair. And something else follows as well. If we can find instances of our author murmuring "a plague on both your houses" at systems of belief with which he is in general sympathy, then we should not be surprised to find him in secret sympathy with that "third force" he so frequently and caustically denigrates—liberalism. The truth of the matter is that sometimes the pounding that Marx and Christ deliver to each other (and, as above, to themselves) leave standing only a figure resembling Matthew Arnold, much as our author might wish to deny it. As we shall see, it is only by examining how Greene continually threads his critical faculties among all three of these competing worldviews that we may sufficiently grasp his particular take on the twentieth century's political tragedies and contradictions.

We can begin to see in how complicated a manner Christianity, Marxism, and liberalism are intertwined by keeping in mind Father Quixote's horrific vision of utter certainty while surveying other sites in Greene's canon temporally far afield from it. *Monsignor Quixote* is one of our author's last novels, but it has been his contention from the period of his earliest that, as he said once in a letter to the editor, "doubt like the conscience is inherent in human nature," and that

---

3. Cassis, *Man of Paradox*, 470.

"perhaps they are the same thing" (*YE,* 225). Take, for instance, the sympathetic Dr. Czinner in *Stamboul Train,* a committed revolutionary who yet understands the moral benefits of doubt. The doctor is himself an atheist on the familiar Marxist grounds that "God [is] a fiction invented by the rich to keep the poor content" (*ST,* 112), but his reaction to young Carol Musker's own denial of God is prompted by an underlying feeling that a thoroughgoing lack of doubt is morally troubling in and of itself: "he was shocked by the ease of her disbelief, which did not come from the painful reading of rationalist writers and nineteenth-century scientists; she had been born to disbelief as securely as he had been born to belief. He had sacrificed security in order to reach the same position, and for a moment he longed to sow in her some dry plant of doubt, a half-belief which would make her mistrust her judgment" (151). Thus Czinner is "the first of Greene's protagonists reluctantly to retain a vestige of faith, while at the same time professing a Marxism he is not quite convinced of, at least in the abstract form it takes in his own final speech."[4] What is interesting about the quasi-Marxist revolutionary Czinner believing in the salutary effects of religious doubts (or half-beliefs) is that doubting, though it may be an inescapable fact of life for both the Marxist and the Christian, is neither a Marxist nor a Christian desideratum—though it *is* one for liberalism. Certainly in Greene's fiction as a whole, the sympathetic Christians and Marxists all doubt the truth of their creeds and causes, or, rather, are sympathetic in proportion to the extent to which they doubt them, as anyone who compares León Rivas's reluctant trigger-finger with the lieutenant's itchy one immediately understands. Greene's account of a kindred soul he met on a trip to East Germany underscores this attitude: "Perhaps the old Catholic convert has something in common with the old Communist convert which makes it easy for the two to get on terms—he has lived through the period of enthusiasm and now recognizes the differing regions of acceptance and doubt. One Communist, who had been an orthodox Jew, said to me, 'I gave up my faith when I was eighteen and joined the party. Now at fifty one realizes that everything is not known'" (*RE,* 212). But to encourage doubt for its own sake—to describe it as in itself ethically desirable—is to buy into, or at least to tacitly align oneself with, the liberal

4. Pendleton, *Conradian Masterplot,* 70–71.

project of evenhanded adjudication between different and even incommensurable notions of social good, none of which are credited, from the system as a whole's point of view, with possessing absolute truth. Liberalism always gets itself into difficulty when it attempts to assimilate true believers of any stripe, and thus "God save me from such a belief" and "save him too from belief" might be the only credo to which the self-conscious liberal could give unqualified assent.

And where there is doubt, there is failure, or at least failure's shadowing specter, for only those who are without doubt as to the absolute justice of their cause are without fears that it may not somehow triumph in the end. This goes to the heart of Greene's quarrel with Christianity and Marxism's eschatological confidence, for whether one claims the sanction of holy scripture or that of the immutable "laws" of history, the Christian and the commissar are both comforted by a future whose chronicle has always already been written. It is in connection with this long-term hubris concerning what is to be that Greene draws an audacious yet convincing historical connection between classical liberalism and the Marxism that is sworn to destroy it, using something like the Christian conception of original sin to tie the damning knot. Commenting on Diego Rivera's mural entitled "Creation" in *The Lawless Roads,* he reports that it is "all outstretched arms and noble faces, white robes and halos" and represents an attempt to "adap[t] Christian emblems to a vague political idea." He then goes on to ask, "but the Son in Rivera's 'Creation'—what is he but Progress, Human Dignity, great empty Victorian conceptions that life denies at every turn?" (*LR,* 70). This criticism of socialist realism in its pictorial mode echoes another aimed at its literary expression, also from the thirties, where he calls the philosophy behind such writings "that dreadful shadow of Victorian progress and inevitable victory" (*RE,* 66). Of course it is undeniable that Marxism—or rather, the writings of Karl Marx—are productions of the Victorian age, but clearly Greene has something much more inflammatory in mind here. He is in fact provocatively linking the kind of art that, according to Marxist criticism, is the very definition of *bourgeois*—that is, the productions of liberal Victorian optimism—with those produced from the pens and brushes of a later, and supposedly supersessionary, revolutionary "science." And note too that what he accuses both of harboring is nothing other than eschatological certainty, a linear view of history that radically underestimates human incorrigibility and wrongheadedly yearns for a millennium (of either progress or revolution) without political sin and thus devoid of narrative interest. It is also ironic that what Greene is doing here—pointing out that two supposedly incompatible discourses actually serve to promote the same deep but false assumptions about human nature—is very similar to what Marxist criticism prides itself on doing.

Greene continues to draw attention to the Victorian tone of dialectical materialism as late as *The Comedians,* where Dr. Magiot, whose call to commitment the novel wholeheartedly endorses, is gently satirized for the "period" aspect of the politics he espouses. Having summoned Brown to his home, the doctor "wait[s] for [him] in his Victorian sitting-room with a decanter of port," and while Brown thinks that "it might seem an odd setting for a Marxist," he "remember[s] hearing of the lace curtains and the china cabinets in the early Ilyushin jets." Still, the protagonist "fe[els] that after dinner we should have joined other members of the Browning Society for a discussion of *Sonnets from the Portuguese.* Hamit lay in his drain a very long way from here" (*TC,* 247–48). That last sentence seems once more to lump Marxism and liberalism derogatorily together, for it suggests a body of optimistic theory as detached from tragic experience as Pyle's ideas garnered from the college lectures of York Harding.

As if to refute the eschatological certainties of Marxism, Greene portrays all his revolutionaries as failures, though not in a way that discredits the justice of their cause, for in Greeneland it is the hopeless causes that are the most worthy of allegiance, while the ones that succeed are almost always morally suspect by the very fact of their success. Indeed failure for Greene is in a sense the only legitimate form of victory, for to fail in a good cause is to have committed oneself to it without appearing to confirm its eschatological boasts. Dr. Czinner, in what will set a pattern for Greene's later revolutionaries (and his later Catholics), is beatified only after his failure. When he hands the hectoring Mabel Warren a newspaper account of how his revolutionary hopes have been crushed by the forces of reaction, she reads of "a failure which has put him completely out of her power" (*ST,* 69), for now that "he [is] beaten," he is "triumphant" and invulnerable. Deciding to go on to Belgrade and confront the authorities anyway, he becomes divested of many of the moral ambiguities that have hitherto attended his revolutionary actions: "I am alive again, he thought, because I am conscious of death as a future possibility, almost a certainty. . . . I am afraid, he told himself with triumph, I am afraid" (73). The list of those who are ennobled despite, or because, they "fail" to lead their secular or religious cause to triumph includes the whisky priest, the guerrillas of *The Comedians,* and León Rivas. As Terry Eagleton indicates, this penchant for showing the protagonist to be "at once worthless and better than he thinks by finding his best qualities in the way he faces his worthlessness" is itself part of an ambivalent struggle in Greene's mind between liberal humanism and a religious view of man as radically fallen. The novels see "God as incarnate, not in human creativity, but in human failure," a state of affairs that follows naturally from the conception of a weakened deity we have heretofore traced. And so "the more men are exposed as broken and corrupted failures, the more one can love them and so have one's 'humanism,' but the more, by the same token, they endorse an anti-humanist view of their fallenness."[5] The failure of Greene's heroes is thus a critique of the "empty Victorian conceptions" of progress that infect both liberalism and Marxism, but one that, because it demands that we pity all who are doomed to fail, nevertheless smuggles in a scattershot liberal-humanist compassion at the same time.

An aversion to millennial claims is not the only reason that failure in a political cause is no crime in Greeneland. As we have seen in the previous chapter, what counts in the highest court is the individual's decision to risk him- or herself through commitment, not the practical consequences of that commitment—thus Magiot's breezy reply to Brown's suggestion that if his mother were now fighting with the rebels she would be fighting "uselessly": "Oh, yes, uselessly, of course" (*TC,* 234). This notion also prevails in *The Honorary Consul,* where "the individual act of charity is more important . . . than successful political action." One can safely say that, in Greene's conception of political commitment, it is not a matter of whether you win or lose or even primarily of how you play the game—rather, it is largely just a matter of *whether* you play the game. As Sharrock declares concerning the later novels, "Marxism, as a cause, is ultimately justified as a means for the self to realize itself," or, to put it another way, leftist causes are chiefly important because

---

5. Eagleton, "Reluctant Heroes," 109, 114; on the ennobled revolutionaries, see Adamson, *Dangerous Edge,* 175.

they engage our charity, not because they are going to remake our world anytime soon. Just how Victorian—nay, Dickensian—this all is can be seen in the convincing ring of Georg Gaston's comment that "what really matters in Greene's world is whether or not his characters experience a change of heart."[6] That Greene's characters pick up a Bren rather than opening their strongboxes does not wholly disguise the fact that in both cases a personal drama takes precedence over a social one.

Somewhat counteracting this insistence that private salvation is more important than social transformation is Greene's avoidance of what might be termed "Nathaniel Hawthorne's bonfire." In a short story entitled "Earth's Holocaust," Hawthorne explains how the people of the world, "overburdened with an accumulation of worn-out trumpery," decide to burn all useless and antiquated things in a huge bonfire, thereby freeing themselves to live a brighter future. The first to go are the coats of arms and badges of knighthood, followed by crowns and scepters, alcoholic drinks, stimulants, weapons of war, gibbets, marriage certificates, literature, religious regalia, and finally the Bible itself. It is at this point that a "dark-complexioned personage," carrying more than a whiff of brimstone, emerges from the crowd and declares that "there is one thing that these wiseacres have forgotten to throw into the fire, and without which all the rest of the conflagration is just nothing at all—yes; though they had burnt the earth itself to a cinder!" The bewildered onlookers then ask what this essential missing item might be.

> "What, but the human heart itself!" said the dark-visaged stranger, with a portentous grin. "And, unless they hit upon some method of purifying that foul cavern, forth from it will re-issue all the shapes of wrong and misery—the same old shapes, or worse ones—which they have taken such a vast deal of trouble to consume to ashes. I have stood by, this live-long night, and laughed in my sleeve at the whole business. Oh, take my word for it, it will be the old world yet!"[7]

What is interesting about this story is the unusually clear way in which it puts forward a classically conservative argument against all

6. Adamson, *Dangerous Edge,* 174; Sharrock, *Saints,* 222; Gaston, *Pursuit,* 23.
7. Nathaniel Hawthorne, "Earth's Holocaust," 158–59.

progressive politics. Man is radically fallen and all social remedies for the human condition are therefore futile unless preceded by a spiritual conversion in each and every individual. This conversion experience may be specifically Christian, or it may be as vague as the Victorian change of heart: the real, if unspoken, point is that, however the conversion is defined, it is too much to expect from more than a few scattered recipients of grace in any age, and thus a conservative politics of order, discipline, and denial is the only one that corresponds to the immutable spiritual condition of the mass of mankind. Now for his part, Greene undeniably views human beings as radically fallen creatures in need of conversion, but interestingly, he steers completely clear of the conservative corollary to that belief outlined above. He can do so because he defines the necessary conversion experience as nothing other than the individual's decision to join, broadly speaking, a leftist political enterprise, for only progressive causes arouse and utilize our charity. Such causes are thus anything but futile, though, as noted before, his primary interest is their effect on the individuals who participate in them rather than their social impact.

True, there is a moment in *The Power and the Glory* where the priest, in debate with the lieutenant, seems to echo Hawthorne's sentiments: "That's another difference between us. It's no good your working for your end unless you're a good man yourself. And there won't always be good men in your party. Then you'll have all the old starvation, beating, get-rich-anyhow. But it doesn't matter so much my being a coward—and all the rest. I can put God into a man's mouth just the same—and I can give him God's pardon. It wouldn't make any difference to that if every priest in the Church was like me" (*PG*, 195). What the priest is really saying here is that the leader of *his* movement is an incorruptible being, while those who run the lieutenant's are continually open to corruption. This skepticism about *professional* leftists—the people who run the movement or the party—appears to continue into Greene's later period, since in both *The Comedians* and *The Honorary Consul* the attractiveness of the rebels is owing in part to their status as amateurs; both Philipot and Rivas's band don't quite know what they're doing and wind up making fatal mistakes. Furthermore, in the latter novel, El Tigre, "the one who gives the orders" (*HC*, 104) but with whom "only those in Rosario are in touch" (36), is at best an ambiguous figure, whose safe distance from the dangers incurred by his "instruments" (99) arouses suspicion. In truth, if there is any aspect of Greene's thought that reeks of Hawthorne's conservative conflagration, it is this chronic distrust of success in any form. As Allott and Farris long ago pointed out, "there is social criticism and hatred of avoidable cruelty and injustice in Greene's novels, but such injustice is always seen as part of a wider reference to the 'injustice' of life as a whole."[8] Obviously for our author there is something deeply amiss with the very fabric of reality, and thus all those who rise and prosper in this world must bear the taint of being in sympathy with an injustice that precedes any particular political regime or economic system, of being the beneficiaries of a universal misalignment. Where Greene differs from the conventional Christianity of Hawthorne is in seeing this "aboriginal calamity"—a phrase from Cardinal Newman cited by Greene—as having engulfed and debilitated God as well as the tempted hearts of his creatures: aboriginal indeed, such a calamity. In the practical, everyday sphere the result is that *all* political eminencies—even those of the left—are dubious ones, though for those amateurs who decide to fight and fail for the people's cause, redemption is at hand.

Of course all this focus on the individual has significant implications for Greene's ability to assimilate Marxist thought into his own political vision in anything like its original or undiluted form. As Robert Pendleton rightly says, Greene follows his mentor Conrad in focusing again and again on "the more private motivations behind an individual's political actions." Indeed, rightly speaking, there are for Greene *only* private motivations for political engagement. Certainly none of his protagonists are pricked into action by abstract appeals in behalf of the suffering masses or our brothers in arms; rather, their commitment arises only as the result of a "deep recognition of another human being's needs and rights,"[9] and indeed the novels leave us in no doubt that it is Rowe's love for Anna Hilfe, Brown's for Joseph, Plarr's for his lost father, and Fowler's violent ambivalence toward Pyle that prompt the heroes to accept the dangerous wager of engagement. Consequently there is no need in Greeneland for the didactic role of the party, for only the searing emotions of love

8. Allott and Farris, *Art*, 18.
9. Pendleton, *Conradian Masterplot*, 67–68; Adamson, *Dangerous Edge*, 196.

and hate—up-close and personal, as it were—can penetrate the thick carapace of our indifference, while the manifesto and the soapbox speech reach only the ears of the choir. As Rowe himself declares, "One can't love humanity. One can only love people" (*MF*, 184).

Nor is there any embarrassment on Greene's part about the essentially private genesis of his protagonists' commitments, for he not only depicts their engagement as continuing to be sustained by personal motives, but insists that such motives are the only adequate guardian of a political movement's essential morality. When the private reason for "going into the streets" is lost or forgotten, then expediency becomes the director of actions and the liberators begin to resemble the oppressors. This idea emerges in *It's a Battlefield*,[10] where Surrogate and Bennet, rivals within the Communist party's leadership, both ignore the suffering individual victim of political oppression, Drover, in their pursuit of wider agendas. Surrogate, for instance, feels that "personalities" have "always betrayed him" and distracted him from the "lovely abstractions of Communism" that "had lured him into the party. . . . He resented even Drover's intrusion as an individual to be saved and not a sacrifice to be decked for the altar" (*IB*, 44). For his part, Bennet, the supposed scourge of do-nothing intellectuals like Surrogate, insists that "this meeting's got more to attend to than Drover. Who's Drover anyway? I've never 'eard 'im do anything for the party. We've got a big job on now that can't wait for Drover" (45). Largely because of attitudes like these, the text portrays the party as merely one more entity driven by expediency, one more isolated company on the battlefield, fighting for nothing more selfless than its own self-promotion.

Greene's most powerful articulation of the need to always keep the political personal, however, occurs in *The Power and the Glory* and stands as perhaps his most potent critique, from a recognizably Christian perspective, of the moral temptations inherent in secular progressive politics. Here the whisky priest is attempting to convince his prematurely worldly daughter that her personal fate is of enormous interest to him, but not only to him:

> He went down on his knees and pulled her to him, while she giggled and struggled to be free: "I love you. I am your father and I

10. See Pendleton, *Conradian Masterplot*, 67.

love you. Try to understand that." He held her tightly by the wrist
and suddenly she stayed still, looking up at him. He said, "I would
give my life, that's nothing, my soul . . . my dear, my dear, try to
understand that you are—so important." That was the difference, he
had always known, between his faith and theirs, the political leaders
of the people who cared only for things like the state, the republic:
this child was more important than a whole continent. He said,
"You must take care of yourself because you are so—necessary. The
president up in the capital goes guarded by men with guns—but my
child, you have all the angels of heaven—" (*PG*, 82)

This scene is juxtaposed with the lieutenant's speech to the village
a few pages earlier, where he also attempts to convince the peasants
of their true worth, though in the ironizing context of choosing a
hostage to be taken away and likely executed: "He broke out suddenly, 'Why won't you trust me? I don't want any of you to die. In
my eyes—can't you understand—you are worth far more than he
is. I want to give you' he made a gesture with his hands which
was valueless, because no one saw him—'everything.' He said in
a dull voice, 'You. You there. I'll take you'" (77). It is expedient to
take hostages, and thus the lieutenant winds up killing those he
would usher toward the secular millennium; the priest's waverings
between weakness and principle is the opposite of expedient, and
yet, as the timely arrival of his replacement in the book's final pages
suggests, it is his army that may eventually win the war, one person
at a time.

What is a stark contrast in *The Power and the Glory* becomes a game
of inches in *The Honorary Consul,* where a considerable amount of
tension centers on the question of whether León Rivas, the revolutionary Catholic priest, will or will not kill the innocent hostage
Charley Fortnum for the sake of a political objective. The orders
of El Tigre, the "all too distant leader"[11] of León's guerrilla group,
seem clear: whether the right or the wrong man has been taken, if
the Paraguayan prisoners are not released, Fortnum must be killed
to prove the seriousness of the rebels' intent and thus presumably
expedite the organization's next operation. Whether Rivas will follow
these instructions goes to the heart of Greene's political vision, for

11. Salvatore, *Greene and Kierkegaard,* 63.

over the course of the novel León articulates a worldview that is the closest approach in the canon to a workable synthesis of Marxism and Christianity: "I never told you I had left the Church. How can I leave the Church? The Church is the world. The Church is this *barrio,* this room. There is only one way any of us can leave the Church and that is to die. . . . Not even then, if what we sometimes believe is true" (*HC,* 198). In like manner, when Rivas speaks of his eschatology, Greene crafts his phrases in such a way as to make it impossible to say whether León is espousing primarily a politics of secular liberation or a religion of salvation:

> "Christ was a man," Father Rivas said, "even if some of us believe that he was God as well. It was not the God the Romans killed, but a man. A carpenter from Nazareth. Some of the rules He laid down were only the rules of a good man. A man who lived in his own province, in his own particular day. He had no idea of the kind of world we would be living in now. Render unto Caesar, but when *our* Caesar uses napalm and fragmentation bombs . . . The Church lives in time too. Only sometimes, for a short while, for some people—I am not one of them—I am not a man of vision—I think perhaps—but how can I explain to you when I believe so little myself?—I think sometimes the memory of that man, that carpenter, can lift a few people out of the temporary Church of these terrible years, when the Archbishop sits down to dinner with the General, into the great Church beyond our time and place, and then . . . those lucky ones . . . they have no words to describe the beauty of that Church." (218, Greene's ellipses)

The careful and eloquent splitting of hairs—a Church not beyond time, but beyond *our* time—alerts us that this passage represents a kind of culmination of Greene's lifelong desire to put Marxism and Catholicism into fruitful dialogue.

But there is one hair that cannot be split—will Rivas actually take the life of his hostage for the sake of political expediency? At one point, in conversation with Fortnum, he "mutter[s] a cliché absent-mindedly, 'They say one man has to die for the people.'" This would indeed seem to be the crux of the matter, though here Charley quickly reminds the priest that "that was what the crucifiers said, not the Christians," which prompts León to admit that he "was not thinking when [he] spoke" (117). The issue also comes to involve

León's conception of a God who suffers but evolves along with his human creations, for Plarr tauntingly asks if killing Fortnum will aid the Deity's progress:

> "No. I pray all the time I shall not have to kill him."
>
> "And yet you will kill him if they don't give in?"
>
> "Yes. Just as you lie with another man's wife. There are ten men dying slowly in prison, and I tell myself I am fighting for them and that I love them. But my sort of love I know is a poor excuse. A saint would only have to pray, but I have to carry a revolver. I slow evolution down."
>
> "Then why . . . ?"
>
> "Saint Paul answered that question, 'What I do is not that which I wish to do, but something which I hate.' He knew all about the night-side of God. He had been one of those who stoned Stephen."
>
> "Do you still call yourself a Catholic believing all that?"
>
> "Yes. I call myself a Catholic whatever the bishops may say. Or the Pope." (227)

Of course, as it turns out, Father Rivas does not end up killing his hostage. Choosing to go suicidally to the wounded Plarr's aid instead of carrying out the orders of El Tigre, he declares with his penultimate breath that he is "quite safe" now because he "could not kill a mouse," and admits that he "was never made to be a killer" (250). The implication of this scene is wide ranging: when push comes to shove, and Marxism is to be interwoven with Christianity, the latter's claims concerning the primacy of the individual trump the former's commitment to a supposedly greater collective good—the leftist priest will not slaughter even one innocent for the sake of a better future.

II

But what, we are entitled to ask, would a Marxism that must incorporate within itself a primary and unwavering concern for the individual look like? Greene's answer in *The Quiet American* is that it would simply look like Marxism as it is actually practiced on the ground. Here Fowler makes an assertion that Greene later echoed in an interview:[12]

12. See Cassis, *Man of Paradox*, 184.

> . . . who cared about the individuality of the man in the paddy
> field—and who does now? The only man to treat him as a man is the
> political commissar. He'll sit in his hut and ask his name and listen
> to his complaints; he'll give up an hour a day to teaching him—it
> doesn't matter what, he's being treated like a man, like someone of
> value. Don't go on in the East with that parrot cry about a threat to
> the individual soul. Here you'd find yourself on the wrong side—it's
> they who stand for the individual and we just stand for Private
> 23987, unit in the global strategy. (QA, 97).

This is a comfortable answer, but it avoids a lot of questions about the
differences between Marxism in an insurrectionary and a governing
mode, between a heroic Communist struggle and a day-to-day Communist polity. I believe that the uncomfortable answer—uncomfortable for Greene, anyway—would be that such an individual-centered
Marxism, should it ever actually emerge and govern, would look a
lot like social democracy, which would in turn—and here's the rub—
only differ from liberal reformism in matters of degree, not kind. I
think that at some level, perhaps at an unconscious level, Greene understands this. As Neil McEwan puts it, our author "respects Communists as far as he can see them as idealists, more aware of social evil
than are the complacent majority of people," while at the same time
he is "opposed to Communism as it exists." Greene has thus "dreamed
of a Communism that does not and could not exist, and . . . if he were
frank he would confess to the liberalism which marks all his work."[13]

    There are in fact aspects of Greene's biographical record that
suggest that his allegiance to something like a recognizably liberal
outlook may have lived on, like a repressed forbidden desire, despite
all his virulent rhetoric denouncing it. When, for instance, our author
briefly joined the Communist party during his Oxford days, his friend
Joseph Macleod was shocked at such behavior from someone he
considered a dyed-in-the-wool liberal: "I couldn't believe this. It was
a surprise beyond all words. And I said 'What for?' and he replied,
'Well, I think it's the only future.' It shook me to the core. Graham was
more stirred and activated by individual victimization than by class
or wage exploitations." If the evidence from Greene's fictions is to
be any guide at all, Macleod was apparently quite right about what

13. Neil McEwan, *Modern Novelists: Graham Greene,* 14.

at bottom "stirred and activated" his schoolmate; at any rate, it is certainly always the plight of individuals and only that which moves his fictional creations toward political commitment. This idea of a liberalism spurned early, which nevertheless claimed the author's unwilling and perhaps unconscious allegiance, is also suggested by Greene's reminiscences about his father: "I started to grow fond of him [only] when I was an adult, while I was up at Balliol. I think I behaved a bit roughly towards him then, for he was very liberal—not only in the political sense, belonging as he did to the Liberal party— but in the true liberal sense, while I was being tempted by extremes: I mean the Communist party, with which I flirted briefly. In 1923 one could still believe in the October Revolution."[14]

I have taken as my central subject in this book the detailed nature and overall tendencies of Greene's extremity of mind and temper- ament, but an attraction to extremes *because* they are extremes— which our author certainly harbored—can mean that one may occasionally embrace two extremes that cancel each other out. Per- haps Greene's desire to recognize the Marxist masses and the invio- lable Christian soul simultaneously left him in possession of nothing more extremist than the familiar liberal subject. And, in the same vein, what about our author's attitude toward that other unliberal tenet, the need for revolutionary violence? As we have already seen, armed revolutionaries don't seem to get very far in Greene's fictions. León Rivas is an interesting figure in this respect, for while his death testifies to the sincerity of his revolutionary beliefs, he not only refuses to use his gun, but also articulates a vision of political struggle that has a decidedly gradualist ring to it: "You believe in evolution, Eduardo, even though sometimes whole generations of men slip backwards to the beasts. It is a long struggle and a long suffering, evolution, and I believe God is suffering the same evolution that we are, but perhaps with more pain" (*HC*, 226). This is seemingly progress without apocalypse, reform without revolution, and as such it is a political vision that might not be all that shocking to the sensibilities of Lloyd George.

And yet if Greene's insistence on the inviolability of the individ- ual and his implied political incrementalism do strike us as liberal

---

14. Macleod quoted in Norman Sherry, *The Life of Graham Greene,* 1:161; Allain, *Other Man,* 33.

commonplaces, what then do we make of the withering scorn directed at the likes of Ida Arnold, York Harding, and the Entrenationo Academy, liberal pillars all? What is it, specifically, about liberalism that so enrages Greene? The relationship between the liberal mindset and the mediated mode of life was discussed in our first chapter, and it need not be revisited here, though it must surely account for much of our author's supposed detestation of political middle-of-the-roadism. There is in addition, however, an aspect of liberal reformism seemingly despised by Greene that is more germane to our present discussion. This is, paradoxically, its lack of a transformative eschatology—the presence of which he finds anathema in the repertoires of Christianity and Marxism.

If Ida Arnold is, as Neil Nehring suspects, "the namesake of Matthew Arnold,"[15] then her lack of a compelling teleology may be seen as representative of the social philosophy she makes flesh. For Ida, "death [is] the end of everything," and thus "life," defined in purely sensual terms as "sunlight on brass bedposts, Ruby port" and "Fred's mouth pressed down on hers in the taxi" must be preserved at all costs, and "she [is] prepared to cause any amount of unhappiness to anyone in order to defend the only thing she believe[s] in" (*BR*, 36). Her vision of the future is really an endless repetition of the present, and a false one since it willfully ignores the entropic decline of the body: "no real sense of danger could lodge behind those large vivacious eyes. Nothing could ever make her believe that one day she too, like Fred, would be where the worms. . . . Her mind couldn't take that track; she could go only a short way before the points automatically shifted and set her vibrating down the accustomed line, the season ticket line marked by desirable residence and advertisements of cruises and small fenced boskages for rural love" (144). Indeed, Ida, in her good-humored, hail-fellow dullness, refuses to acknowledge the transformative potential of human beings. When Rose declares that "people change," Ida replies, "Oh, no they don't. Look at me. I've never changed. It's like those sticks of rock: bite it all the way down, you'll still read Brighton. That's human nature" (198). To have no eschatology is apparently as bad as having an overly ambitious one, for Ida's incarnate liberalism also sentences us to a kind of plotlessness, though this time it is the plotlessness of

15. Nehring, "Revolt," 229.

endless sensual repetition and a denial of the tragic master narrative of entropy's eventual triumph, the only narrative that can spark our redemptive pity and charity. The liberal vision promises a future of more money and more gadgets, but a society that has only this story to tell itself about itself has, to Greene's way of thinking, banished all the potential *mystique* from its *politique.*

It is also apparently Greene's belief that liberalism's vague and un-compelling eschatology leads liberals into serious confusions about how to attain it. In this respect, *The Confidential Agent* and *The Quiet American* can be seen as examples of, respectively, the feckless and dangerous extremes to which liberal chiliasts are driven. On the harmless but pitiful side resides Dr. Bellows, founder of the Entrenationo Academy, where "everyone lives in an atmosphere of unreality . . . in an ivory tower, waiting for miracles" (*CA,* 132). With his "weak and noble face" (126) and "old liberal eyes . . . full of tears" (132), Bellows believes that the better communication provided by an international language will bring on the shining future of uni-versal peace, though the meager condition of his academy shows up the impossibility of his dream. It is significant that here Greene compares him to the Christian saint, that class of person who comes closest to realizing a postmillennial life here on earth.

> "Love of all the world. A desire to be able to exchange—ideas—with—everybody. All this hate," Dr. Bellows said, "these wars we read about in the newspapers, they are all due to misunderstanding. If we all spoke the same language . . ." He suddenly gave a little wretched sigh which wasn't histrionic. He said, "It has always been my dream to help." The rash unfortunate man had tried to bring his dream to life, and he knew that it wasn't good—the little leather chairs and the draughty waiting-room and the woman in a jumper knitting. He had dreamt of universal peace, and he had two floors on the south side of Oxford Street. There was something of a saint about him, but saints are successful. (43)

The more sinister side of liberal idealism is represented by York Harding and his acolyte, Pyle. Here the goal of establishing "national democracy" is pursued "out of a book" (*QA,* 157) at a level of theoretic abstraction that is as humorous as the workings of the Entrenationo Academy—until people start to die as a result of it:

I was to learn later that he [Pyle] had an enormous respect for what he called serious writers. That term excluded novelists, poets and dramatists unless they had what he called a contemporary theme, and even then it was better to read the straight stuff as you got it from York.

I said, "You know, if you live in a place for long you cease to read about it."

"Of course I always like to know what the man on the spot has to say," he replied guardedly.

"And then check it with York?"

"Yes." Perhaps he had noticed the irony, because he added with his habitual politeness, "I'd take it as a very great privilege if you could find time to brief me on the main points. You see, York was here more than two years ago." (24)

What makes Pyle an intriguing character is that his murderous bomb campaign emerges not from viciousness or anger, but from the very atmosphere of heady abstraction in which he has been schooled, from the fact that he has "punted down into Phat Diem in a kind of schoolboy dream" (162). That such a detached state of mind can often allow the aggressor to ignore or disown the pain he causes his victims is simply intolerable to Greene. As one critic puts it, Pyle "is not so much a 'child' as a 'liberal,' which to Greene is a person with a willed ignorance of the world." What also angers our author is the dishonesty of liberalism's dirty war for a "clean"—in the American, antiseptic sense—body politic. Communists make no bones about the need for killing if the world is to realize Marx's millennium, just as Christians are (nowadays, and in theory at least) not confused about the futility of violence in bringing about God's, but liberalism's endtime is so vague that one may talk peace and make war simultaneously without contradicting any specific liberal doctrine. Fowler, for instance, answers Pyle's anticolonial effusions by insisting that the French in Indochina "aren't leading these people on with half-lies like your politicians—and ours. I've been in India, Pyle, and I know the harm liberals do. We haven't a liberal party any more—liberalism's infected all the other parties. We are all either liberal conservatives or liberal socialists: we all have a good conscience. I'd rather be an exploiter who fights for what he exploits, and dies with it" (96). Greene, a man fascinated with, and often sympathetic to the violence inherent in ideological extremes, takes special umbrage when the supposed center has recourse to force. As he stated in an interview, "I would go to almost any length to put my feeble twig in the spokes of American foreign policy. I admit this may appear simplistic but that's how it is. Some time ago there was an article in *The Spectator* about *The Quiet American,* which said that it made little difference whether I inclined to the Right or the Left, since what I truly detested was American liberalism. That wasn't far wrong."[16] Liberal eyes can weep copiously, but in contrast to those of the priest and the politburo member, they don't see clearly and unsentimentally what kind of business they are ultimately about. Our author can forgive almost anything except chronic obtuseness, especially if such myopia is backed by the power of the state.

One final fault that Greene finds with liberalism is its success— specifically its material success. As he says of Ida Arnold, "there [is] no place in all the world where she fe[els] a stranger" (*BR,* 72), for "behind her [are] all the big battalions" (221) and she "belong[s] to the great middle law-abiding class" (80). Liberalism enjoys such a wide circle of friends because it promises—and in some cases delivers— material riches in, relatively speaking, the short term. Greene, for his part, shares with the saints to which he so frequently makes reference an almost visceral hatred of conspicuous accumulation. Thus, while "his sense of justice doubtless sees the merits of the postwar Welfare State," his "fiction is underpinned by disgust with the endless gratification of consumer tastes" and of "a civilization that panders to human acquisitiveness," an attitude best revealed in *The Quiet American*'s disparaging catalog of American convenience foods and sanitary aids. And thus, as Anthony Burgess shrewdly divines, it may have been the Communist bloc's inability to match the West frozen dinner for frozen dinner that kept drawing Greene eastward, in spirit and body, over the Berlin Wall: "a political doctrine that is committed to improvement of the material lot of the people, yet signally fails to do so, seems to have been visited by an ironical paraclete: it is not yet clogged with butter and drowning in Coca-Cola vats; it is nearer the angels than it wishes to be."[17] If, for Greene, all success is suspect, then material success is the most suspect of

16. Chace, "Spies," 167; Greene quoted in Allain, *Other Man,* 90.
17. Maria Cuoto, *Graham Greene: On the Frontier: Politics and Religion in the Novels,* 108; Anthony Burgess, "Politics in the Novels of Graham Greene," 97.

all, for it dulls the edges of the moral issues and stark choices that make for life's compelling narratives.

But does our author then secretly wish that people remain impoverished merely so they may retain their narrative potential? Let us revisit, in this regard, what must count as the whisky priest's weakest argument in his debate with the lieutenant:

> "But there was one thing always puzzled me about men like yourself. You hate the rich and love the poor. Isn't that right?"
> "Yes."
> "Well, if I hated you, I wouldn't want to bring up my child to be like you. It's not sense."
> "That's just twisting . . ."
> "Perhaps it is. I've never got your ideas straight. We've always said the poor are blessed and the rich are going to find it hard to get into heaven. Why should we make it hard for the poor man too?"
> (*PG,* 199)

This is indeed "just twisting," and Jesuitical, and falsely ingenuous—if, that is, we take it only as expressing the priest's Christian orthodoxy in a particularly unimaginative form. If, on the other hand, we view this momentary lapse in the conservation of character as a bit of Greene's own idiosyncratic theology spilling through, we may catch a glimpse of the dread with which he contemplated a world of material abundance—liberal or Marxist—in which lives weighed down with burdens of gold can no longer act out the stories of risk and commitment that are the only delight of a wounded and suffering God. The lieutenant's political philosophy doesn't seem likely to deliver its promised poisoned chalice to the people, but Ida's just might, and therein, to Greene's mind, lies its danger. And herein, for Greene's readers, is a poignant irony, for to some extent our author's progressive politics are at war with his chosen aesthetic object—to the extent to which the miserable of the earth are relieved of material want and social injustice, they cease to be of narrative interest. A prosperous and democratic Greeneland is no Greeneland at all.

III

The irregular shape of the preceding argument, which has followed Greene back and forth among Christianity, Marxism, and liberalism, leaving dents in each and lighting nowhere for long, suggests that our author's political vision is not the straightforwardly ecumenical and synthetic one it is sometimes portrayed as being. And yet—speaking only for the moment of Christianity and Marxism— we do see much evidence of a lifetime's effort to devise a workable combination of the two. As early as *The Lawless Roads,* for instance, we hear him musing that "Catholicism . . . ha[s] to rediscover the technique of revolution" (*LR,* 29), while as late as the middle 1960s he still appears to believe in the possibility of "some kind of accord between Communism and Christianity." Even in later years, his interviews and public speeches resonate with a fading, though persisting hope. On the one hand, he is cheered by the spread of liberation theology in Latin America, proclaiming at a Moscow conference that "we are fighting—Roman Catholics are fighting—together with the Communists, and working together with the Communists. We are fighting together against the Death Squads in El Salvador. We are fighting together against the Contras in Nicaragua. We are fighting together against General Pinochet in Chile. . . . There is no division in our thoughts" (*RE,* 316–17). On the other hand, when queried about his politics he wearily admits to harboring only "the hopeless hope of a human face of Communism."[18] When we turn to the novels, however, both the hope and the skepticism seem to be there from the beginning, dialogically affirming and denying the possibility of synthesis in the selfsame breath. Consider, for instance, the whisky priest's halting attempt to describe the kingdom of heaven to his peasant congregation.

"One of the Fathers has told us that joy always depends on pain. Pain is part of joy. We are hungry and then think how we enjoy our food at last. . . . That is why I tell you that heaven is here: this is a part of heaven just as pain is a part of pleasure. . . . Pray that you will suffer more and more and more. Never get tired of suffering. The police watching you, the soldiers gathering taxes, the beating you always get from the jefe because you are too poor to pay, smallpox and fever, hunger . . . that is all part of heaven—the preparation. Perhaps without them, who can tell, you wouldn't enjoy heaven so much. Heaven would not be complete. And heaven. What is heaven?

18. Cassis, *Man of Paradox,* 184, 302.

" . . . Heaven is where there is no jefe, no unjust laws, no taxes, no soldiers and no hunger. Your children do not die in heaven. . . . You will never be afraid there—or unsafe. There are no Red Shirts. Nobody grows old. The crops never fail." (*PG,* 69–70)

What is noteworthy about this passage is its volatile ambiguity, for the speech occupies a point of unstable equilibrium between a pacifist and indeed quietist version of Christianity and a full-blown liberationist theology. On its surface the address appears to counsel a meek acceptance of—or even an obsequious wallowing in—earthly suffering in the hope of an eventual posthumous reward where the last shall be first. At the same time, however, the starkly local, material, and minimally transcendent account of heaven insinuates that such a paradise is, given an overthrow of the current political order, graspable in this life if only people will struggle to achieve it.[19] It is thus a passage that seems at loggerheads with itself, pointing in two diametrical directions simultaneously: like the atmosphere of entropy that envelops all the novel's enactions of grace, it suggests that the whisky priest and the lieutenant are both right and both wrong simultaneously. And precisely because it is a palimpsest affirming both ecumenical cooperation and partisan exclusion, the scene is remarkably emblematic of Greene's fitfully and ambivalently synthetic political enterprise as a whole. Furthermore, when we stand back and view this early masterpiece alongside his last, a continuity of confliction emerges, for what *The Power and the Glory* attempts (but is unable) to put asunder, *The Honorary Consul* joins—but again in a way that cancels as much as it constructs. León Rivas, on one level, is a composite of the whisky priest and the lieutenant, the noble yet fallible embodiment of a vigorous liberation theology. As we have seen, though, on another level he exemplifies the very impossibility of Greene's supposed Marxist-Christian concordat, since blending the two systems seems to dissolve the distinctive aspects of both into an individual-centered, nonviolent, gradualist ideology whose eschatology is almost entirely a matter of this world, all of which hearkens back to an earnest Victorian liberalism that was, in the 1930s, supposedly the problem in the first place.

And it is in such ambivalences and mutual cancellations, I think, that we can once again clearly see Greene the political thinker

19. See Sharrock, *Saints,* 128.

clashing with Greene the storyteller, for what the Christian and Marxist myths offer him is not only—and perhaps not even primarily—a transformative politics, but rather an intellectual and emotional milieu conducive to transformative plots and characters susceptible to radical changes of heart. When he tried hardest to imagine the synthesis at practical work in the world, the result was at most a liberalism cognizant of both the fall of man and the class war—a social-democratic liberalism, in other words—but otherwise one largely unchanged from that he was force-fed on both sides of the green baize door. "We all seem to live with dead fathers, don't we?" remarks Dr. Plarr in that novel of Greene's which most deliberately attempts to blend the philosophies of Christ and Marx. As far as our author's political vision is concerned, it certainly does seem that way.

But to simply accuse Greene of being, underneath all the leftist rhetoric, an entirely unconscious liberal and to leave it at that—as some have done with obvious relish[20]—is to paint too simple a picture, for his disagreements with the left were often open and direct. When discussing his attitude toward Marxism in the early 1960s, for instance, Greene took pains to make a distinction: "here in Cuba it is possible to conceive a first breach in Marxist philosophy (not in Marxist economics)—that philosophy as dry as Bentham and as outdated as Ingersoll." Furthermore, he says, "there is no inherent opposition between Marxist economics and Catholicism, and in Cuba . . . Marxism . . . is less philosophical" (*RE,* 219, 218). Here again, we have the equation of Marxist thought with Victorian fustiness, but now it is only the "philosophy" and not the "economics" that is tarred. Something of the same sort of distinction appears to account for the author's gentle treatment of *The Comedians'* belated Victorian communist, Dr. Magiot, who also discriminates between different aspects of leftist orthodoxy: "Yet I have grown to dislike the word 'Marxist.' It is used so often to describe only a particular economic plan. I believe of course in that economic plan—in certain cases and in certain times, here in Haiti, in Cuba, in Vietnam, in India. But Communism, my friend, is more than Marxism, just as Catholicism—remember, I was born a Catholic too—is more than the Roman Curia. There is a *mystique* as well as a *politique.* We are humanists, you and I" (*TC,* 286). The word that Magiot chooses to

20. See Adamson, *Dangerous Edge.*

express what Marxist philosophy *should* be—*mystique*—as well as his mention of his Catholic upbringing, clearly suggests that, for Greene, what Marxism needs is a philosophy that is the opposite of the atheist and determinist one put forward by that "old bore" Karl Marx.[21] But what form could this philosophy take? Must it be, as we have suggested, no more than a kind of tough-minded liberal twig grafted to a Marxist economic trunk? Certainly Greene wishes us to believe that it might be something more, because to his mind, liberal capitalism is not really a philosophy at all, properly understood—and it certainly provides no *mystique* capable of engaging the deeper chambers of the heart:

> Belief, like it or not, is a magnet. Even what seem the extravagant claims of a belief are magnetic. In a commercial world of profit and loss man is hungry often for the irrational. I do not believe that the little knots of people who gather near Check-point Charlie are there to demonstrate repugnance, as do the bus loads at the Brandenburg Gate. Part of Berlin has become a foreign land and they are staring into the strangeness, some with enmity, others with apprehension, but all with a certain fascination. Behind them lies the new city, the smart hotels, the laden stores; but capitalism is not a belief, and so it is not a magnet. It is only a way of life to which one has grown accustomed.
>
> To take the few steps beyond Check-point Charlie can be compared with the acceptance of the last difficult dogma—say the infallibility of the Pope. There are moments when the possible convert is in a state of rebellion; he can see the wall and nothing but the wall. There are moments when he will gladly stretch his faith to the furthest limits. Perhaps there is always one moment when he shuts his eyes and walks into the wide ruined spaces beyond the check-point. He looks back over his shoulder and the dogma has suddenly changed. What had been a threat can even appear like a protection. (*RE*, 209)

There are several things to be said about this extraordinarily suggestive passage. The first is that, in its metaphorical blending of Marxist and Catholic dogma, it implies that what Marxism needs to import from Christianity is not only a concern for the individual,

---

21. Cassis, *Man of Paradox,* 362.

but the sense of mystery itself, for "even what seem the extravagant claims of a belief are magnetic" and "there are moments when [the possible convert] will gladly stretch his faith to the furthest limits." A Catholic accepts that some things are simply unexplainable or unknowable, and thus there is about Catholicism—despite all its dogmas—a chink of contingency in the panorama of providence, a toleration of paradox as the occasional best answer to a desperate question, and a knowledge that the last word about the world has not yet been written, even in scripture. This is certainly the message that Greene's choruslike priests convey as they close his major novels: "You can't conceive . . . nor can I or anyone the . . . appalling . . . strangeness of the mercy of God" (*BR*, 246); "the church knows all the rules" but "it doesn't know what goes on in a single human heart" (*HM*, 272); "I would rather be wrong with St. Thomas than right with the cold and the craven" (*TC*, 283). In other words, certainty killeth, while mystery giveth life, for what finally separates the Christian millennium from the Marxist is that the former will involve the consummation of mysteries as well as of laws and prophecies. If in fact "man is hungry . . . for the irrational" and we all "star[e] into the strangeness . . . with a certain fascination," then only a political system that does not claim to possess all the answers can inspire an allegiance that engages the complete human being. When, for instance, León's wife Marta asks him with anxiety whether all his ideas about an evolving God are in the catechism, León replies that "the catechism is not the faith" but "a sort of two times table" (*HC*, 227). Thus if any worldview, secular or religious, is to prevail, it must recognize that the most important things it is capable of bearing witness to will forever escape what it can codify and explain about itself. "Do you know what happens," asked Greene of an interviewer, "when you wish the world to be neat and orderly and precise, a closed, untroubled place? You try to make it that way. And when people don't respond (and they don't), you end up with Belsen."[22] What Marxists—and liberals—crucially lack, then, are reasons to believe a thing *because* it is absurd.

Second, I think the passage—again because of its conflated portrait of the Christian and Marxist pilgrim—provides us with a crucial hint as to why, in the 1930s, Greene was drawn to Catholicism

22. Ibid., 101.

instead of, as was the prevailing fashion among young writers of the day, becoming a Marxist[23]—a move for which he was never forgiven in some quarters. Those critics who believe that Greene's conversion never carried the full engagement of his heart or head—among whom I unreservedly count myself—sometimes point to his desire to marry Vivien Dayrell-Browning as an important reason for his taking instruction and eventually submitting to baptism.[24] While recognizing the plausibility of such conjectures, I would like to nominate an additional motivation: his intense hatred of capitalism and the liberalism that legitimated it. But, it will immediately be asked, if he did despise the endemic injustice of the economic and political status quo—and his novels of the thirties give us little room to doubt it—why not opt for the Marxism so readily available at that place and time? He didn't, I think, because Marxism was simply insufficiently *different* from liberalism. Insufficiently different, that is, in the ways that mattered to him: in its being at base just another economic model dragging a vision of social morality behind it, in its overly optimistic assumptions about human nature, and especially in its desire to muster and organize the whole of life under the tyrannical writ of reason. Greene, ever the intellectual and emotional traveler, looked around him at the world of the Depression and decided that he wanted to change it not by crossing what he perceived to be a merely provincial boundary into Marxism, but by entering that part of a familiar city which was yet "a foreign land," for "in a commercial world of profit and loss man is hungry often for the irrational." Greene's conversion to Catholicism—whatever his eventual heresies—was seen at the time, and for a good long while, as a kind of defection from the left. What I think such observers failed to realize was that in joining the Church of Rome the author felt himself to be walking through a Check-point Charlie and into an alien land more inimical to the bourgeois West than any eventually erected during the Cold War.

And so perhaps, in the final analysis, the best single word to describe the politics of Graham Greene is "Christian." This is so not because Greene routinely espoused, within his fictions or elsewhere, sympathy for specific political causes supported by the Catholic

23. See George Watson, *Politics and Literature in Modern Britain,* 88–91.
24. See Sharma, *Search for Belief,* 31–32; and Adamson, *Dangerous Edge,* 189.

Church or other Christian groups—indeed, the opposite was just as frequently the case. Rather, his political instincts betray a Christian coloration because they are almost always arrayed against the powers and principalities of this world. León Rivas is right, of course, when he says that the Caesar of biblical times is not the Caesar of napalm and fragmentation bombs, but, in the context of Greene's novels as a whole, he is also wrong. Wherever power congregates in the fictions, there the face of Caesar appears also, multiple and the product of a specific history but yet in an important way always the same, for power—whether it be of the right, left, or center—is always the expression of a success, and therefore by definition of something ungodly. God has power, of course, but He is differentiated from Caesar because unlike Caesar, God is a failure. And, insists Greene, we must each of us struggle against Caesar, even if we too are all but doomed to fail, because in that failed striving resides all our dignity, charity, and pathos, and because by accepting a call to martyrdom we place ourselves and—perhaps, someday—our society, on the road to secular and divine redemption. Graham Greene chose as his baptismal name that of the apostle Thomas, whose name has become synonymous with doubt (*SL,* 169). And it is the words of that figure—who doubted and yet who nevertheless committed himself wholly to a cause (and who went on to write gospels deemed uncanonical)—that best capture Greene's vision of both our political duty and our political destiny: "Let us go up to Jerusalem and die with Him."

Bibliography

Adamson, Judith. *Graham Greene: The Dangerous Edge: Where Art and Politics Meet.* New York: St. Martin's, 1990.

Aisenberg, Nadya. *A Common Spring: Crime Novel and Classic.* Bowling Green: Bowling Green University Popular Press, 1979.

Allain, Marie-Françoise, ed. *The Other Man: Conversations with Graham Greene.* Trans. Guido Waldman. New York: Simon and Schuster, 1983

Allott, Kenneth, and Miriam Farris. *The Art of Graham Greene.* London: Hamish Hamilton, 1951.

Atkins, John. "Sex in Greeneland." In *Essays in Graham Greene: An Annual Review.* Vol. 1, ed. Peter Wolfe. Greenwood, Fla.: Penkevill, 1987.

Auden, W. H. "The Heresy of Our Time." In *Graham Greene: A Collection of Critical Essays,* ed. Samuel Hynes. Englewood Cliffs, N.J.: Prentice Hall, 1973.

Austen, Jane. *Mansfield Park.* New York: Penguin, 1985.

Bakhtin, Mikhail. *Problems of Dostoevsky's Poetics.* Ed. and trans. Caryl Emerson. Minneapolis: University of Minnesota Press, 1984.

Boardman, Gwenn R. *Graham Greene: The Aesthetics of Exploration.* Gainesville: University of Florida Press, 1971.

Brock, D. Heyward, and James M. Welsh. "Graham Greene and the Structure of Salvation." *Renascence* 27 (1974): 31–39.

Brontë, Emily. *Wuthering Heights.* 1847. Reprint, New York: Norton, 1972.

Burgess, Anthony. "Politics in the Novels of Graham Greene." *Journal of Contemporary History* 2, no. 2 (April 1967): 93–103.

Cassis, A. F. "The Dream as Literary Device in Graham Greene's Novels." *Literature and Psychology* 24, no. 3 (1974): 99–108.

Cassis, A. F., ed. *Graham Greene: Man of Paradox.* Chicago: Loyola University Press, 1994.

Chace, William M. "Spies and God's Spies: Greene's Espionage Fiction." In *Graham Greene: A Revaluation,* ed. Jeffrey Meyers. New York: St. Martin's, 1990.

Chapman, Raymond. "The Vision of Graham Greene." In *Forms of Extremity in the Modern Novel,* ed. Nathan Scott. Richmond: John Knox Press, 1965.

Christensen, Peter G. "The Art of Self-Preservation: Monsignor Quixote's Resistance to Don Quixote." In *Essays in Graham Greene: An Annual Review.* Vol. 3, ed. Peter Wolfe. St. Louis: Louis Hall Press, 1992.

Conrad, Joseph. *Heart of Darkness.* 1899. Reprint, New York: Penguin, 1986.

———. *Lord Jim.* 1900. Reprint, New York: Norton, 1968.

Craig, Randall. "Good Places and Promised Lands in *The Comedians.*" *Renascence* 39, no. 1 (fall 1986): 312–24.

Cuoto, Maria. *Graham Greene: On the Frontier: Politics and Religion in the Novels.* New York: St. Martin's, 1988.

Daleski, H. M. *The Divided Heroine: A Recurrent Pattern in Six English Novels.* New York: Holmes and Meier, 1984.

DeVitis, A. A. "Greene's *The Comedians:* Hollower Men." *Renascence* 18 (spring 1966): 129–36.

———. "The Later Greene." In *Essays in Graham Greene: An Annual Review.* Vol. 1, ed. Peter Wolfe. Greenwood, Fla.: Penkevill, 1987.

———. "Religious Aspects in the Novels of Graham Greene." In *Modern Critical Views: Graham Greene,* ed. Harold Bloom. New York: Chelsea House, 1987.

Diemert, Brian. *Graham Greene's Thrillers and the 1930s.* Montreal: McGill-Queen's University Press, 1996.

Eagleton, Terry. "Reluctant Heroes: The Novels of Graham Greene." In *Modern Critical Views: Graham Greene,* ed. Harold Bloom. New York: Chelsea House, 1987.

Erdinast-Vulcan, Daphna. *Graham Greene's Childless Fathers.* New York: St. Martin's, 1988.

Evans, Robert O. "The Satanist Fallacy of *Brighton Rock.*" In *Graham Greene: Some Critical Considerations.* Lexington: University Press of Kentucky, 1963.

Ferns, C. S. " 'Brown Is Not Greene': Narrative Role in *The Comedians.*" *College English* 12, no. 1 (winter 1985): 60–67.

Foucault, Michel. *Discipline and Punish: The Birth of the Prison.* Trans. Alan Sheridan. New York: Random House, 1977.

Friedman, Alan Warren. " 'The Dangerous Edge': Beginning with Death." In *Graham Greene: A Revaluation,* ed. Jeffrey Meyers. New York: St. Martin's, 1990.

Gaston, Georg M. A. *The Pursuit of Salvation: A Critical Guide to the Novels of Graham Greene.* Troy, N.Y.: Whitston, 1984.

Greene, Graham. *Brighton Rock.* 1938. Reprint, New York: Penguin, 1977.

———. *A Burnt-Out Case.* 1961. Reprint, New York: Penguin, 1977.

———. *Collected Essays.* Reprint, New York: Viking, 1969.

———. *Collected Short Stories.* New York: Penguin, 1986.

———. *The Comedians.* 1966. Reprint, New York: Penguin, 1976.

———. *The Confidential Agent.* 1939. Reprint, New York: Penguin, 1971.

———. *The End of the Affair.* 1951. Reprint, New York: Penguin, 1975.

———. *A Gun for Sale.* 1936. Reprint, New York: Penguin, 1974.

———. *The Heart of the Matter.* 1948. Reprint, New York: Penguin, 1978.

———. *The Honorary Consul.* 1973. Reprint, New York: Penguin, 1974.

———. *The Human Factor.* New York: Simon and Schuster, 1978.

———. *In Search of a Character.* New York: Penguin, 1961.

———. *It's a Battlefield.* 1934. Reprint, New York: Penguin, 1977.

———. *The Lawless Roads.* 1939. Reprint, New York: Penguin, 1982.

———. *The Ministry of Fear.* 1943. Reprint, New York: Penguin, 1978.

———. *Our Man in Havana.* 1958. Reprint, New York: Penguin, 1971.

———. "Places." TS with author's revisions. Letters and Papers of Graham Greene. Harry Ransom Research Center, University of Texas at Austin.

———. *Monsignor Quixote.* New York: Simon and Schuster, 1982.

———. *The Power and the Glory.* 1940. Reprint, New York: Penguin, 1991.

———. *The Quiet American.* 1955. Reprint, New York: Penguin, 1977.

———. *Reflections.* Ed. Judith Adamson. London: Reinhardt, 1990.

———. *A Sort of Life.* New York: Simon and Schuster, 1971.

———. *Stamboul Train.* 1932. Reprint, New York: Penguin, 1975.

———. *The Third Man* and *The Fallen Idol.* 1950. Reprint, New York: Penguin, 1977.

———. *Travels with My Aunt.* 1969. Reprint, New York: Penguin, 1977.

———. *Ways of Escape.* New York: Simon and Schuster, 1980.

———. *Yours, Etc.: Letters to the Press.* Ed. Christopher Hawtree. London: Reinhardt, 1989.

Haber, Herbert R. "The End of the Catholic Cycle: The Writer versus the Saint." In *Graham Greene: Some Critical Considerations*, ed. Robert O. Evans. Lexington: University Press of Kentucky, 1963.

Hardy, Thomas. *Tess of the d'Urbervilles*. 1891. Reprint, New York: Penguin, 1985.

Hawthorne, Nathaniel. "Earth's Holocaust." In *Nathaniel Hawthorne's Tales*, ed. James McIntosh. New York: Norton, 1987.

Helsa, David H. "Theological Ambiguity in the 'Catholic Novels.' " In *Graham Greene: Some Critical Considerations*, ed. Robert O. Evans. Lexington: University Press of Kentucky, 1963.

Hoggart, Richard, "The Force of Caricature." In *Graham Greene: A Collection of Critical Essays*, ed. Samuel Hynes. Englewood Cliffs, N.J.: Prentice Hall, 1973.

Hughes, R. E. "*The Quiet American:* The Case Reopened." *Renascence* 12, no. 1 (autumn 1959): 41–49.

Hynes, Joseph. "Two Affairs Revisited." *Twentieth-Century Literature* 33, no. 2 (summer 1987): 234–53.

Kaplan, Carola. "Graham Greene's Pinkie Brown and Flannery O'Connor's Misfit: The Psychopathic Killer and the Mystery of God's Grace." *Renascence* 32, no. 2 (winter 1980): 116–28.

Karl, Frederick R. "Graham Greene's Demonical Heroes." In *Modern Critical Views: Graham Greene*, ed. Harold Bloom. New York: Chelsea House, 1987.

Kelly, Richard. *Graham Greene*. New York: Fredrick Ungar, 1984.

———. *Graham Greene: A Study of the Short Fiction*. New York: Twayne, 1992.

Kermode, Frank. "Mr. Greene's Eggs and Crosses." In *Graham Greene: A Collection of Critical Essays*, ed. Samuel Hynes. Englewood Cliffs, N.J.: Prentice Hall, 1973.

Kubal, David L. "Graham Greene's *Brighton Rock:* The Political Theme." *Renascence* 23, no. 1 (autumn 1970): 46–54.

Kunkel, Francis L. *The Labyrinthine Ways of Graham Greene*. Rev. ed. Mamaroneck, N.Y.: Paul P. Appel, 1973.

———. "The Theme of Sin and Grace in Graham Greene." In *Graham Greene: Some Critical Considerations*, ed. Robert O. Evans. Lexington: University Press of Kentucky, 1963.

Kurismmootil, K. C. Joseph, S.J. *Heaven and Hell on Earth: An Appreciation of Five Novels of Graham Greene*. Chicago: Loyola University Press, 1982.

Laitinen, Kai. "The Heart of the Novel." In *Graham Greene: Some Critical Considerations,* ed. Robert O. Evans. Lexington: University Press of Kentucky, 1963.

Larson, Michael. "Laughing till the Tears Come: Greene's Failed Comedian." *Renascence* 41, no. 3 (spring 1989): 177–87.

Lawrence, D. H. *St. Mawr* and *The Man Who Died.* New York: Vintage, 1953.

Levin, Gerald. "The Rhetoric of Greene's *The Heart of the Matter.*" *Renascence* 23, no. 1 (autumn 1970): 14–20.

Lewis, R. W. B. "The 'Trilogy.'" In *Graham Greene: A Collection of Critical Essays,* ed. Samuel Hynes. Englewood Cliffs, N.J.: Prentice Hall, 1973.

Malamet, Elliott. "Graham Greene and the Hounds of *Brighton Rock.*" *Modern Fiction Studies* 37, no. 4 (winter 1991): 689–703.

———. "Penning the Police/Policing the Pen: The Case of Graham Greene's *The Heart of the Matter.*" *Twentieth-Century Literature* 39, no. 3 (fall 1993): 283–305.

McEwan, Neil. *Modern Novelists: Graham Greene.* New York: St. Martin's, 1988.

Miller, D. A. *Narrative and Its Discontents: Problems of Closure in the Traditional Novel.* Princeton: Princeton University Press, 1981.

Miller, J. Hillis. *The Disappearance of God: Five Nineteenth-Century Writers.* Cambridge: Harvard University Press, Belknap Press, 1963.

Miller, R. H. *Understanding Graham Greene.* Columbia: University of South Carolina Press, 1990.

Mills, John. "The Dog in the Perambulator." *West Coast Review* 23, no. 2 (fall 1988): 79–91.

Nehring, Neil. "Revolt into Style: Graham Greene Meets the Sex Pistols." *PMLA* 106, no. 2 (March 1991): 222–37.

O'Prey, Paul. *A Reader's Guide to Graham Greene.* New York: Thames and Hudson, 1988.

Orwell, George. "The Sanctified Sinner." In *Graham Greene: A Collection of Critical Essays,* ed. Samuel Hynes. Englewood Cliffs, N.J.: Prentice Hall, 1973.

Péguy, Charles. *Basic Verities: Prose and Poetry.* Trans. Anne Green and Julian Green. New York: Pantheon, 1948.

Pendleton, Robert. *Graham Greene's Conradian Masterplot: The Arabesque of Influence.* New York: St. Martin's, 1996.

Polhemus, Robert. *Erotic Faith: Being in Love from Jane Austen to D. H. Lawrence.* Chicago: University of Chicago Press, 1990.

Poole, Roger C. "Graham Greene's Indirection." In *Graham Greene,* ed. Harray J. Cargas. Christian Critic Series. St. Louis: B. Herder, n.d.

Rowe, Jan Tips. "The Heart of the Matter: Blasphemy by Allegory." *Linguistics in Literature* 6 (1981): 1–21.

Salvatore, Anne T. *Greene and Kierkegaard: The Discourse of Belief.* Tuscaloosa: University of Alabama Press, 1988.

Scott, Carolyn. "Review of R. H. Miller's *Understanding Graham Greene.*" In *Essays in Graham Greene: An Annual Review.* Vol. 3, ed. Peter Wolfe. St. Louis: Louis Hall Press, 1992.

Sharma, S. K. *Graham Greene: The Search for Belief.* New Delhi: Harman Publishing House, 1990.

Sharrock, Roger. *Saints, Sinners, and Comedians: The Novels of Graham Greene.* Notre Dame: University of Notre Dame Press, 1984.

———. "Unhappy Families: The Plays of Graham Greene." In *Graham Greene: A Revaluation,* ed. Jeffrey Meyers. New York: St. Martin's, 1990.

Sherry, Norman. *The Life of Graham Greene.* Vol. 1, *1904–1939.* New York: Penguin, 1989.

Shuttleworth, Martin, and Simon Raven. "The Art of Fiction: Graham Greene." In *Graham Greene: A Collection of Critical Essays,* ed. Samuel Hynes. Englewood Cliffs, N.J.: Prentice Hall, 1973.

Silverstein, Marc. "After the Fall: The World of Graham Greene's Thrillers." *Novel: A Forum on Fiction* 22, no. 1 (fall 1988): 24–44.

Smith, Grahame. *The Achievement of Graham Greene.* Totowa, N.J.: Barnes and Noble, 1986.

Spurling, John. *Graham Greene.* New York: Methuen, 1983.

Thomas, Brian. *An Underground Fate: The Idiom of Romance in the Later Novels of Graham Greene.* Athens: University of Georgia Press, 1988.

Unamuno, Miguel de. *The Tragic Sense of Life in Men and Nations.* Trans. Anthony Kerrigan; ed. Anthony Kerrigan and Martin Nozick. Princeton: Princeton University Press, 1972.

Walker, Ronald G. *Infernal Paradise: Mexico and the Modern English Novel.* Berkeley and Los Angeles: University of California Press, 1978.

———. "World without End: An Approach to Narrative Structure in Greene's *The End of the Affair.*" *Texas Studies in Literature and Language* 26, no. 6 (summer 1984): 218–41.

Watson, George. *Politics and Literature in Modern Britain.* Totowa, N.J.: Rowman and Littlefield, 1977.

Wiesenfarth, Joseph. *Gothic Manners and the Classic English Novel.* Madison: University of Wisconsin Press, 1988.

Williams, Trevor L. "History over Theology: The Case for Pinkie in Greene's *Brighton Rock.*" *Studies in the Novel* 24, no. 1 (spring 1992): 67–77.

Wolfe, Peter. *Graham Greene the Entertainer.* Carbondale: Southern Illinois University Press, 1972.

Index

afterlife, 16–17, 43, 87, 143–44, 149
anti-Americanism, 41–42, 46–47, 160,
 189
anti-Semitism, 7
Arnold, Matthew, 5, 26, 172, 186
Austen, Jane, 12–13, 17
authorship, 47–48, 158–59, 169

betrayal, 106
Blake, William, 3
bourgeois ethos, 1, 11–16, 23, 27, 32,
 35–37, 41, 43, 46–48, 50–54, 56, 96,
 174, 186, 196
Brönte, Emily, 5, 11–17, 19, 96, 104–5,
 137–38
Browning, Robert, 5

Camus, Albert, 12
Catholic Church, 3–4, 5, 10–11, 23, 49,
 53–59, 87, 121–22, 170–74, 180–83,
 191–97
Christ, Jesus, 71, 87, 88, 149
Conrad, Joseph, 8, 11–14, 17–20, 23,
 26, 36, 40, 54, 179

Dante, 136
De Quincey, Thomas, 5
deus absconditus, 4–5, 59–60, 88, 97
Dostoyevsky, Feodor, 8, 13
doubt, 172–74

Eco, Umberto, 142
entropic decline, 24–26, 31–32, 61,
 65–70, 83, 85–86, 95, 97, 104, 105–8,
 114, 115, 135, 186–87
espionage, 43–46
evil, problem of, 71, 73–77, 84–89
evolution, moral, 85–87
extremity, attractions of, 1–2, 7–8,
 30–32, 34–35, 36–46, 48, 50–59, 96,
 133–34, 147–58, 185, 188–89

failure as victory, 175–76, 179, 197

free will, 80–82

gender, 6–7, 102–3
grace, divine, 29–30, 61–65, 68,
 130–32, 147, 150–53
Greene, Graham:
—Brighton Rock, 6, 10, 23–37, 38, 39,
 44, 51, 57–58, 61, 64, 77, 129–38,
 147, 186–87, 189, 195
—Burnt-Out Case, A, 42, 51, 84, 89,
 108–9, 124–26, 138, 139, 164
—Collected Essays, 1, 106, 135
—Comedians, The, 6, 46, 84, 108, 111,
 112, 113, 126, 128, 129, 138, 139,
 140–59, 160, 161–65, 166, 175, 176,
 178, 195
—Confidential Agent, The, 37–40, 41,
 45, 187
—End of the Affair, The, 16, 51, 67,
 70–71, 77–83, 102–8
—Heart of the Matter, The, 6, 51,
 67, 70–77, 85, 86, 88, 90, 93–99,
 100–102, 104, 114, 119–22, 132, 138,
 166, 195
—Honorary Consul, The, 42, 77, 84–87,
 88, 108–11, 134, 139, 164, 165–66,
 167, 176, 178–79, 181–83, 192, 193,
 197
—Human Factor, The, 43, 44–46, 47,
 126–27
—It's a Battlefield, 11, 118, 180
—Lawless Roads, The, 51, 174, 191
—Ministry of Fear, The, 43–44, 90–92,
 99–100, 104, 115–18
—Monsignor Quixote, 170–71
—Our Man in Havana, 44, 118
—Power and the Glory, The, 6, 20,
 49–70, 73, 83, 96, 138, 147, 171, 176,
 178, 180–81, 190, 191–92
—Quiet American, The, 40–42, 47,
 84, 97, 108, 112–13, 122–24, 138,
 139, 148, 150, 160–61, 167, 183–84,
 187–89

—*Reflections,* 173, 174, 191, 193
—*Sort of Life, A,* 197
—*Stamboul Train,* 173, 175–76
—*Travels with My Aunt,* 42–43
—*Ways of Escape,* 102, 129
—*Yours, Etc.,* 51

Haggard, H. Rider, 135
Hawthorne, Nathaniel, 177–78, 179
hell, impossibility of, 25–26, 32–33,
  129–39
heresy, 3–4, 67–68, 71–72, 89, 170–72,
  179
Hopkins, Gerard Manley, 5

innocence, 159–64, 167

James, Henry, 8, 82, 106

Lawrence, D. H., 11–14, 20–23, 104
liberalism, 26–28, 169, 172–76,
  184–90, 192, 193, 194, 195, 196
love: as agape, 30, 90, 101–2, 106–7,
  114, 120; as caritas, 28–30, 51–52,
  90, 111–14, 115, 124, 127–28, 153,
  162, 166, 178, 187, 197; as eros,
  3, 26, 28–30, 90, 91–101, 102–11,
  113–14, 124–25, 127–28, 162

Marlowe, Christopher, 138
Marxism, 87, 169, 170–76, 179–85,
  190, 191–96
miracles, 82–83
Modernism, 5, 7, 20

Newman, John Henry, Cardinal, 179

peace, 95, 114–28, 162
pity, 72–73, 84–85, 90–104, 105, 107,
  115, 117, 134–35
political commitment, 139–68,
  175–76, 178, 197
Postmodernism, 7

Romantic era, 4–5

sin, 132, 137–38
Stevenson, Robert Louis, 11, 135

Victorian era, 4–5, 88, 174–75, 176,
  177, 178, 193